The Management of a Student Research Project

2nd Edition

The Management of a Student Research Project

2nd Edition

John A. Sharp and Keith Howard

Gower

1st Edition first published in 1983 and reprinted 1985, 1986, 1987, 1989 (twice), 1991

2nd Edition published 1996

Published by
Gower Publishing Limited
Gower House
Croft Road
Aldershot
Hants GU11 3HR
England

Gower
Old Post Road
Brookfield
Vermont 05036
USA

Reprinted 1996, 1998

John A. Sharp and Keith Howard have asserted their right under the Copyright, Designs and Patents Act 1988 to be identified as the authors of this work.

Sharp, John A., 1942–
   The management of a student research project. – 2nd ed.
   1. Research – Management 2. Universities and colleges – Graduate work
   I. Title II. Howard, Keith, 1931–
   001.4'2

ISBN 0 566 07706 X

2nd Edition edited, designed and typeset from authors' disk by Bill Ireson, Norwich.
Printed and bound in Great Britain at the University Press, Cambridge

Contents

List of Figures and Tables

TABLES

Preface To The First Edition

The expansion of tertiary education during the last twenty years has seen a significant growth in the number of courses during which the student is expected to undertake project work of one form or another. Although not always designated as 'research' a large proportion, if indeed not the majority, of projects require independent enquiry on the part of the student which would qualify for that description. It is hoped that this book will have something for all students whose aim is to write up and present for examination the results of projects which may last from a month or two to several years.

The aim of the book is to assist such students to manage their projects both more efficiently and more effectively. The motivation to write the book came over three years spent by the authors as Chairman and Vice-Chairman of the large doctoral programme at the University of Bradford Management Centre and their experiences as supervisors and examiners of full and part-time students working on doctoral and master's theses, master's dissertations, and undergraduate projects.

Responsibility for the co-ordination of the activities of well over 100 research degree students during these three years made it clear that although the students may be working on widely differing topics they shared many problems in common. By reflecting on the experiences of students in various fields and at various levels the authors concluded that a book which was concerned with the management of a student research project rather than with the problems arising from a particular field of research itself should have general relevance. Although the discussion must cater for the highest (that is doctoral) level it was felt that much guidance could be obtained by selective reading of the book by the student working at first degree level.

For projects which are given a mark or must be completed if a qualification is to be awarded the objective of the student is quite clear. At research degree level however, the situation, until quite recently, has been very different, with the so-called 'apprentice model' influencing attitudes. At its best the apprentice model involves a student working under the direction of a single academic who in addition to being an expert in the area of the study is skilled in research methodology and is able to motivate students to complete their thesis within a prescribed time. At its worst it implies incompetent and inadequate supervision with both student and supervisor being responsible to no-one in particular and resulting in yet another 'failure to complete'.

Although there is a slow trend to central direction or co-ordination of student research it remains the case that the vast majority of students will depend largely for success on their own resources and, as stated, it is the aim of the authors to improve both the standard of the research and the probability of timely completion of the written report by promoting self-management. Our current working environment means that we draw heavily on the social sciences for examples but hope that our earlier backgrounds in engineering and mathematics (together with not a few years in industry) will enable us to establish credibility to student researchers in a much wider field.

We have tried out our ideas on a number of colleagues and would like to express our sincere thanks to Dr Stephen Sobol and Virginia Hayden in particular who caused us to do quite a bit of rethinking. Our gratitude is extended also to Pat Corby and Nigel Howard who were kind enough to criticise certain passages, and to Anne Bennett who offered us some advice on reproduction. Additionally we recognise the valuable assistance received from the Management Centre Librarian, Neil Hunter.

A quite separate and distinct expression of thanks should be made to Marjorie Richards who compiled the first draft of the manuscript for us. Coping with contributions from two authors is by no means easy, and quite apart from typing the text she did on occasions undertake duties of a sub-editorial nature.

Our thanks are similarly extended to Majorie Kay for undertaking the heavy work involved in incorporating the final amendments into the text.

As a final point we hope that our female readers will not be offended by our use of the masculine form.

K. Howard

J. A. Sharp

1983

Preface to the Second Edition

Somewhat more than a decade after the publication of the first edition the authors are in a position to reflect on changes of significance which have occurred during the period.

In the first instance both of the authors have moved to other institutions and have been exposed to a range of additional approaches to project work.

The greatest impact on the execution of research has, however, been through developments in information technology which have enabled the process of research to be facilitated and enhanced by access to personal computers and information networks.

A further change of significance has been the growth of part-time study, of distance learning through correspondence, and distance teaching where faculty from one institution in one country spend short periods overseas in direct contact with students following their institution's programmes. All of this has led to a considerable increase in students being required to draw upon their own resources to complete their projects. Although nothing can equate with an effective supervisor, immediately accessible, we hope that the written guidance that we offer will help to compensate for any difficulties such students encounter in project work.

A notable intellectual change in the 1980s, as far as this book is concerned, has been the rise of postmodernism with its denial of the existence of a single, human-value free, 'objective' form of knowledge. From its initial beginnings in the humanities and in critical social science its ideas have found increasing support even in the philosophy of natural sciences. From the point of view of research, especially outside the hard sciences (the latter accounting for a diminishing proportion of student researchers) this has led to a discernible tendency towards 'anti-positivist' attitudes to research which emphasise the subjective nature of the interpretation of the individual researcher's research findings. Although the intellectual arguments for this position are of considerable interest at the higher levels of research, at least, they are, in our view, of limited use to the student researcher because they presuppose a familiarity with positivist approaches to science. Indeed, one of the major reasons for requiring students to undertake a research project is to provide familiarity with this approach. This book undoubtedly has a positivist orientation which is intended to support such training. We accept that student researchers may eventually go beyond positivist views but remain convinced that they do need first to familiarise themselves with what traditionally constitutes good research practice.

The continued success of the first edition and the comments of many of our colleagues who have used it encourages us in the belief that this view remains widely shared and that there is a very real need for a second edition. More even than the first it has benefitted from the comments of our students, our immediate colleagues, and colleagues in other institutions both within and outside the UK. To single out particular individuals would be invidious but we would like to dedicate this second edition to all of them.

J. A. Sharp

K. Howard

1996

Part A

Preparation

1

Research and the Research Student

THE AIM OF THIS BOOK

Many degree and diploma students become involved in projects of one kind or another. In some instances the project forms a relatively minor part of a course, in other instances the project is virtually the whole basis on which an award is made. At either extreme, the primary purpose in making a research project part of the qualification is to foster the personal development of the student. With a research project, at whatever level, the agenda is set by the student to a greater extent than is possible in the ordinary taught course. Similarly, the student bears responsibility for the quality of learning that takes place in the project and for the eventual written outcome.

Whether the student is seeking to write a report at undergraduate level, a dissertation at master's level, or a thesis at doctoral level, two key factors which must be borne in mind are timing and quality. In some instances the time constraint is inflexible. If the report is not presented by a particular date the qualification sought is not obtained. When deadlines of this nature apply, compliance with them can lead to content which is sub-standard if an ineffective approach is adopted.

Recognition that PhD and masters' theses must be of high quality sometimes results in inordinate lengths of time being taken for completion. Indeed, the task of finishing theses proves to be too much for many students and has been the subject of some discussion in the UK for many years. A survey[1] conducted in the UK during the early 1980s found that although achievement was a little better in the subject areas covered by the, then, Science Research Council – now the Engineering and Physical Sciences Research Council (EPSRC) – only about 30 per cent of students who had been researching full-time in the social sciences were awarded higher degrees (in some cases up to a decade after commencing their studies). A consequence of findings such as these was to generate substantial pressures to ensure more timely completion by publicly funded research students. Later in the decade, as pressures for quality audit in higher education grew, it was realised that similar problems of unwarranted delays in the completion of research projects were also occurring in many coursework based degrees and diplomas. This problem of delay in completion is, then, a general one, which is one of the major issues with which we are concerned.

It is assumed that admission procedures ensure that student entrants have the potential to complete their studies satisfactorily. What, therefore, are the reasons why sub-standard work is submitted or students fail to complete? Much of the explanation must lie in the inability of students to plan and control – that is, to manage – their work. By 'manage' we mean the manipulation of all resources available to students, both material and human. The most important of the human resources being the person who is, in many cases, designated to supervise the student.

Our aim is to provide degree and diploma students (and their supervisors) with guidance in the identification of feasible research projects and on how to complete them.

It is recognised that the demands made of students in terms of training and quality will vary enormously according to the level at which the research is undertaken, but also it is recognised that all research projects have certain features in common. We feel, though, that it would be unsatisfactory to adopt an 'average' approach and thus we will attempt to satisfy the needs of the highest level of student research. It is hoped that students working at other levels will be able to find the guidance apposite for them, skimming over those sections of the chapters that are particularly pertinent for research degree students and concentrating on those sections directed to lower levels of study. To that end we have indicated in the summary which appears at the end of each chapter the major differences between research students and course-based students as far as the material of that chapter is concerned. Where possible, the book is addressed to all types of student researcher and will often refer to the 'research report' rather than to 'thesis, dissertation, or report'. If the remarks are directed specifically to the research degree student 'thesis' will be employed, while 'dissertation' will be used to refer to the type of research report produced in connection with taught courses.

Some of the particular needs of the part-time student are considered where these differ from those of the full-time student.

THE STRUCTURE OF THE BOOK

Almost by definition, research is not a straightforward process made up of a series of distinct steps each of which is part of a clearly defined sequence. Quite apart from opportunities to undertake several activities at the same time, blind alleys will from time to time necessitate a return to an earlier stage.

This does not mean, however, that students should use the inevitability of uncertainty as an excuse for not adopting a systematic and logical approach to their work. The latter is the essence of planning, a process demanded by all project work.

This book has been divided into three parts, each of which is concerned with a broad aspect of student research. It can be argued that certain activities are more or less common to research regardless of the field in which it is pursued. Thus, all students have to select (or at the very least understand the implications of) a topic. They will then need to use the particular skills and techniques which the specific nature of their research demands. Finally, they will have to undertake their work within a certain environment before reporting upon the outcome of their studies. Figure 1.1 shows the extent to which it is possible to cover, in a book aimed at student researchers in general, the range of problems encountered by the student at each of these stages of their research.

The inference to be drawn from Figure 1.1 is that both the preparation and production phases of student research have (for a given level) much that is common across all research fields. That which primarily distinguishes one type of research from another is the activities needed to track down, collect, and analyse data. These activities, as depicted in Figure 1.1, are the subject of Part B which comprises the chapters on analysing the data, and gathering the data. In addition to the present chapter the other chapters to be found in Part A are selecting and justifying a research topic, planning the research project and literature searching. Part C, which is concerned with research output, includes chapters on executing the research and presenting the results of the research.

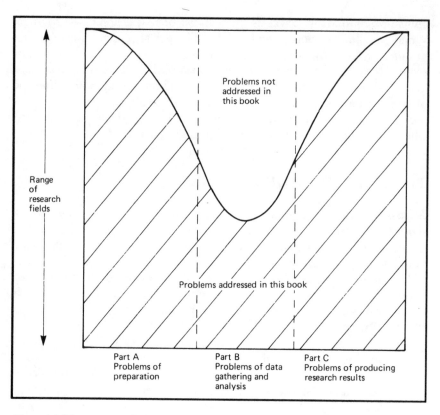

Figure 1.1 The extent to which problems common to a range of student research are addressed in this book

Part B presented the greatest difficulty in our attempt to be relevant to the broad field of student research. We have, however, concentrated on the management of data gathering and analysis. In our coverage of analytical methods we recognise our bias towards the social sciences but would claim that many of the techniques referred to have a broader application not least because of the growing importance of subjects such as management in fields of study like engineering or environmental studies.

We do not propose that this book should be read from cover to cover at one go: much will depend on the experience which has been accumulated by the student. Sections of the book have been designed to impart skills (such as those needed in literature searching and formal planning), others to add to the student's knowledge (for example, the chapter on analytical techniques), and still others to describe the environment in which the research will be conducted (for example, the problems encountered in executing research). Thus, the book may be seen as a reference work, to be picked up at intervals during the course of the study.

WHAT IS RESEARCH?

Most people associate the word 'research' with activities substantially removed from day-to-day life and which are pursued by outstandingly gifted persons with an unusual level of commitment. There is, of course, a good deal of truth in this viewpoint, but we would argue that the pursuit of research is not restricted to this type of person and indeed can prove to be a stimulating and satisfying experience for many people with a trained and enquiring mind.

It is the case that the major contributions to knowledge do tend to come from highly intelligent and committed investigators. Significant advances are, however, the 'tip of the iceberg' insofar as the total volume of effort is concerned. Indeed, top-class investigators often fail to achieve firm conclusions, while by far the greatest amount of activity is much less ambitious in nature. Fundamental additions to knowledge frequently draw upon prior studies of restricted scope carried out perhaps by workers of limited research experience.

Thus, if it is accepted that lower level work and training are prerequisites for the expansion of knowledge it would seem that 'research' is an activity which can be undertaken at any time in an individual's life when reasoned thinking is possible.

We define research as

> seeking through methodical processes to add to one's own body of knowledge and, hopefully, to that of others, by the discovery of non-trivial facts and insights.

At the higher levels of student research a necessary condition of success is that the research actually adds to existing knowledge rather than simply leading to an increase in an individual's understanding of previous work. This requirement will be considered at some length in the next chapter.

SOME FEATURES OF STUDENT RESEARCH

The concern of this book is, then, with student research projects and, although a commonness of process is evident, account must be taken of constraints which are imposed by the particular environment in which the student will be working. For example, all or some of the following factors may be relevant.

1. The research topic may be imposed on the student.
2. The research (if it is to be rated a success) must be completed within a given time period: for example, four weeks, six months, or three years.
3. Funds for experiments, travel, postage and so on may be limited or even non-existent.
4. The results of the research must be presented in a specified manner.
5. The student may possibly have to relate to an academic supervisor who is not interested in, or may lack competence within, the field of study chosen.

Research work outside the educational system is primarily concerned with adding to knowledge. Within the educational system, however, an additional factor is present, namely the need to demonstrate research competence. Indeed, at all levels except the higher degrees by research, the need to demonstrate research competence outweighs that of adding to knowledge. Short comments on the various levels are apposite at this stage. A closer look at the criteria to be satisfied at each level will be taken in Chapter 8.

First Degree and Diploma Projects

This category includes studies which form part of courses at the first level of higher education, many of which are referred to as 'degree equivalent'. Although analytical rigour is not usually demanded, independent enquiry and exercise of judgement is expected as, too, is a reasonable standard of presentation of the results. In some cases, students will be expected to display competence in specific areas – for example, the ability to collect data. It is customary for the projects to comprise part of the student's assessment. Rarely will projects represent less than 10 per cent of a particular year's assessment. In some instances (for example, the sandwich course with a whole year in industry) the project may be the only academic assessment made during a part of the course.

It may be argued that if students are capable of independent enquiry they should also be capable of planning how the enquiry should be pursued. There is some force to this argument but what is often not appreciated by tutor or student is that there is much more to research methodology than may initially be supposed. Time devoted to studying the research process is therefore a worthwhile investment.

Although research is a vital element of further education it should not be assumed that all tutors have had direct research experience. True, academic staff may have been overseeing first degree or diploma projects for many years but this does not guarantee competence in research methods.

Postgraduate Dissertations

A feature of recent decades has been the growth in masters' degrees obtained by 'study and dissertation'. Thus, typically, a one year full-time course may comprise nine months of taught courses, with three months being available for a project to be written up as a dissertation. A period of the order of three months is insufficient to enable tasks to be undertaken which will form a sufficient basis for the 'thesis' required for the master's or for doctoral research degrees. Little more than a descriptive account can be given of some line of enquiry and the absence of validation and generalisation distinguishes dissertations of this type from the thesis of the pure research degrees.

Where the elapsed time made available for a postgraduate dissertation is rigidly controlled, students need to plan their project very carefully and in particular should avoid being over-ambitious. There are, however, some courses which permit a student to take much longer over their dissertation (possibly to include an additional two or more years of part-time study). Although the dissertation may then be more substantial due to a greater opportunity to collect data, the probability of completion can be reduced by the competing demands of employment.

Masters' Degrees by Research

The requirements for the successful completion of projects at master's degree level are in some respects difficult to establish. In particular, the degree of originality needed and the extent to which generalisation of the results is possible may be unclear. At the very least any conclusions which are reached must be capable of validation even if no attempt to generalise them is made. Certainly, the contribution to knowledge of a master's thesis should be of some significance, particularly in view of the fact that it is likely to serve as a reference work.

The thesis will probably be externally assessed when attention will be given to the thoroughness of the research as indicated by the bibliography, in addition to the analysis, conclusions, and the standard of layout.

Doctoral Projects

This is the highest level of student research activity and, although students may go on into careers in research itself, the doctoral project will probably be the last occasion when they are formally assessed on the grounds of both research competence and originality. The major aim is to present a thesis for external assessment which will prove to be satisfactory in both respects. A subsequent aim may be, through publication, to become recognised as an expert in the field of study chosen. The requirements are, inevitably, more demanding than those of the master's degree by research: for example, the University of Kent (1995) requires that:

> The thesis should be an original contribution to knowledge or understanding in the field under investigation and should demonstrate the candidate's ability to test ideas, whether his/her own or those of others, and to understand the relationship of the theme of investigation to a wider field of knowledge. It should be of such scholarly merit as would on that ground justify its publication either as submitted or in an abridged form.

The achievement of a doctorate in any subject will represent a major investment in terms of time and effort. Usually, the process requires at least three years and there is no guarantee of a successful outcome. Failure to complete is a disturbing feature of doctoral study; a major aim of this book, as stated earlier, is to reduce the chances of this occurring.

Projects and the Part-time Student

During the 1980s, the number of part-time programmes in higher education, particularly at master's level, increased dramatically in the UK. By implication, students in this category devote part of their non-leisure time to academic study and the remainder usually to employment. Predominantly, they are managers or professionals who wish to add to their career potential by supplementing a qualification at degree or equivalent level with a higher degree.

Although there is a significant trend towards the inclusion of formally assessed projects within first degree programmes, which has exposed students to aspects of the research process, an equally important trend has been the growth of masters' projects undertaken by part-time students in employment. The dual status of student and employee provides opportunities not hitherto available, as the researcher might well be in a position to move beyond recommendations to assuming responsibility for change within the organisation. If this is the case, *action research*, rather than *applied research* is in prospect. In the following section, 'Classifying Research', comment will be made on this approach which enables students to cause change within an organisation.

Whilst positive advantages can be created by part-time study, difficulties can arise, often created by the absence of a high measure of contact with faculty and fellow students. The motivation needed to sustain research effort over, possibly, a five-year period has to be of a high order. Access to facilities and supervisors is much more restricted than is the case with full-time students and the value of self-management of the research project is therefore greater. (Further comments are made on this aspect in Chapter 7; see 'Working with a Supervisor'.)

CLASSIFYING RESEARCH

The majority of student research projects are completed without much thought being given to the type of study which has been followed. In this section we examine research from four points of view:
1. The field of research.
2. The purpose of research.
3. The approach to research.
4. The nature of research.

Each of the four will have a different bearing on the successful management and completion of a study.

The Field of Research

Research is most frequently classified by field but this is largely little more than a labelling device which enables groups of researchers with similar interests to be identified.

Fields are often grouped for administrative purposes into categories such as the social sciences, life sciences, physical sciences, engineering, and the humanities. A small proportion of research may fall into more than one of these categories. This is particularly so at the higher levels of research where the project may often involve the translation of ideas from one field to another.

As far as this book is concerned, classification by field is of the least relevance. This does not mean that researchers do not need a comprehensive knowledge of their own subject. Rather, it reflects our intention to concentrate on those aspects of research that are common to most fields and the majority of research projects.

The Purpose of Research

A research project has many different purposes. Four common ones are:

a) to review existing knowledge;
b) to describe some situation or problem;
c) the construction of something novel;
d) explanation.

The review of existing research findings is a very common type of student research project, particularly in diploma, undergraduate and taught masters' courses. It can provide excellent research training with the added advantage that it requires little by way of resources save access to a good library.

Although descriptive research may appear to be less demanding than other types this is often far from the case. However, due to the lack of knowledge of a subject or research methods, or both, it is quite possible that the purpose of a student's first study will be to describe something, particularly if there has been little previous research in the field.

The construction of something which is useful is an outcome of research which increasingly is being favoured by sponsors. In the physical sciences and engineering, students may be recruited to pursue a particular line of research such as the construction of a new type of optical system.

Explanation is the ideal of all professional research workers. It is only when causal rather than statistical relationships are identified that generalisations may be made or laws formulated.

The Approach to Research

Another way of classifying research is by the major research approach used. Approaches that are frequently used in student research are the laboratory experiment, the field experiment, the case study, and the survey.

The laboratory experiment is relevant to all the major research subject groupings (with the possible exception of the humanities) but is primarily used in physical science, life science and engineering research.

In the context of research method a field experiment suggests that an investigation subjected to certain controls is conducted in non-laboratory conditions. For example, a new detergent may have been developed as a result of laboratory research and a field experiment may be set up to see how well it works in actual use.

The case study is often the basis for student projects, particularly in the social sciences. In this type of research students may spend a period in an organisation and the comments and conclusions which emerge will be based solely on their experiences in that setting.

There is some connection between the survey and the field experiment in that techniques relevant to the latter may be used in the former. However, whereas the field experiment implies controls and need not necessarily involve people the survey is viewed separately here as a method of extracting attitudes and opinions from a sizeable sample of respondents.

The Nature of Research

Our fourth view of research is by nature and type of contribution to knowledge. A further label is the 'level' at which research is conducted. Figure 1.2 includes classifications proposed during a period of approximately twenty years culminating in 1992. We have made an attempt to categorise by the three levels proposed by Grinyer (1981), Clark (1972), and the UK Universities Funding Council (1992), but we make no claim for exact comparability.

Grinyer suggests that the opportunity of a truly original contribution to knowledge (which is related to our concept of value to be presented in Chapter 2) decreases as we go down the list, whereas the prospect of successful completion increases. Both Clark and Grinyer were mainly concerned with research in the social sciences, whereas the definition proposed by the UK Universities Funding Council is intended to cover all fields of research.

Our three levels of research indicated in Figure 1.2 are, then, defined as follows.

Level 1
This is concerned with the development of theory, without an attempt being

Clark	Grinyer[†]	UK Universities	Level
Pure Basic Research	Pure Theory	Basic Research	1
Basic Objective Research	Testing of Existing Theory	Strategic Research	2
Evaluation Research	Description of the State of the Art	Applied Research	3
Applied Research	Specific Problem Solution		
Action Research			

Figure 1.2 Classification by the nature of research. After: Clark (1972) as elaborated by Bennett (1983); Grinyer (1981); UK Universities Funding Council (1992). [†]Professor P. H. Grinyer, suggested this classification at the 5th National Conference on Doctoral Research in Management and Industrial Relations, University of Aston Management Centre on 6/7 April 1981

made to link this to practice. The findings are usually reported in learned journals.

Level 2
This might take the outputs from Level 1 and seek to draw general conclusions about the prospects for application. Academics will be interested in the findings, but so too will be relevant professionals working in industry, commerce or government who will wish to evaluate the potential for transfer of the findings to their own settings.

Level 3
This embraces research undertaken with a specific practical objective in mind. For some purposes, as Grinyer suggests, it may realistically be divided into three sub-levels with the 'Evaluation/Description' sub-level possibly overlapping our Level 2. 'Applied Research', at the middle of Level 3, is an activity in which professional and student researchers might be involved, with the output being recommendations for action by others. The final sub-level, 'Action Research', as its name implies, leads to change, and the researcher is a participant in the change process rather than an observer of it. Clearly, this will demand skills and experience which many students will not possess.

THE PROCESS OF RESEARCH

Deeper understanding of research will come from consideration of the process by which it is conducted and, of course, from embarking upon an actual study.

We would argue that, despite the wide variety of field, purpose, and approach, some common features of the research process can be identified, and that if a student departs significantly from a general systematic approach the research will be inefficient and quite possibly ineffectual.

Several conceptual models designed to serve as a basis for a systematic approach to research have been proposed. Rummel and Ballaine (1963), drawing upon suggestions made by J. L. Kelly and J. Dewey, proposed a model with six steps: a felt need; the problem; the hypothesis; collection of data; concluding belief; and, general value of conclusion.

The model outlined in Figure 1.3 demonstrates some similarities with Rummel and Ballaine's proposal but contains different emphases. Steps 1 to 4 of the model may be described as the planning phase, with the remaining steps, numbers 5 to 7 as the effectuation phase. Much work, notably a search of the literature, is involved in the planning phase, and this should be highly

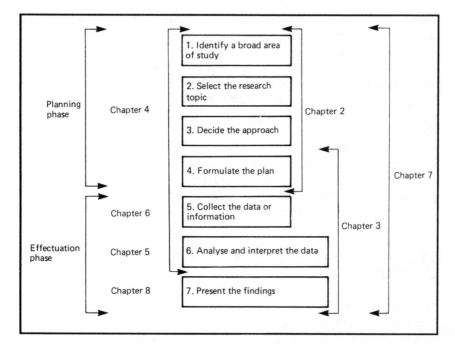

Figure 1.3 A systematic approach to research – a process model. (The chapter numbers indicate where each step is discussed in this book.)

relevant to parts of the effectuation phase. Until the end of Step 4 it is often the case that the researcher finds it necessary to return to one of the earlier steps before proceeding further. Reversion from the effectuation to the planning phase may, however, prejudice the prospects of completion given the time constraints within which most students must work.

Each step should be viewed as being less reversible as progress is made from the beginning of the project to the end. A research project, however, always involves novelty – at least for the student – and the researcher will frequently find a need to return to an earlier step because later experience has shown how the project can be more closely defined. It will be appreciated that such a return, though it may expedite future work, does not constitute progress. Too frequent reversion to earlier steps is a sure sign that the initial steps of the planning phase have been inadequately carried out.

The seven steps in Figure 1.3 should be comprehensible to all students though the relative importance of individual stages will differ from one project to another according to the aims and approach as we shall see later. The figure contains reference to Chapters 2 to 8 indicating where each of the steps will be considered in some depth. Although during a project the research plan will precede data collection and analysis, an initial treatment of these two latter steps is given earlier in this book so that students will have some understanding of the methodology and tools of research before they decide upon the direction and duration of their study.

Careful compliance with the model should considerably improve the prospects of successfully completing a piece of research. It is difficult to avoid the temptation to skip steps or to proceed having only partially completed stages. Thus, though the research topic may have been only vaguely formulated a student may commence to organise a project in the hope that an appropriate topic will emerge after data have been collected; or a researcher may reach conclusions after collecting only part of the data planned and, as a result, discontinue further collection, only to find that the initial interpretation was incorrect.

THE SUCCESSFUL COMPLETION OF STUDENT RESEARCH

One immediate question is: 'What is success?'

Below master's level success is measured by formal recognition that examination requirements have been satisfied. At master's and doctoral level, when dissertations and theses are to be displayed in libraries, success often means also that students are satisfied that their own standards have been met.

A further question is: 'What are the factors that affect success as thus defined?'

A useful vehicle for providing an answer is a survey of PhD students in which the authors were involved. Stimulated by the widespread concern over completion rates (particularly in the social sciences) the Doctoral Committee at the University of Bradford Management Centre devised a questionnaire and sent it to 45 students whose full-time studies had terminated and to 28 full-time students who were currently doing research. From the former category 19 replies (42 per cent) were received and 18 (64 per cent) were received from the latter category. The 19 students who had ceased to research full-time included 10 who had transferred to part-time registration in an endeavour to complete their studies.

Students were asked to indicate for 20 factors whether these had affected research progress beneficially, neutrally, or adversely. The factors included:
a) the subject chosen;
b) the research design;
c) quality of supervision;
d) quantity of supervision;

e) availability of funds;
f) teaching;
g) running tutorials;
h) writing papers;
i) attending conferences;
j) own level of motivation;
k) own abilities.

The implications of these and other factors will be examined in other parts of this book, particularly in Chapter 7.

In order to effect a measure of interpretation, beneficial responses were scored +1, neutral responses O, and adverse responses –1. By simple addition a total score was obtained for each factor, and factors were on this basis assigned to the categories of those having an adverse effect on progress and those having a beneficial effect. The results are shown in Figure 1.4 ranked for each category in descending order.

In Chapter 7 obstacles to successful completion are examined under four

Category of respondent		
Students who had completed their doctorates	Ex full-time students who had not yet completed	Current full-time students
Adverse Effects		
None	Availability of funds	Teaching Running tutorials
Beneficial Effects		
Own level of motivation	Writing papers	Attending conferences
Own abilities	Own abilities	Own level of motivation
Writing papers	Quality of supervision	Quality of supervision
Attending conferences	Quality of supervision	Writing papers
Quality of supervision	Own level of motivation	The subject chosen

Figure 1.4 A survey response indicating factors which influence student research progress

different types of problem: individual centred; supervisor related; research related; and general support (see Figure 7.1).

Different perceptions will be noted from the above rankings where, for example, successful students rated four individually centred activities as having been most beneficial to completion. It should be borne in mind that the rankings were derived from a total of 37 responses and that the point of the exercise was to provide, rapidly, a basis for action. Nevertheless, the information derived was interesting and reference will be made again to the survey later in this book.

Of some interest here is that only in the case of students who were currently researching full-time was the subject chosen fairly beneficial to progress. Even for those who had successfully completed their studies the factor was located no higher than the mid-point of the rankings and thus does not appear in Figure 1.4. As might be expected the nature of the subject chosen was ranked even lower (twelfth of twenty) following the aggregation of the responses of erstwhile full-time students who had yet to complete their research.

TYPES OF RESEARCH AND THIS BOOK

Having examined research from four different viewpoints it will be noted that only in one case was it necessary to refer to the subject of the research. Even when research is classified by field, there are still many acceptable styles of research project.

This in our view justifies our attempt to produce a book that meets the large number of needs that are common to most student researchers. In particular we have drawn heavily on the process model of research (Figure 1.3) in the organisation of the remaining chapters.

This chapter commenced with a reference to the two key factors of timing and quality, and the implications of being unable to satisfy the former are readily apparent – that is, no report, no qualification. We believe that by the adoption of careful management the prospects of earlier and successful completion will be much enhanced.

What is more difficult to grasp is how the quality criterion can be satisfied and, indeed, how it can be measured. It should be evident from studying the different types of research that many varieties exist. There are, for example, combinations of research approach and purpose that are legitimate in a particular field and each combination will carry with it different implications in terms of constraints and opportunities for research with potential quality. Which is selected will depend in part on student preference and attitude towards risk. An important point to stress is that, where research degrees are

18

concerned, as far as is possible the topic should be chosen by students rather than being foisted upon them, otherwise motivation (which was rated highly in the survey referred to above) will be difficult to sustain.

In Chapter 8 we shall be considering the range of requirements which need to be satisfied at the different levels of research. These will provide a fairly specific list of criteria against which a prospective topic can be evaluated. A rather different view of quality will be taken in Chapter 2 when we will suggest that research may be judged in terms of its potential value and the surprise element which will arise from a change in previously held beliefs. Clearly, research which is likely to be rated lowly in terms of both value and surprise will have limited prospects of success at research degree level, even though the methodological quality proves to be high.

An important factor that needs to be taken into account in assessing quality is that value and surprise do not exist in isolation – they are subjective. This points to a need for the student to give some thought to the person or the type of person who will assess the research.

The aim should be, therefore, to maximise the probability of timely and successful completion by identifying as soon as possible a research topic with high potential quality. This, taking account of the resources available to the student, should appear, with good management, capable of being concluded within whatever period is available. As in good management, the identification and control of quality is just as important as the planning and control of resources. All of these aspects are examined in the chapters which follow.

THE REQUIREMENTS TO BE SATISFIED

At several points in this chapter we have stressed that forward planning should feature throughout the research. It is, sensible, however, that before embarking upon what we describe in Figure 1.3 as the effectuation phase the student should reflect at some length on the activities to be undertaken and the requirements to be satisfied. As far as is possible a clear and unambiguous vision of what will be needed should be sustained throughout the research.

As the student moves beyond planning there is a clear prospect that immersion in literature searching, primary data gathering and analysis will cause sight to be lost of the totality of the research. We suggest that writing should commence as soon as is realistically possible but would argue strongly that the student should view the separate chapters as an integral part of a final whole. Far too frequently examiners are presented with reports, dissertations, or theses which are disjointed, inconsistent or fall short on logical and coherent argument.

In Chapter 2 a logical structure of a thesis is proposed in which content is allocated into six sections. Here, a few words are appropriate on what constitutes a good thesis, etc., a standard which the student should seek to attain.

The Aim of the Research

A good deal of the book up to this point has addressed this issue. The researcher and, subsequently, the reader should be convinced that the study is well worth undertaking. Throughout the programme the student should never lose sight of the aim; everything that is written should be subordinated to this.

Appropriate Use of the Literature

At lower levels of research recognition may be given to an effective review of the literature on its own account, albeit that it must be linked to the study. Research theses demand full integration of existing literature at all stages of the thesis. It is likely that a chapter of a thesis will be devoted to establishing the existing state of knowledge as a datum but references to the works of others should, as appropriate, appear throughout the chapter.

If full impact is to be achieved the student must actively seek conflicting views on a particular issue. Evaluating and synthesising the views of others when embarking upon an attempt to add to knowledge in a given field calls for considerable critical insight – and in historical studies may, indeed, be the whole basis for satisfying a research objective.

Research Methodology

This must be justified. The researcher has now to identify different and potentially applicable designs and then explain the reasons for choosing a particular methodology – which may involve several different approaches. Thus, an in-depth case study may be supplemented by a mailed question-naire, or a number of interviews may be followed by a series of research workshops.

The researcher must address the question: 'What bias might arise from conclusions reached by adopting a certain methodology?', not least because that might well be a matter raised by an examiner.

Presentation of the Research Results

The completion of the data gathering phase (which it is to be hoped will not involve too much revisiting) will see the researcher in the possession of a substantial, even vast, amount of data, intelligence and information. The seeds of the analysis are contained herein and no small measure of skill is needed to order and present the results in a form which is consistent with the thesis or dissertation.

Clearly, it is impossible to include the primary data whether, for example, these be instrument readings or questionnaire responses within the writing; but it must always be understood that examiners may insist upon, and other researchers might request, access to the data collected. The argument will be sustained if simple data are included in appendices, but it is customary to process and present data in such a way that their interpretation is possible from the text. Graphics, tables and the outcome of mathematical or statistical analysis may be employed to achieve the desired effect.

Analysis of the Results

Although the analysis will have commenced with the initial processing of the primary data the value of the research will be dependent upon the researcher's interpretation, leading to conclusions and recommendations. It will need to be appreciated that only rarely is the researcher confronted with a 'puzzle', for which there is a solution. More often there is a 'problem' in respect of which a number of conclusions might be possible.

In a large part the ability of the researcher will determine what conclusions are drawn from the data. It is possible that quite different findings would be reached in certain cases by different analysts. An example is the range of sub-optima encountered in complex simulations. The quality of a thesis, in particular, would be undermined if there was evidence that the researcher had adopted a 'blinkered' approach and had failed to review and explore alternative possibilities.

It is always sensible to comment on the limitations of the analysis. At higher levels this may be due to a rather limited response rate to a questionnaire; at lower levels it could be that the student felt that the research aim could be satisfied by employing simple rather than more advanced statistical techniques. The student should, however, never leave the analytical phase without feeling confident that the aim of the research has been satisfied sufficiently for the qualification being pursued.

Conclusions and Recommendations

The thesis or dissertation ends with conclusions reached by the researcher. These should be presented with clarity and emphasis and should be related to the aims as stated at the outset. It is the duty of students working at postgraduate level to identify prospects for further research to provide impetus for those who will tread the same path.

Using 'level' as defined in Figure 1.2, conclusions should be followed by recommendations for application for those categories of research falling within Level 3 – for example, 'Applied Research' and 'Action Research'.

At this stage it is suggested that the student should refer to Figure 8.1 which lists the criteria to be satisfied for successful completion of the different levels of degree. In addition to satisfying the requirements through logically ordered writing in the six areas referred to above it behoves the student be aware continuously of the relevant qualitative criteria included in Figure 8.1.

CHAPTER SUMMARY

RESEARCH IS: a process by which researchers extend their knowledge and possibly that of the whole community. Student research is encountered from first degree or diploma level through to doctoral level.

It involves the development of research competence and additions to knowledge. In general the former is more important at lower levels, the latter at higher levels.

RESEARCH CAN BE CLASSIFIED:
    by field
    by purpose
    by approach
    by nature
Combinations of these categories create a large number of different types of research project. Not all are feasible given the student's expertise and the resources and time available.

THE IDENTIFICATION OF A GOOD RESEARCH TOPIC: requires that thought be devoted to its quality which will be assessed by taking into account such factors as standards, value and the element of surprise.

A SUCCESSFUL OUTCOME TO THE RESEARCH PROJECT: is more likely if it is conducted as a series of logically ordered steps which in large part are common to all types of student study. A range of factors (many of which are under the personal control of the student) will have a bearing on the outcome.

UNDERSTANDING THE REQUIREMENTS: of theses, etc., is essential to a successful outcome.

2

Selecting and Justifying a Research Project

Because of the very different time-scales of research degree and dissertation projects there are significant differences in the way that the choice of research topic is made. Accordingly, we will treat the two types separately. Before doing so, however, it is worth noting a common factor concerned with benefit to the student which should be taken into account irrespective of the type of research project.

PERSONAL VALUE OF THE TOPIC

The educational benefit of conducting a research study has already been noted. However, it is up to the individual student to obtain the maximum self-development from the research project. A key factor in this respect is the choice of research topic. Other things being equal, a project that is closely allied with the student's career aims is better than one that has no obvious relevance. Thus students who intend to pursue careers as, for example, consultants, are clearly well advised to familiarise themselves with the 'state of the art' in some field which has high relevance to the future rather than studying a topic which has little interest to practitioners.

SELECTING A DISSERTATION TOPIC

The primary aim of a dissertation is to develop the individual student's ability to conduct independent research. It is not expected to make a significant contribution to knowledge; indeed, many good dissertations do no more than review systematically, and impose some structure on, a field of interest.

We have already suggested that, in many cases, the student who is involved in a research project for a taught course will find that a list of topics is made available by academic staff. The student can choose from this list in the light of personal interest, career plans, etc. In such cases, it is safe to assume that the topic is viable provided that the research project is conducted competently.

In other cases, especially where the course is part-time and students are sponsored by their employers, the dissertation is often expected to provide a solution to some problem in their own organisation. In our experience, the selection of a dissertation topic under these circumstances has something in common with the topic selection process for the research student as discussed below. Considerations of novelty are not important because the topic will be specific to the sponsoring organisation. There is, however, a need to ensure that the dissertation topic is consistent with the academic aims and standards of the course.

RESEARCH DEGREE TOPIC SELECTION IN OUTLINE

Until a topic has been selected the research cannot be said to be underway. Despite this obvious comment it is not uncommon to find full-time research students who have yet to make a real start on their study a year after commencement. True, they may have done an enormous amount of reading, thinking, or travelling, but in no sense could this be seen as making significant progress, which only really occurs from Step 3 of Figure 1.3 onwards. Research plans may founder because of the unexpected but this possibility should not be confused with an inability to identify an appropriate topic with reasonable speed; yet, in our experience, this is one of the most common problems encountered in student research.

The prospects of selecting a suitable topic will be enhanced if a systematic approach is adopted. Figure 2.1 expands primarily upon Step 3 of Figure 1.3. In the first place the broad area of study will suggest likely supervisors, who normally will prefer to supervise studies in fields which are related to their main interests. Thus, a lecturer in marketing who has inclinations towards quantitative methods may be prepared to undertake supervision of a student who wishes to develop a mathematical advertising model but may not be prepared to supervise a student who wishes to research into the development of consumerism.

The significance of the various stages included in Figure 2.1 will vary considerably according to the level at which the research is to be undertaken. An undergraduate may be presented with a research topic (such as an analysis of a company's distribution system) which would obviate the need for thought to be given to any of the stages. By contrast, each of these stages will feature prominently during the early part of a doctoral study, consuming perhaps 20 per cent of the time ultimately spent on the research.

APPOINTING THE SUPERVISOR

Most books on research methods pay little regard to the role of the supervisor in research studies. In part, this is because such books are addressed to all researchers, many of whom are solely accountable for the work they do. Almost by definition, however, any 'student' within a formalised education system must be complemented by a 'teacher'. In the particular context of student research activity the 'teacher' is usually referred to as the 'supervisor', although other descriptions such as 'project director' may be encountered. In this book 'supervisor' will be used to imply the individual to whom the student will turn for regular guidance. It is, nevertheless, appreciated that many students will receive a minimum of supervision during their projects and we will seek to provide guidance in these situations.

More is written in Chapter 7 on the relationship between the student and the supervisor. Comments in this chapter will be limited to the supervisor's role up to the point when the topic is finally agreed and the research proposal accepted. The extent of the dialogue between student and supervisor will normally be related to the level at which the research is being undertaken. Thus, academic staff may have a list of topics which are appropriate for students below research degree level whereas research students are more likely to have a clearer idea as to what they would like to do. Although topic selection at research degree level may be an arduous process the likelihood is that the precise topic which eventually emerges will in large part have been identified by the student, and as such will provide an opportunity to establish an academic reputation in a specific area.

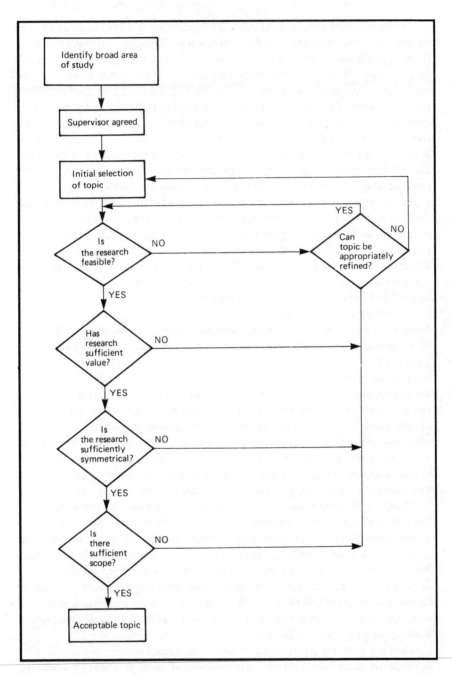

Figure 2.1 The process of topic selection

The 'apprentice model' in which a doctoral student relates directly to one, occasionally two, but rarely more, supervisor(s) throughout the whole of the project (with which the supervisor is concerned from the outset) is traditional in the UK educational system. By contrast, North American doctoral students attend taught courses for the first half or even two-thirds of their period of study before commencing their projects under the direction of a member of staff. This model is increasingly being adopted in the UK with the first year of PhD studies being devoted primarily to taught courses. Indeed, this process has been given some encouragement by the introduction of one year Master of Research degrees aimed at providing research training as proposed in the 1993 UK White Paper on science policy.[1]

At the outset, however, doctoral research students should recognise that the thesis eventually written should be seen as their work. Whereas craftsmen may work alongside their apprentices throughout the period of their indenture, and may well be associated with the output of their joint endeavours, academic supervisors must gradually 'stand back' from doctoral students' research as it progresses; it is not their contribution to knowledge that will ultimately be assessed but that of the students themselves.

In the case of undergraduate and postgraduate taught course projects, it is normal for the student to have only limited access to a supervisor. A 'budget' of a few hours of a supervisor's time is usually the best that can be expected. The input of a supervisor, at this level, is usually confined to ensuring that the student conducts the research satisfactorily and that the research report is properly structured. It is relatively rare that there is any need for the supervisor to have a deep knowledge of the subject under study. At research degree level, however, both student and supervisor should share common interests. The problem of matching the interests of student and supervisor is a feature of the apprentice model and can result in strong candidates being lost to research or, equally unsatisfactorily, embarking upon a line of research to which they are not fully committed. A clear advantage of models of study which delay the setting up of a formal student/supervisor relationship is the opportunity which arises for 'breaking the ice' before commitment is made.

The opportunity cost of pursuing a research study full-time for from one to three years (that is the 'cost' of not doing what otherwise might have been done) may be very high if a successful outcome is not achieved. In this respect the importance to research students of obtaining an appropriate supervisor cannot be overstated. It would be the first indication of bad management of their research if students were not to obtain answers to the following questions about prospective supervisors:

1. What are their records in terms of student completions?
2. What are their views on the management of student research – and, in particular, the supervisor's role in it?

3. How eminent are they in their specialisms?
4. In addition to being knowledgeable about their subjects have they high competence in research methodology?
5. How accessible are they likely to be?

Since individuals respond in different ways to the uncertainties of research, students will need to base their decision, in part, on the type of relationship to which they respond best. Thus, the highly creative, independent student might put most emphasis on Question 3, whereas a student who responds best to a fair degree of direction will probably place more weight on Questions 2 and 4.

If students are intending to conduct their studies part-time they should recognise that supervisors will often feel less committed. Although, in the UK, the apprentice model will still normally apply, it will need to take account of the greater duration of the research which will render the findings both remote and uncertain. Part-time study can be very demanding but can be much facilitated if students are prepared to sustain a strong initiative in their dealings with their supervisor.

INITIAL SELECTION OF A TOPIC

It would be almost tautological to claim that the eventual successful completion of a research study will be seen to have depended on the selection of an appropriate topic. For each student however a range of possible topics will exist and some will prove to be more 'appropriate' than others. The possibility that a student who has been accepted by an institution should fail due to an inability to identify a workable topic is wholly inconsistent with the responsibility which the institution has itself in this matter. Nevertheless, the student, particularly at the higher levels, has a significant part to play in topic selection and it is our contention that by adopting a thorough and well ordered approach the chances of selecting a topic which will enhance completion prospects will be much improved. In what follows we are proposing a mechanism which should greatly assist in the identification of a line of study which will be consistent with the student's interests and abilities.

Figure 2.1 suggests that a logical sequence should be followed before a topic is finally selected. In practice, researchers will probably subject their ideas to the tests indicated without necessarily being aware that they are doing so in a particular order. Nevertheless, before finally selecting a topic it should be rigorously exposed to the tests listed.

The first step is to identify areas which seem to have potential. The super-

visor should, of course, be involved at this stage and may in fact have a ready-made topic which appeals to the student. If this is not the case, then students must, particularly at research degree levels, meet two requirements.
1. Identify an apparently novel topic.
2. Be able to convince themselves and others of the novelty of the topic.

In this, Requirement 1 implies a degree of creativity, the extent of which will relate to the level at which the research is to be undertaken; and Requirement 2 will involve a systematic search of the literature along the lines to be described in Chapter 4. It is customary to consider several topics during the selection process and it is sensible that students should identify as many potentially rewarding lines as they can.

Only at the level of the research degree does it become necessary to add to the body of knowledge to any significant extent. Therefore, at this level, an early step must be to determine what the body of knowledge is. The supervisors have an obvious contribution to make at this stage.

There are numerous sources of ideas for research. It is assumed that the supervisors will discharge their responsibilities appropriately at this stage by being both proactive (putting forward their own suggestions) and reactive (responding to the student's findings).

Suggestions for research topics may arise from the following sources.
1. Theses and dissertations.
2. Articles in academic and professional journals.
3. Conference proceedings and reports generally.
4. Books and book reviews.
5. Reviews of the field of study.
6. Communication with experts in the field.
7. Conversations with potential users of the research findings.
8. Discussions with colleagues.
9. The media.

The type of study being followed will affect the extent to which students use the sources listed above. PhD students must expect to cover most if not all of them as it is vital to establish that their work is original. At other levels convenience and access are likely to dictate the action taken.

Sources 1 to 5 imply access to a high-quality library – the quality being measured in terms of the library's stock of literature and the ability of the library staff to procure texts from other libraries. In similar vein, the local library staff should be able to suggest to the student which other libraries could be visited with advantage.

All theses, many dissertations and other student reports will generally contain suggestions for additional research. Journal articles sometimes include recommendations for further work and, as they are reasonably up to date (appearing a year or so after the completion of a study), should be given careful attention by the researcher. Reports, particularly of government sponsored bodies, although often the outcome of protracted enquiries, are usually published with some speed. Again, these often contain recommendations on which research can be based. Books give a detailed account of particular fields and consequently will figure prominently in a researcher's studies; books do, nevertheless, possess the disadvantage that they are not as up to date as the other written sources mentioned, and their contents may have become known to other researchers. It will be noted that Source 4 in our suggestion list above includes book reviews as well as books. The reviewers of a book are usually able to evaluate the extent of its contribution to knowledge and can provide a useful service for students seeking ideas for topics. Citation indexes (see Chapter 4) provide listings of book reviews and may well be worth consulting for this purpose alone. The essential step of gaining access to relevant published material will be examined in depth in Chapter 4.

Reviews of the field of study (Source 5) provide a very useful guide to the researcher as to what is known in the field and what are still matters of conjecture; and of what has been discovered by previous researchers and where research is needed. There seems to be a definite trend with the proliferation of research subjects for academic journals to publish review articles by leading experts in the field.

Sources 6 to 8 require rather more initiative than does a mere search of the literature. The notion that research can be pursued from behind a desk may appeal to some students (and indeed may be all that is expected for a dissertation) but whatever the field, at research degree level, much advantage may be gained from discussions with others. Active researchers are usually sympathetic towards students who are undertaking studies in an area of mutual interest. Ideas for research can sometimes be tested during a brief conversation on the telephone or at conferences and seminars but ideally an appointment should be sought where potential topics can be discussed more fully. These comments apply with particular force to doctoral level students who are able to identify individuals from other institutions or organisations who are obviously leaders in their field. In these circumstances a journey of some distance may well prove to be a highly useful investment.

The growing practice of electronic conferencing can assist students who wish to expose their thoughts on prospective topics to those researching round the world in specified fields. Increasingly, use is being made of systems such as the Internet (see Chapter 4), Compuserve and America Online for this purpose.

Although there will be some circularity in the sense that the nature of the research will not be defined until the topic has been selected, the field in which the student is working will probably favour certain categories of research which might be linked to potential users. Thus, a research student in biochemistry might make contact with the research departments of companies manufacturing pharmaceuticals, or an engineering student could initiate discussions with a company making hydraulic valves.

Much may be gained when a few ideas have been generated by discussing them informally with colleagues (students and staff). In this respect the advantage of working within a research group is obvious and the need for greater initiative on the part of the lone research student is highlighted.

The media should not be ignored as a potential source of topics. Researchers are disinclined to publish their findings until they have been sufficiently substantiated but newspapers, popular journals, and radio and television may report on research progress which is felt to be of general interest. Additionally, findings may be reported by the media perhaps twelve months before scholarly accounts appear in learned journals. Students in the social sciences in particular may through awareness of the media be able to identify issues within which research topics might be located.

TECHNIQUES FOR GENERATING RESEARCH TOPICS

Experience suggests that methods of evaluating topics, and suggestions as to where to look for them, are often ineffective. Students need specific methods that will guide them in the topic selection process. These methods should be capable of providing useful guidance for two very different types of student: the 'underfocused' whose ideas of a subject area are not specific enough to form the basis of a viable topic and the 'overfocused' who has a singleminded aim of pursuing a particular topic. Underfocused students need ways of refining rather vague and often somewhat grandiose notions of a research area. The methods that are useful to them are those enabling them to identify a researchable 'niche' which they are capable of exploiting with the time and resources at their disposal. The overfocused student might seem, by contrast, to have the ideal attitude for successful research. It must be remembered, nevertheless, that research is a specialised business and that it is by no means unknown for research students who have a clear idea of the research they wish to do to find, belatedly, that it has been done already, or is not feasible, a fact of which they are unaware simply because of unfamiliarity with the frontiers of the subject. Where a supervisor has indicated an area for study this is less likely to be a problem but the implication of Figure 2.1 is that there are occasions when the best decision a student can make about a possible research topic is to drop it. For both types of student there is virtue in having methods that are capable of suggesting alternative themes given a starting subject. The techniques that are helpful in topic selection are essentially part of the field of 'creativity or problem-solving theory'. Useful detailed discussions of these fields can be found, for instance, in Tarr (1973), de Bono (1976), and Ackoff (1978).

Three approaches of considerable use to the researcher will be discussed here in more depth: the use of analogy, relevance trees and morphological analysis.

The Use of Analogy

Analogy plays an important role in many types of research. It aids the research process in two ways: firstly, it may suggest a fruitful line of enquiry in a particular subject area based on a perceived resemblance to some other area; or, secondly, it may suggest methods of analysis devised for use in one field which may profitably be employed in another. This latter role is exemplified by certain statistical techniques and will be discussed further in Chapter 5.

The use of analogy in topic formation is the principal interest here. As an example of this process take the case of the researcher with an interest in small business innovation who notes that many experts have suggested that the advanced equipment used in the West is inappropriate in developing countries and that the latter need 'intermediate technology' better suited to their less developed technical infrastructure. On reflection, the researcher perceives that the gap between the most advanced small businesses and the least is by no means dissimilar to that between the West and certain of the developing nations. From there it is a short step to speculate about 'intermediate technology' in the small business and the forms it might take (for example, in production management methods).

Relevance Trees

Though 'relevance trees' originated in the field of research and development management, their attraction is that they are excellent models of one of the ways people think about problems. Essentially, a relevance tree suggests a way of developing related ideas from a starting concept. To be most effective, the starting concept should be fairly broad. The relevance tree then serves as a device, either for generating alternative topics or for fixing on some 'niche'. The importance of both functions has, of course, already been noted.

Figure 2.2 shows an example of a relevance tree. Starting from the broad

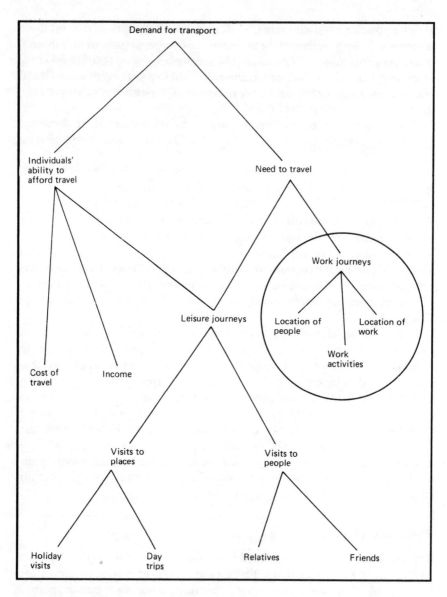

Figure 2.2 Example of a relevance tree

area of 'Demand for transport' the researcher first identifies two major factors affecting it, 'Need to Travel' and 'Individuals' ability to afford travel', which in turn can be related to 'Income' and 'Cost of travel'.

The first factor splits again into 'Leisure journeys' (also affected by the ability to afford travel) and into 'Work journeys'. Determinants of the latter factor are seen to be 'Location of work' (where it is carried out), 'Location of people' (where they live) and 'Work activities'. This last set of ringed variables might suggest to the researcher a possible topic, namely the extent to which changes in the forms of work activity will affect in the longer term where people live and how far and how frequently they travel to work.

Morphological Analysis

Morphological analysis is another technique originally developed for use in industrial research and development. It relies upon a threefold process.
1. Defining the key factors or dimensions of a particular subject.
2. Listing the various attributes of the factor or ways it can occur.
3. Defining all feasible combinations of the attributes.

Figure 2.3 shows an example of morphological analysis for defining valid types of management dissertation. It is supposed, for the purpose of illustration, that the body of knowledge to be used is already known but that it is

FOCUS	OBJECTIVES	DESIGN
Issue	Description	Desk Research
Management Function	Identify Key Dimensions	Mail Questionnaire
Market	Post Audit, Lessons for Management	Questionnaire Survey
Markets	Identify Barriers/Benefits	Case Study
Organisation	Forecast	Comparative Analysis
Several Organisations	Develop Tool	Modelling
Technology	Technique Development	
Decision	Technique Application	
Project	Develop Business Plan	

Figure 2.3 Example of morphological analysis. Types of management research dissertation

desired to identify a topic of sufficient potential for a master's degree. The researcher has selected three major factors defining type of management research:

1. Focus; the group or activity which is to be researched.
2. Objectives; what it is for.
3. Design; which methodology is employed.

Various possible attributes of each factor are listed and different types of research project can then be generated by taking one attribute from each of the three columns of Figure 2.3. For example,

Several Organisations / Identify Key Dimensions / Comparative Analysis

which, clearly, would involve the researcher in attempting to determine the key dimensions of some phenomenon by comparative analysis of data drawn from several organisations.

In practice, not all combinations are feasible: for example, the limited scope for comparative analysis within one project. However, it will often be found that combinations involving two or more attributes of one or several factors are attractive. For example,

Modelling

Issue / Technique Development /

Case study

a design frequently encountered in practice because of the opportunity it gives for testing the performance of techniques developed in actual situations.

Morphological analysis is capable of generating a very large number of alternatives. For this reason it is necessary to define only a few key dimensions or factors and to restrict the aspects of each that are considered. This forces the user to structure the problem and is thus particularly useful to the under-focused student who finds it difficult to get to grips with topic selection.

FEASIBILITY OF THE RESEARCH PROPOSED

There is little purpose in attempting a full evaluation of a topic unless the research to which it leads is feasible. The student should therefore consider the following factors.

1. Access to and availability of data and information.
2. Opportunity to pursue a particular research design.
3. The time needed to complete the research.

4. The technical skills needed.
5. Financial support.
6. The risk involved.

The six factors may be relevant to all levels of research and the first two can be insurmountable obstacles.

Access and Availability

The first factor may be exemplified by a student who has selected as a research topic variation in manufacturing costs in different countries within multinational car firms. Some car companies may be prepared to state in which countries costs are particularly high but it is unlikely that sufficient companies, if any, would disclose detailed data. This may be an obvious example but students should satisfy themselves that there is reasonable prospect of access before proceeding further. A more difficult assessment for the student to make at this stage is whether data or information which will be essential to the research actually exist. Clearly, planned approaches involving the analysis of secondary data (which are not gathered by the researcher) will be impossible if the data have not been recorded or are unreliable.

Opportunity for Research Design

The student may be inclined towards a topic in which a laboratory features and in many cases, such researchers will be able to set up experiments in their own institution's laboratories. If, however, the student intends to conduct a field experiment, some degree of co-operation will normally be needed. For example, pricing policy for academic journals may well be felt to be a suitable topic for research but it would be unlikely that a publisher could be found who would agree to handing over control of pricing to a student. Similar difficulties may be encountered in attempts to arrange a survey. Thus, a researcher may wish to study member/officer relationships within a particular local authority. Before proceeding further, permission must be sought to approach the subjects of the investigation. To attempt to proceed without approval is likely to lead to complete frustration of the plan.

Time Available

A prime aim of this book is to assist students to complete their research within the time available to them. In some instances, research is designed without proper thought being given to the time needed for its completion.

For example, the development of an anti-corrosive paint could be an appropriate outcome of a research study but the time required to assess the anti-corrosive properties added to the development period may far exceed the time available to a student researcher. Another question is whether too much is being attempted within the time available for research. When the topic has been selected, much is to be gained by drawing up a research plan which will indicate whether the deadlines can be met.

Technical Skills

It is reasonable to assume that student research at any level is more likely to succeed if the topic chosen will utilise skills and knowledge already possessed. There would, for example, seem to be greater prospects of satisfactory completion if a student with a first degree in physics were to research in this subject rather than in botany. In some instances, however, it is impossible to avoid having to acquire new skills if a topic is to be researched effectively. This is particularly so in the social sciences where skills often require to be developed in statistics, mathematics and computing. Students should, therefore, consider very carefully whether the topic chosen matches the skills they possess or will have time to develop during the course of their study. If doubt exists, the supervisor should be able to give guidance.

Financial Support

Much research has foundered because of a lack of resources. In student research where the prime resource is the individual concerned, it is essential that the financial support needed for the study should have been resolved before work is started. The student's budget will include funds to support normal research expenditure which may involve travelling, purchase of books, cost of typing and so on. Many students are, however, unclear as to what expenditure will be covered by their sponsor[2] but this is unlikely to cover the purchase of expensive equipment or materials or unlimited travel and subsistence and may not extend to postal questionnaires. Before a topic is finally selected, therefore, the question of cost must be examined. Inability to undertake certain activities due to a shortage of funds may prejudice a potentially successful study if the problem is not anticipated and resolved at the outset.

The Risk Involved

As a final point, the student should consider the risk that for any reason the project will prove impossible to complete. It will be remembered that, in discussing the nature of research in Chapter 1, we made the point that some types of research are perhaps inherently more risky than others; the student should, therefore, at least decide whether the risk of the project proposed is acceptable.

These above comments on our six factors have been made particularly with full-time research in mind. They apply with even greater force to part-time researchers with the one exception that in longitudinal studies involving an evaluation of some phenomenon over time the part-timer may have an advantage because of the longer duration of the study. In the UK, for example, most degree awarding bodies although preferring a part-time doctorate to be completed within five years would be tolerant towards a student registration of up to a decade, providing evidence of progress could regularly be given and there was no threat of the research becoming out of date. Social, economic, or political 'experiments' often need lengthy periods of evaluation, and as such would exceed the two or three years available to full-time research students.

No apology is made if the observations appear to be somewhat negative. By giving systematic consideration to the feasibility of the topic and the risks it entails the student will be forced to think carefully about the purpose of the research and the approach to be adopted. If the topic can satisfy the demands of feasibility, as described, the student will be well equipped to complete the planning phase (see Figure 1.3); if not, the prospect of a future disaster can be avoided by refining the topic or selecting another.

SOCIAL VALUE OF THE RESEARCH

Having satisfied themselves that the topic is feasible, students next need to consider whether it has sufficient social value. In some respects the student is in a privileged position in that the value of research may be judged purely on its contribution to academic knowledge with the question of its wider, social utility being unimportant. At the level of the undergraduate or the postgraduate dissertation, the question of value may be resolved even more easily as the prime aim is to demonstrate a measure of research competence or problem solving ability (through, for example, a literature search or a case study).

The right of researchers to select topics which have no apparent value for the community at large is, however, being increasingly questioned. For example, the 1993 UK White Paper on science policy[3] lays upon the UK Research Councils the duty of taking account of the need of publicly funded research to support the wealth creation process.

There is little point in studying apparently irrelevant and trivial topics if alternative topics of 'importance' can be identified. A further advantage of working on a topic of some significance is that the student is much more likely to be motivated; a frame of mind essential for successful completion. In addition, the supervisor (and ultimately any external examiner) is likely to take a greater interest if the research outcome is of undoubted value to the community. The student who elects to pursue a topic that has little obvious social value must expect in today's research climate that this aspect of the research will at examination receive much more attention than hitherto.

It is, of course, indicative of a thorough approach to a study if the student is convinced that a topic of social value has been identified. In realising this situation advice will normally have been taken from experts in the area in addition to that offered by the supervisor. The model depicted in Figure 2.1 is, however, an idealised one and it is possible that changes made to the topic for one reason (for example, infeasibility) may fundamentally alter its ability to satisfy other requirements including social value. For example, it may have been agreed initially between a doctoral student and a supervisor that the research would focus on the relationship between local authorities in England and central government. The student, after considering the extent of the fieldwork involved, may have decided to examine the relationship between one local authority only and central government. Although studies in depth have their own attractions and advantages, value would probably be lost because of the restricted scope for generalisation afforded by a single case study. In order to avoid such an eventuality it is evident that second opinions should be sought at each new stage or redirection.

There is, unfortunately, no easy way to measure the social value of research, and indeed its importance in student research is related to the level of the activity, being much more important in the case of doctoral studies. The best advice to students is probably for them to continue to search for an alternative topic if the one under consideration seems to be of doubtful social value.

RESEARCH SYMMETRY

Even though a student may be satisfied that research is both feasible and potentially valuable, Figure 2.1 suggests that there are still two stages of the idealised process to go through before a topic is finally selected. The first of these stages requires that the alternative outcomes of the study should be identified. Although below research degree level there may be only one outcome – for example, the writing up of a literature search or a case study – in more advanced research two or more outcomes may be possible: firstly, a hypothesis may be accepted or rejected, or, secondly, an experiment may provide a definite result or may be inconclusive. Preferably each of the outcomes should represent acceptable findings in which case the risk involved in the research will be reduced.

The extent to which the outcomes are of similar value is an indication of the symmetry of the research. The research student should seek to select a topic which promises high symmetry, but the prospects will be affected by the research approach which is adopted. Thus, some research work of an experimental nature undertaken in laboratories by scientists and engineers may be highly asymmetrical and may ultimately fail to achieve a positive result. Alternatively, a student may be unable to validate an econometric model which has been developed, perhaps mainly from theory. In both of these instances this would lead to there being no basis for the award of a research degree.

Symmetry depends in large part on prior beliefs about a topic which are held within a field of study. If, for example, there is strong support for the view that the eating of sweets damages children's teeth or there is little belief that the phases of the moon affect work output, experiments which confirm strongly held opinion will not be rated highly even though the design and conduct of these experiments cannot be criticised. Obviously, if the research findings were to contradict current belief they would be of potential value but this is unlikely in both cases cited. An example of a symmetrical research topic would be one concerned with the effect on career progress of students who attain the degree of Master in Business Administration (MBA). If it were found that the MBA had no effect on career progress this conclusion would be of considerable value as would the contrary finding (although note should be taken of 'Scope for Research' as discussed in the next section).

One possible outcome of research is that the findings are inconclusive. Research students should satisfy themselves that the probability of this type of outcome is sufficiently low. As an example, we can consider a student seeking to establish whether a theory of leadership based on research within a number of companies in the private sector is applicable also to management in the public sector. If a hypothesis to this effect were to be confirmed or rejected either finding could be of considerable value. Although the topic may be symmetrical with regard to conclusive outcomes the research student may feel that there is a distinct possibility of an inconclusive outcome and that this makes the research insufficiently attractive to pursue.

It is evident that, at doctoral level, symmetry is to be preferred if the research lends itself to it, because it reduces the risk of an unsuccessful outcome to the research. In this way research which satisfies all other criteria should lead to a successful outcome. We do not wish, however, to imply that success or failure always involves symmetry. Research which is of an exploratory or descriptive nature will normally have only one outcome which will be assessed at some point on a scale ranging from acceptable to unacceptable.

SCOPE FOR RESEARCH

The final test of a research topic, as is suggested in Figure 2.1, is that of assessing whether sufficient scope exists. In large part, scope will be related to work already completed in related areas. As a result of such work prior beliefs will be held and these will affect the reaction to the research outcome in terms of novelty and surprise. Prior beliefs may range from certainty (for example, that the earth moves round the sun) to complete uncertainty (for example, whether life exists elsewhere in the universe). Scope should be seen as the opportunity to increase, reduce, or even confirm (if these are based on analogies) current beliefs.

In considering scope, research students should reflect also on the value of their potential topic. If this is high there may be sufficient scope even if prior beliefs are strongly held (for example in the case of the effect of dietary fat on health). It goes without saying that findings which overturn strongly held beliefs on matters of importance will be rated highly but these opportunities will present themselves only rarely to the student researcher. The topics to be avoided are those which are potentially low in both surprise and value (here in the broadest sense). Thus, a researcher might select as a topic the speed of learning of a foreign language by child expatriates. It would come as no surprise, and would be of little apparent value, to find that British children in families living in France or Germany gain a more rapid command of the languages of these countries than do their counterparts living in the UK. On the other hand, there may be both surprise and value in finding that the same children demonstrate higher competence in mathematics than do children of similar ages in the UK. Though the standards required vary from one level of research to another students should satisfy themselves that the topic has sufficient potential along the dimensions of both scope and value.

DEVELOPING A RESEARCH PROPOSAL

At all levels of study considerable benefit can be gained by systematic planning. A process in which many of the answers to questions raised will be vague and uncoordinated and are probably held within the mind of the researcher is represented in Figure 2.1. The aim, then, must be to develop a realistic plan of action with clear objectives which, taking account of resources and constraints, has a high probability of being achieved. The planning process itself is discussed in the next chapter but at this point reference is made to certain documents which research students should be prepared to compile: topic analyses and the research proposal.

It is recommended that research degree students should undertake preparation of both types of document. Dissertation students can usually content themselves with preparing an abbreviated research proposal. Topic analyses and the research proposal will contribute to the achievement of the first major milestone; namely when both supervisor and student have agreed the study to be pursued.

Experience shows that the step of preparing and submitting views in writing for consideration by supervisors and others can be highly beneficial for students. Redirection of research can be accommodated much more readily at earlier rather than later stages and yet some students are reluctant to commit themselves to paper.

Both topic analyses and the research proposal are of similar structure and the latter is in fact an elaborated version of a topic analysis. The sections of each are shown in Table 2.1

The Topic Analysis

Topic analyses are convenient ways of summarising various aspects of one or more potentially acceptable topics. A topic analysis should not exceed a few pages in length. It should contain summaries, following careful consideration of each of the sections of Table 2.1, rather than a set of speculative observations.

One factor which causes some research students much concern in the early stages of their research is the hypothesis. Simon (1969, p. 37) defines a hypothesis as 'a single statement that attempts to explain or to predict a single phenomenon' (as opposed to a theory which is an entire system of interrelated thought). If a novel hypothesis can be substantiated there will be an addition to the body of knowledge and hence the attraction to the researcher of identifying an appropriate hypothesis. In many instances, however, the purpose of the research does not lend itself to other than trivial hypotheses. Thus, a chemist may hypothesise that a single dye can be developed which will provide a colour that varies with time of day but this would be stated much more sensibly as a research objective. There is no reason why more than one hypothesis should not be formulated. Thus, a study of innovation might incorporate hypotheses on the effects of organisation size and the managerial style of R and D departments. In general however it is preferable to avoid too detailed a specification of the research. It is usually better to identify a single hypothesis with considerable potential for testing.

Section	Topic analyses (2 to 5 pages)	Research proposal (20 to 50 pages research degree; 2 to 10 pages dissertation)
Summary		X
Research objectives/hypotheses	X	X
Prior research in the area/literature review	X	X
Value in terms of the possible outcomes	X	X
Research design or approach to the research	X	X
Tentative schedule	X	X
Provisional chapter details		X

Table 2.1 Content of topic analyses and the research proposal

The section of the topic analysis dealing with research value will be highly significant when research degrees are involved and will encompass the comments made above on social value, symmetry and scope of the research. It will be strengthened if evidence can be provided that authorities in the field agree that there is a need for the research proposed.

If more than one topic proves to be acceptable to both student and supervisor the final choice will most probably depend upon the weightings attached by the student to the value of the research and the approach likely to be adopted. Some students react positively to the challenge of higher value (but often higher risk) studies whereas others wish to maximise the chances of completing their research and hence select the topic most consistent with this aim.

Those students for whom the completion of a topic analysis is an essential part of the planning phase may wish to model their approach on the example which is presented at Appendix 1.

The Research Proposal

Whereas a topic analysis should contain just sufficient information for a decision to be reached on the line of research to be pursued, the research proposal should be seen as the document which finally establishes both the need for the study and that the researcher has or can acquire the skills and other resources required. Students should in fact imagine that they are tendering for a research contract through the medium of the research proposal. In reality it is highly probable that the latter will need to be refined, possibly more than once.

The final version of the research proposal for a research degree might be 20 to 50 pages in length, whereas two to five pages is usually enough for dissertation purposes. In those sections which are common to both the topic analysis and the research proposal the main elaboration in the latter case will be on prior research and probable methodology. Students working for higher degrees will accumulate many additional references during the course of their research and writing but before embarking on the execution phase they must be able to satisfy themselves and their advisers that they are wholly familiar with previous and current work in the area of their planned study. In addition to guaranteeing novelty this will be a major factor in assessing the value of possible outcomes. Thus, the account of prior research as indicated by the list of references and the bibliography contained within the research proposal should be comprehensive.

The proposal will need to describe in sufficient detail the approach which the student will use. In large measure this will indicate whether or not the line of study planned is feasible. The factors identified in the section of the research proposal labelled 'Feasibility of the research proposed' should be addressed. Thus, descriptions will need to be given of such matters as the sampling frame and method, type of equipment needed, the data to be collected, the nature of the experiment, the methods of analysis to be employed, the resources and the time required to carry out the project. This will probably be the most difficult section of the research proposal to write and there should be much resort to expert advice. Inevitably there will be questions still to be resolved. Students must, however, ask themselves the question: 'Dare I risk proceeding when significant uncertainty remains?' In some instances the answer must be 'No'. It would, for example, be ridiculous to write up a proposal which did not guarantee the opportunity to pursue a particular research design. On the other hand it would be reasonable for a student who is familiar with one computer programming language to assume that it would be possible to acquire skills in another.

Although only tentative, it is desirable that a schedule should be incorporated in a research proposal. It is important that, with limited time at their disposal, students should become used to thinking in terms of deadlines. Such a schedule will be beneficial to the research student when drawing up the research plan. Given the tight nature of the deadlines involved and the other calls on their time – the search for a job, for instance – a schedule of this nature is essential to the dissertation student.

Similarly, much is to be gained by including within the research proposal details of the chapters, in the form of, say, 6–12 main section headings per chapter. The chapters themselves will normally accord with a standard and logical structure. An example (Howard, 1978) which relates to doctoral theses is as follows:

1. The introduction describing the general problem area, the specific problem, why the topic is important, prior research, approach of the thesis, limitations and key assumptions, and contribution to be made by the research.

2. A description of what has been done in the past. This is a complete survey of prior research which, if very nominal, might be combined with Chapter 1. If there is extensive prior research, the results might preferably be broken down into two or more chapters. It is normally an important section of the thesis because the description of what has been done provides background and also documents the fact that the candidate's research is unique as the thesis is not duplicating earlier work.

3. A description of the research methodology. One or more chapters may be used to describe the research method. For example, the chapter(s) might describe a simulation model, a data collection technique, a measurement technique, an experiment, or an historical method of analysis. In essence, this section describes how the research was conducted.

4. The research results. The results of the chosen methodology are reported: the data are presented, the conceptual framework is described, the historical analysis is defined, or the comparative studies are explained.

5. Analysis of the results. This may be included with earlier chapters depending upon the type of thesis. This is a key section because it explains the conclusions that can be drawn from the data, the implications of a theory and so on.

6. Summary and conclusions. The thesis is summarised with emphasis upon the results obtained and the contribution made by these results. Any suggestions for further research are also outlined.

The purpose of a research proposal should not be forgotten. It should not be seen as a progress report to be filed but as a document for decision. For the dissertation student it is essential to get the research proposal agreed by the supervisor as early as possible. In the case of a research degree student, although the supervisor should be encouraging the student to submit the proposal the decision to be taken is of sufficient importance for the student to take the initiative in arranging a formal presentation/seminar which preferably will be attended by other researchers as well as the supervisor. The result of this presentation should be general agreement that the researcher should now be able to proceed with some confidence. If such agreement does not materialise it is to be hoped that sufficient constructive criticism will have been obtained for a revised proposal to have a good chance of acceptance on the next round.

CHAPTER SUMMARY

TOPIC SELECTION: is a process which differs considerably for dissertation and research degree students.

Dissertation students with help from their academic institution will often select their topic without great difficulty but should always take into account potential value. Where a dissertation is carried out in an organisation care needs to be taken to ensure that the topic is of sufficient academic merit.

For a research degree student, topic selection can absorb a significant proportion of a research study. Certain steps can, however, be recognised which enable a systematic approach towards topic selection to be adopted; this should reduce the probability of excessive time being spent on this stage.

Research degree students are likely to find it useful to prepare one, or more, topic analyses before embarking on a fully fledged research proposal..

THE SUPERVISOR: Dissertation students normally only receive limited amounts of supervision directed to ensuring the research project is carried out competently. Detailed knowledge of the field is rarely needed by the supervisor and should not be expected.

For research degree students supervisor(s) should be appointed as soon as possible and should be heavily involved during the topic selection process.

THE GENERATION OF RESEARCH TOPICS: may be facilitated by a number of techniques which include analogy, relevance trees and morphological analysis.

FOR RESEARCH DEGREE STUDENTS THE ACCEPTABILITY OF A RESEARCH TOPIC: may be judged by giving consideration to its feasibility, value, symmetry, and scope.

A RESEARCH PROPOSAL: should be developed when a topic has been provisionally agreed so that the full implications of the study will emerge from detailed planning.

Although the broad content of the Research Proposal is the same whether it relates to a dissertation or a research degree, it is much longer and more detailed in the latter case. In particular, both types of research proposal need a schedule.

3

Planning the Research Project

There are a number of reasons why students experience difficulty in research. The most important of these are:
1. Difficulties in selecting a suitable topic.
2. The problem of selecting an appropriate analytical framework.
3. Inability to manage available resources, in particular, time.

This third reason is common at all levels of research, the inability being often symptomatic of the previous two. Where students experience problems in planning content these often reflect themselves in wasted time and lack of progress.

THE NEED TO PLAN

The aim of this chapter is very simple. It is to present students with a tool for planning their own research project which will enable them to realise when they have run into serious difficulties. More importantly, perhaps, this chapter is also intended to function as a motivational device by enabling students to see that they are achieving goals they have set themselves, since experience shows that the best way to successful completion of the research as a whole is through acquiring the habit of successful completion of intermediate stages.

Although the type of planning to be described is in itself a useful process, through which desirable courses of action are identified and potential pitfalls are anticipated, a major justification is that it serves as a basis for control. What is required is not a loose collection of estimates of what the research will involve but a comprehensively analysed schedule of activities against which research progress may be assessed. The planning referred to in this chapter is not that concerned with the nature of the research itself but with the management of the research project which will be seen as a number of distinct but interrelated stages or activities all of which must be completed before the study is finished. Although the activities will differ in importance each will be planned to the same degree to indicate when, ideally, they should take place.

The major purposes of such planning are to:

a) clarify the aims and objectives of the researcher;
b) define the activities required to attain these aims and the order in which they take place;
c) identify various critical points or 'milestones' in the research at which progress can be reviewed and the research plan reassessed;
d) produce estimates of times at which the various milestones will be reached so that progress can be clearly measured;
e) ensure that effective use is made of key resources; in particular the researcher;
f) define priorities once the research is underway;
g) serve as a guide for increasing the likelihood of successful completion on time.

If this list seems needlessly elaborate and more relevant to the construction of, say, a motorway bridge than the conduct of a student research project, the reader should remember that the fewer the resources of time and money the greater the need for careful planning and that in any research project the key resource is always the student's own time. Furthermore, planning is most necessary where the activities involved are non-routine so that possible difficulties can be anticipated.

A major difference between the planning of research and the construction of a bridge is that in the former case the work content of the various stages cannot always be readily estimated. It is presumed, however, that students will have selected a topic which can be researched within the time available and that, although creative thought and deadlines conflict to some extent, the implied time constraints will be accepted.

NETWORK PLANNING

In planning a research project, an approach should be adopted which will serve as a basis for control of projects of various lengths but will also be sufficiently flexible to accommodate the unpredictabilities of research. Given the success of network analysis techniques in planning and controlling industrial research projects as well as complex construction programmes some form of network is indicated.

The development of the computer in the 1950s stimulated the application of network analysis particularly to construction projects in which thousands of activities may be involved. Much has subsequently been written about techniques of network analysis (see, for example, Lock, 1988). Their primary purpose is to assist in planning and control in situations in which the mind is unable to cope efficiently with the relationships among the numerous activities. The principles involved can be comprehended within an hour or two and application of the technique can be very beneficial to the completion of the study within the time available.

Thus, although the procedures outlined are rather formal they can be applied by students at any level. As elsewhere, it is argued that research students should employ them unless either they are sufficiently experienced in managing research projects to have their own system (which will inevitably be fairly similar), or they agree with their supervisor that these methods are inappropriate in their case.

Nevertheless, the methods have value in their own right as a model of the process of planning a research project and may therefore be so regarded, if desired.

It is felt that, although the number of activities which can be identified in a student research project will usually be a few dozen at the most, network methods should be used to plan and control any project expected to last more than a few weeks. It may be that in some projects use could be made of one of the smaller network packages to be found on the micro-computers to which many students will have access. Providing, however, the number of activities to be incorporated in the network does not exceed 50 or 60, manual control will be possible and may be preferred.

It should be appreciated that, whatever the number of activities, the network itself must be drawn by hand; the computer undertakes the analysis which leads to an indication of the start and finish times of activities and any spare time which exists.

AN EXAMPLE OF A NETWORK IN PLANNING STUDENT RESEARCH

In this section a hypothetical example will be employed drawing upon the research approach used by many students in the social sciences, namely the analysis of response to a questionnaire-based survey in order to test a hypothesis.

Whatever the level of research and whatever stage has been reached the process of network planning is always the same.
1. Determine the objectives.
2. Identify and list (in any order) the activities that need to be carried out.
3. Order the activities. Establish for every activity, those activities which precede it, those which follow it, and those which may be undertaken concurrently.
4. Draw the network.
5. Estimate the time needed to complete each activity.
6. Analyse the network using the completion times.
7. Check the resources and draw up the schedule.
8. Replan as necessary.

We now look at each of these eight in more detail.

Determine the Objectives

As a first step, students should always decide their objectives since these may well influence many of the activities that appear in the list. In this case it is assumed that the student's primary objective is to pursue a career in social science research and that as a consequence during the first six months of study the following subsidiary aims have been defined.

That is, to:
a) work in an area with considerable research potential;
b) acquire familiarity with certain basic tools of social science research, such as the conduct of surveys and the role of statistics in survey analysis and the use of the computer for processing survey data;
c) successfully complete a PhD thesis in the 2.5 years (130 weeks) that the student expects to remain full-time.

Obviously, the points under b) are reflected in the number of activities on

53

the list, whereas the requirement c) may well necessitate replanning if for some reason the analysis shows that the target cannot be met.

Listing the Activities

The student will next need to decide the level at which the activities should be listed. This depends on the length of the project and the stage which has been reached. In a research project for a taught master's course, there will usually be little difficulty in producing a list of activities at the level of detail shown in Table 3.1, which will probably suffice for the whole project. Indeed, students involved in projects as short as this are cautioned that, if they experience difficulties in drawing up a list of the activities or in assessing the time they will take, it may well mean that the project involves too much uncertainty and needs redefinition.

At the doctoral level however, it will normally be necessary to go through the planning process many times during the project and the level of detail appropriate at the beginning may be very different from that needed once a topic has been selected and the research is well underway. Thus at the very beginning a list of activities such as,

i) attending Professor Brown's lectures,
ii) participating in a 'Smalltalk for beginners' course,
iii) selecting a topic,
iv) drawing up research proposal, and
v) carrying out research,

could well be quite adequate, in that it can serve as a basis for monitoring progress in the earlier stages, whilst not pretending to knowledge that the student does not have prior to topic selection.

Equally a slightly more complex model could be achieved by suitably adapting the stages of the research project shown in Figure 1.3. This would, for example, bring into some relief the time which could reasonably be allotted to the selection of the topic itself. In the present case however it is assumed that a research proposal has been submitted and accepted.

Several activities that have already taken place, for example, 'Topic selection', do not, therefore, appear in the network. Planning is about what has to be done and not about what has been done. This means that as the project progresses and activities are completed the network tends to shrink.

It should be noted that the activities listed in Table 3.1 are typical in that they involve a mix of motivational activities (for example, 'Write paper for presentation at conference'), preparatory activities ('Acquiring statistical skills'), activities specific to the research project ('Carry out survey') and, finally, those required for reasons of health and sanity and not directly related

Activity no.	Activity description	Abbreviation	Estimated Duration (weeks)
1	Written statement of concepts and theories	Concepts and theories	3
2	First draft of questionnaire for pilot study	First draft QA	6
3	Finalising of questionnaire for pilot study	Finalise QA	1
4	Decide likely method of analysing response to survey	Decide analytical method	4
5	Select participants for pilot	Select pilot participants	4
6	Acquire statistical skills	Acquire statistical skills	8
7	Attend course on use of standard computer package	Attend computer course	6
8	Write (say, three) drafts of early thesis chapters	Draft early chapters	9
9	Carry out pilot study	Carry out pilot	4
10	Review pilot study	Review pilot study	3
11	Prepare questionnaire for survey	Prepare QA	4
12.	Decide target population and sampling details	Decide target population	4
13	Carry out survey	Carry out survey	12
14	Process data for computer	Process data	6
15	Interpret computer output	Interpret output	6
16	Evaluate nature and extent of response to survey	Evaluate response	4
17	Write paper for presentation at conference	Write paper	4
18	Relate findings to concepts/theories/ hypothesis	Relate findings	6
19	Decide and carry out any further analysis or research	Decide further analysis	12
20	Complete writing of (say, five) draft chapters	Complete writing	15
21	Review and edit thesis	Review and edit	10
22	Correct thesis and obtain bound copies	Correct thesis	4
23	Prepare for oral examination	Prepare for oral	2
24	Allowance for holidays, job interviews, illness and general contingencies	Contingency allowance	24

Table 3.1 A list of activities for a student research project in the social science field

to the work itself, for example 'Allowance for holidays, etc.'. As far as the latter is concerned there is an element of flexibility in that it is part of the contingency allowance that is added to any time estimate. Thus, in this case the student has not scheduled any summer holiday during the research project proper, preferring to improve motivation to beat the schedule by ear-marking some part of any time savings for holiday purposes.

It is sometimes the case that by slightly redefining the activity the student may considerably reduce the risk that the research will run into major problems. Thus, here, the student, though anticipating a high response rate, might well decide to despatch the questionnaire to a much larger sample in case the response was far lower than expected and, in addition, to incorporate certain features in the questionnaire to make it possible to check for any bias in the eventual replies. Neither of these decisions is likely to have much effect on the time required for the activities they affect. On the other hand, either or both of them considerably reduce the risk of failure through insufficient returns or returns with a serious but unrecognised bias.

As the research progresses and activities are completed, replanning may well necessitate changes to the list. Some activities may be dropped, but more likely, some will be broken down into finer detail as the relevant stage of the project approaches: for example, 'Review and edit thesis' might be expanded to include 'Get figures and tables produced'; 'Review and correct Chapter 1'; 'Review and correct Chapter 2' and so on.

The effect of this type of planning is that it is only activities in the near future that are elaborated in detail. As the project progresses the detailed section of the network advances like a wave and, of course, completed sections of the network disappear. This process has been referred to as 'rolling wave planning'. This is only necessary for activities which involve the coordination of several interlinked, lesser activities. The expansion process is compensated for by the completion of earlier activities so that the list is never much longer than shown here. Alternatively, it is possible to run two networks: a broad brush master network for the project as a whole and, where circumstances warrant it, a sub-network that breaks down a single master network activity into far finer detail, for example, where the analysis stage necessitates a set of interrelated computer runs. Most PC-based packages for network analysis make it very straightforward to carry out rolling wave planning. Thus, an activity such as 'Review and edit thesis' can at any time be broken down into more detail, if required.

Order the Activities

The basic method used for drawing the network is to represent the activities by boxes and the order in which activities must take place by linking the

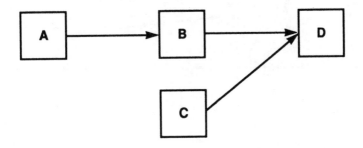

activity boxes by arrows. Thus the diagram is to be interpreted as:

Activity A must be completed before Activity B can start
Activity C must be completed before Activity D can start
Activity B must be completed before Activity D can start and
Activities A and C can start at the same time.

Draw the Network

The network of a research study represented at this level of detail can be drawn very quickly (for further details see, for example, Lock, 1988). The outcome is depicted in Figure 3.1 after consideration has been given to the ordering of activities. It will be noted that the project effectively divides into two stages: Stage 1 comprises research design, data gathering and preliminary analysis. Stage 2 comprises final analysis and thesis preparation. (In the figure, the network has been split at Milestone M4 to reflect this.)

The virtue of such a presentation is that the interrelationship between activities can be clearly seen, particularly where the need for one activity to precede another is not immediately obvious. Furthermore, the first few times this approach is used it may well remind the researcher of activities that have been overlooked. Points in the project at which, in principle at least, the student can be working on several activities at once are indicated by parallel paths through the network – for example, 'Carry out pilot study' and 'Decide target population and sampling details', and these may well be helpful in fitting the project schedule to the resources available. In short, Figure 3.1 shows the 'logic' of the project on which planning must be based and is of

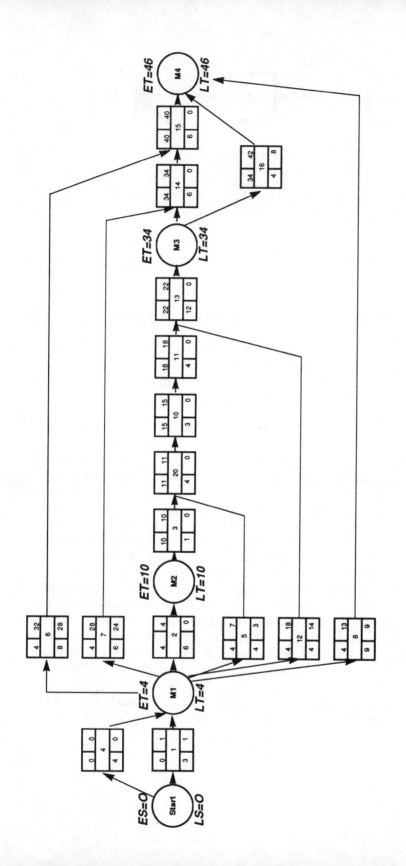

Figure 3.1 Network for a research study: Stage 1 (continued next page)

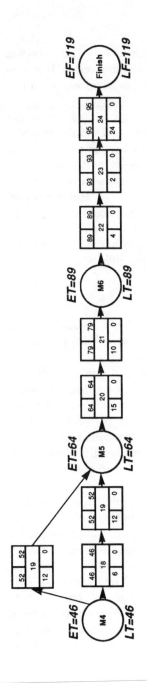

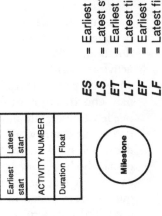

ES = Earliest start time project
LS = Latest start time project
ET = Earliest time milestone
LT = Latest time milestone
EF = Earliest finish time project
LF = Latest finish time project

Network for a research study: Stage 2

very considerable value in itself. Indeed, some researchers use networks solely to indicate the way in which the project activities interact. It is customary to indicate the passage of time by ensuring that all arrows point in a forward (left to right) direction.

So far no reference has been made to activity duration as much value can be gained by drawing the network and thus appreciating the order in which work should be done. Furthermore, a network reduces the probability of overlooking an important stage of the research. There is, of course, no certainty that the study will in execution correspond exactly with the structure of the network, but it should represent the views of the student at the current stage of the research project. Thus, in Figure 3.1, activity number 19 ('Decide and carry out any further analysis or research') might be viewed at the time the network was drawn more as a contingency but in the event may involve several additional stages which need to be carefully planned.

Estimate Activity Times

A major advantage of the network approach is that by undertaking simple calculations a schedule of activities may be prepared and used for controlling the project.

Included in Table 3.1 is an estimate of the number of weeks required to complete each of the 24 activities listed. It should be noted that 'Estimated duration' is the 'elapsed time' – that is, the period required to complete the activity. Usually, this will be longer than the number of weeks of work entailed by the activity, because, say, the activity involves contacting individuals who are not immediately accessible; or, more importantly, when time is needed to integrate information that has been gained into the researcher's conceptual framework. The task of estimation is not an easy one and students will need advice from their supervisors and, ideally, from other students who have completed research in similar areas. Thus, in the hypothetical example it may be possible to identify a researcher who has completed a questionnaire-based survey with considerable similarities to the study envisaged. These experiences would then be translated to assist in estimating the duration of activities 2, 3, 9, 10, 11 and 13 of Table 3.1. The student also, may be reasonably confident in estimating the time to allocate to activities, 1, 5, 12, 17, 20, 21, 22 and 23. It is always necessary (particularly when thinking in terms of a specific individual) to recognise that account must be taken of activities such as holidays and illness which will not further the project work. These are included in activity 24 which it will be seen extends the duration of the project by about 20 per cent. Although, as we have said, allowances need to be built into each activity it is sensible that further latitude is provided to cover activities which are not related to the project.

60

This leaves activities, 4, 6, 7, 8, 14, 15, 16, 18 and 19 which can be roughly apportioned between two groups:
a) those for which the work content may be reasonably estimated but which are undertaken intermittently (activities 7 and 8);
b) those for which there is considerable uncertainty about the work content (activities 4, 6, 14, 15, 16, 18 and 19).

The estimating problem raised by group a) is not too difficult to accommodate. A realistic minimum elapsed time equal to the content of the work should first be assigned to the activity. If after analysis the activity is found to be critical the student will need to establish whether parallel activities are involved and if so the extent to which the total period of the research must be extended. If the activity does not turn out to be critical there will then be scope for stretching it out over a longer period without jeopardising the completion of the project.

The preparation of schedules is made more difficult by the need to accommodate group b) type activities which by definition are incapable of precise estimation. A further complication is the recognition that in some instances the work will be carried out intermittently. Indeed, in the example, only activity 19 ('Decisions on further analysis') will continuously occupy the student's attention. The problem may best be resolved by the student attempting to incorporate work content within 'elapsed time'. Thus, activity 6 ('Acquisition of statistical skills') will require that the student should read certain texts but in order to ensure that the concepts are fully understood an elapsed time of eight weeks may be allocated (as used in Table 3.1) for the comprehension of issues arising from an estimated 50 hours of reading (a standard time of ten hours is sometimes used for each book read but 'heavy-weight' texts are likely to require much longer). In the example used, activity 7 ('Attend course on standard computer package') is placed in group a) as it is not envisaged that the student would need to gain competence in programming. If this were the case the activity would have been more appropriately placed in the group b) category.

A number of general points apply to estimating activity times. Firstly, standard times exist for many unlikely tasks – for example, reading books as cited above. Secondly, students can often reduce the time they require to carry out certain activities and incidentally improve their ability to estimate it by training and preparation – for instance, by taking a rapid reading course before embarking on a literature search. Thirdly, allowances may need to be built in to all activity times to cope with the unexpected occurrences that always seem far more likely to extend the time required rather than reduce it. The need to do this can only be established in the light of the student's own performance on estimating. For this reason, for all except the

61

short research project it is recommended that the student records on a control chart (see Figure 3.2) how long activities actually take as compared with the initial estimate. During the course of the longer research project it may then be hoped to derive a realistic 'correction factor' to apply to the first guesses. Though apparently naive this can be surprisingly effective.

The difficulty of handling uncertainty is probably the major problem in planning. In general single figure estimates are employed (as in Table 3.1) and give a spurious indication of likely accuracy, but in some instances the ensuing errors of estimation are so great that the outcome of the project is prejudiced. An early application of the network approach, which gained a considerable measure of publicity, was to the Polaris programme of the US Navy. The network technique employed was described as PERT (Programme Evaluation and Review Technique) in which pessimistic, most likely and optimistic estimates were made of durations. In this way, in addition to expected project completion times, it became possible to place probabilities upon particular events being completed by a certain date. It is not suggested that the student should go to this length but, even if this was done, the total time taken in this aspect of planning would still be only a very small part of the total study. Some students, having come to appreciate the benefits of the approach, may well be inclined to go as far as they can in order to provide the most effective basis for the control of their study, particularly if it is decided to use a computer package since most incorporate the PERT facility.

Analyse the Network using the Completion Times

Schedule control charts were used for many years prior to the introduction of networks and naturally took some account of the interdependence of activities, although the danger of overlooking a critical interrelationship in complex projects is obvious. The introduction of activity durations into a network enables analysis to be undertaken which leads to the scheduling of activities with an indication of spare time (float) associated with them.

A common convention is that the duration of each activity is contained in the left-hand bottom subsection of each activity box. By working from left to right through the network, 'earliest start times' (the earliest times when activities can be started) are determined and are shown in the top left-hand subsection of each activity box. The latest times when activities may be started if the minimum project completion time is to be achieved (latest start times) are calculated by working backwards from the final project completion time and are shown here in the top right subsection of each activity box.

The computational procedure is simple and can be demonstrated by reference to a number of the activities included in Table 3.1. Assume that the

62

student wishes to give consideration to the milestone which is achieved when the survey is completed (that is, at the end of activity 13). If, for simplicity, activities 6 and 8 are ignored the sub-network will include a total of 11 activities.

By taking account of activity durations it will be seen that the earliest time by which the survey will be completed is 34 weeks (remember that activity 2 cannot start until activity 4 has been completed). If 34 weeks is accepted by the student as the target towards which to work the latest event times can be determined by subtraction. Figure 3.1 also shows a complete analysis of earliest and latest start times.

Whether or not an activity carries float is of great interest to the researcher. Several types of this may be recognised but it is sufficient for our purposes to consider 'total float'. This is the amount of spare time available to an activity if the starting event occurs as early as possible and the finishing event is allowed to take place as late as possible (that is, without delaying the termination of the whole project). Several activities in Figure 3.1 possess total float:

Activity Number	Total Float (Weeks)
1	1
5	3
6	28
7	24
8	9
12	14
16	8
17	2

All of the remaining activities will be seen to have no total float and are said to be 'critical'. Information of this nature can be of the greatest help to students in scheduling their efforts. Of particular concern will be the path through the network which carries no total float (the 'critical path'). If any activities on the critical path take longer than planned the only way in which the project will be completed on time will be a reduction in the duration of a subsequent activity on the critical path. In Figure 3.1 the float for each activity is shown in the bottom right subsection of each box.

It will be seen that 119 weeks is the estimate of the total time needed to complete the project network shown in Figure 3.1, provided there are no resource problems (see next section, 'Resources and Scheduling', below). Given the time required for topic selection and the preparation of a research proposal, this estimate falls comfortably within the requirement of our hypothetical student's third objective of completing the project in about three years from initial registration, given six months have already been spent on preparing the research proposal and so on.

A feature of student research which is frequently alluded to is the scarcity of resources. Thus, apparently parallel activities which would be feasible with freely available resources cannot be undertaken simultaneously. Full consideration must therefore be given to resource availability if realistic schedules are to be compiled.

Resources and Scheduling

In preparation for controlling the project a bar chart is prepared directly from the network diagram of Figure 3.1. This is shown here as Figure 3.2, merely presenting the information contained in Figure 3.1 in a different way.

Indeed, bar charts were used directly for project planning until the 1960s, after which network planning became the preferred method of project planning because it is better at preventing the scheduling of one activity before another that logically precedes it. However, for a simple student project it is possible, with care, to proceed direct to the bar chart if that is what the student wishes.

The bar chart has time in weeks along the horizontal axis. Each activity is represented by a hatched bar starting at the earliest possible start time and with a length equal to its duration in weeks. Where activities have float its extent (being the difference between the latest finish time for the activity and the earliest finish time) is shown as a dashed area. Since critical activities do not have float they are shown as a simple hatched bar. In practice, the bar is labelled to identify the activity concerned. Because of space constraints the labels have been omitted in Figure 3.2.

It is likely that the bar chart will need to be revised at various points during the project. For that reason there is much to be said for producing the bar chart as a by-product of a computer analysis of the network plan. An alternative method where manual analysis of the network is preferred is to produce the bars as strips of card and either attach them to a steel-backed board magnetically or to pin them to a pinboard. In either case, it is then easy to move the bars around for purposes such as resource scheduling. Further details on bar charts and their uses can be found in a standard text on project planning, for example, Lock (1988).

Figure 3.2 permits a number of useful lessons to be drawn. Float is clearly indicated and provides an opportunity to smooth the demand for resources. Here the major resource is the student's time and although the student will be, during the first year, committed to attempting to complete the critical

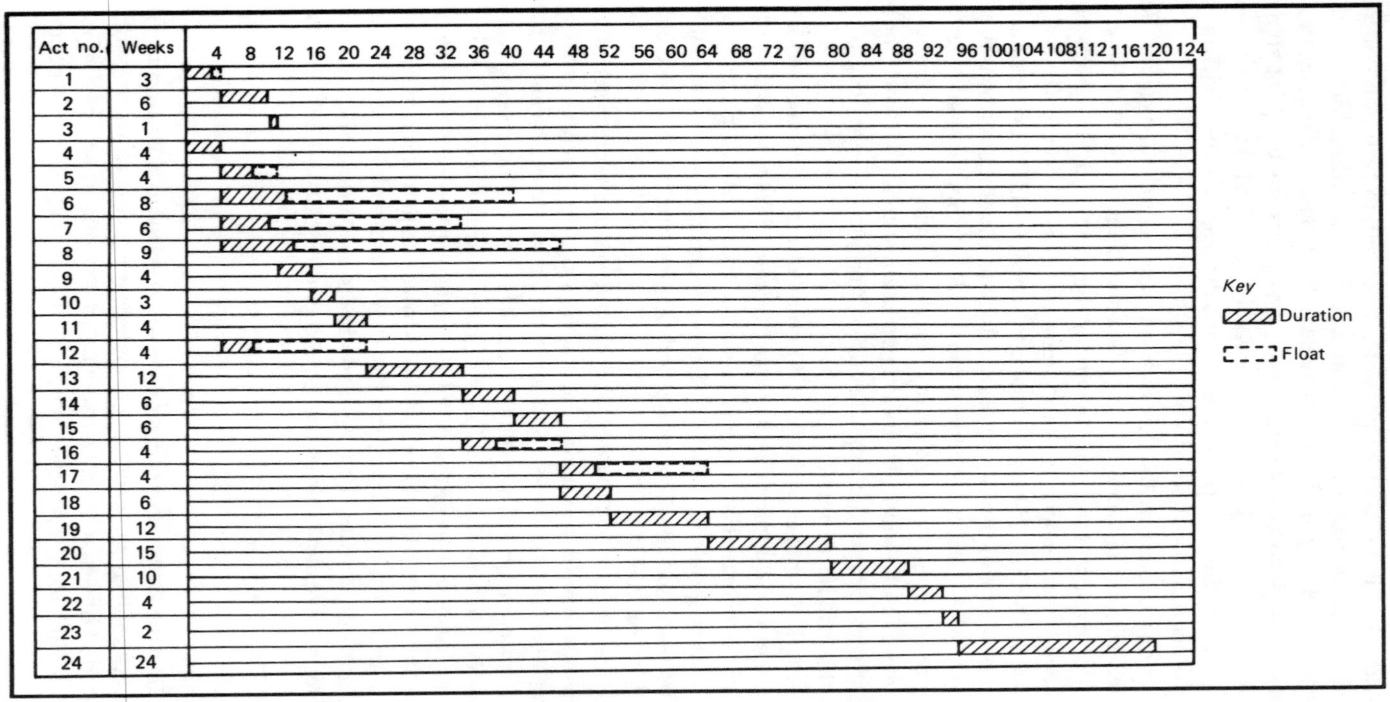
Act no.
Weeks
1 3
2 6
3 1
4 4
5 4
6 8
7 6
8 9
9 4
10 3
11 4
12 4
13 12
14 6
15 6
16 4
17 4
18 6
19 12
20 15
21 10
22 4
23 2
24 24
4 8 12 16 20 24 28 32 36 40 44 48 52 56 60 64 68 72 76 80 84 88 92 96 100 104 108 112 116 120 124
Key
Duration
Float

Figure 3.2 A bar chart based on the network analysis of Figure 3.1

activities on schedule it will also be possible, if desired, to plan non-critical activities so that peak demands on the student's time are reduced. It would, for example, be possible to undertake activities 5, 6, 7, 8 and 12 sequentially. Thus, it might be decided first to select the participants for the pilot study and to follow this, in order, with the acquisition of statistical skills, decisions on target population and sampling procedures, drafting out three chapters and, finally, the acquisition of computing skills.

Of course it may occur that the demands on the student's time cannot be accommodated within the various activity floats available. Under those circumstances the project time will inevitably be extended. In assessing whether this is likely to happen it is important not to over-commit oneself. Experience shows that it is always a mistake to schedule 100 per cent of any resource on a project and this applies particularly to the student's own time during research. The project manager's usual rule of thumb would be to commit no more than 80 per cent of any resource leaving 20 per cent as a contingency margin. Obviously, in drawing up the research plan, each individual student must assess the implications of this idea for the length of working day that will be assumed.

Over any length of time an average of 40 hours effective research work a week would seem to be appropriate for most research projects, particularly since this can be increased if progress is slower than desired. Excessively long hours of work should be confined to times when they are unavoidable and should be restricted to a few weeks with appropriate periods of relaxation allowed afterwards.

The other resource considerations that may affect the project schedule relate to activities that are not under the student's control, such as times at which lecture courses run or to constraints on access to hardware – for example, certain equipment may only be available during university vacations. Only a few such factors should affect any particular research project and these can usually be accommodated by intelligent use of the *bar chart*. Clearly, these and other adjustments which involve the juggling of float are more easily coped with by making the bar chart 'adjustable' in some way. One method is to use a magnetic board; another is to maintain the network on a computer so that new bar charts can be printed out almost instantaneously.

Replanning

It is evident that the seven points dealt with so far relate to the planning of the research. As soon as the project gets underway the role of the network changes from that of being purely a planning tool to one in which it is primarily a control device. Experience indicates that if the project is of any complexity, two outcomes are inevitable. Firstly, activity durations prove to be longer (rarely shorter) than planned and, secondly, the ordering of activities still to be started needs to be amended. The former can be accommodated without too much difficulty; particularly if the basic schedule (that is, before resources are taken into account) is computer generated. The latter can, however, create problems.

Because of the full-time student's need to complete the project by a specific date it is always necessary to have in mind the extent of work yet to be completed. If the order in which activities need to be tackled changes (for example, access to data is delayed) then the student cannot be certain that the target date is still feasible. The only way to satisfy oneself that this is so is to undertake a careful replanning which will involve a revision of the network. As this has to be done manually and as pressure may have arisen because of an unanticipated change foisted upon the student the temptation may exist to put off the re-drawing. This can result in a situation arising in which there is little relationship between the network and the project work (this is often encountered outside the academic world). It is at these points that the student needs the self-discipline to spend some time on an activity (replanning) which does not immediately further the research but which in the longer term may make the difference between completing on time and failing to do so.

RENDERING PROGRESS EXPLICIT: RESEARCH MILESTONES

There is space on the control chart (see Figure 3.2) to enter progress and the state of the study may be indicated by reference to a marker corresponding to the current week. This can be enhanced by filling in the duration allocated to each activity in a distinctive colour and marking the appropriate proportion of the bar below in the same colour as work progresses. This gives an immediate impression of which activities are ahead of schedule and which behind, provides a warning when dates begin to slip and, most importantly, provides a tangible measure of progress which can be very important in maintaining motivation as the project progresses. Alternatively, progress can be indicated by appropriately designed computer output.

A number of events in Figure 3.1 corresponding to the completion of a set of activities were designated as milestones by the student and depicted as circles in *the diagram*. These are particularly important events during a project where progress can be reviewed and will normally be at the end of activities whose outcome is to some extent uncertain. As such they form a natural point at which to assess progress and determine whether the research plan is still feasible or whether it needs modification. Usually, milestones will occur quite frequently but it is recommended that in a longer project no more than three months should be allowed between them. (We have deviated from this in Figure 3.1 for reasons of space.) In a shorter project – a dissertation for example – it is recommended that milestones be fixed at points which enable the feasibility of the project to be reviewed: for example, 'Topic is agreed with the supervisor'.

The achievement of a milestone should be marked by just such a review, involving at a minimum student and supervisor but quite possibly faculty members and students. This matter is discussed at greater length in Chapter 7.

THE ROLE OF NETWORK ANALYSIS DURING THE EXECUTION STAGE

The networks likely to be compiled by students will be much less complex than those used elsewhere and the task of re-drawing should not therefore be too great. Nevertheless, if networks are to be employed throughout the research they should reflect with reasonable accuracy the view which the student has of the sequence of activities likely to be followed until the end of the work. In other words, planning is not something that ceases once execution of the topic selected gets underway. Replanning may well need to be carried out several times in the light of appraisal of previous progress.

THE ADVANTAGES OF NETWORK ANALYSIS

Some students may not be attracted towards the idea of using network analysis. Before rejecting the idea it is argued that consideration should be given to the following advantages.
1. The emphasis on rigorous planning, schedules and milestones is a notion to which students with limited time at their disposal should become accustomed.
2. If a network is used to plan a research study there is little likelihood that significant activities which need to be anticipated will be overlooked.
3. The levelling out of major peaks of demand on the researcher's time or the elimination of *in*feasible requirements for other resources may be possible.
4. In the event that planning indicates that, despite the rough estimates included within the research proposal, there would seem to be little

prospect of achieving an acceptable completion date, major or minor changes to plan may be made.

5. The efforts of the student will be focused on the achievement of the next milestone, thus providing a way of regularly reviewing progress as the project unfolds and identifying situations in which replanning is needed.

6. Motivation is generated by visual evidence of tasks completed, together with an awareness of the extent to which endeavour should be increased.

7. The network and the associated charts provide an excellent basis for communicating to others what activities remain to be completed and how they are linked, achievement to date and the schedule the researcher proposes to follow. The very fact that the supervisor can be made aware of progress is a considerable aid to keeping on schedule. Moreover, the existence of a schedule makes it easier for student and supervisor to coordinate activities such as holidays, attendance at conferences, etc.

PLANNING PART-TIME RESEARCH

Most of the comments made so far in this chapter relate to full-time students. Part-time students have the added problem of planning their research so that it does not conflict with what is usually perceived as a full-time job. If the research is to be part of a mixed course involving study and project, it is beneficial if the topic can be related to the nature of the student's full-time occupation. If this is not the case students will need to give careful attention to the extra workload they are assuming.

Research for higher degrees, in particular, with its need for extensive background reading, implies that this must be undertaken in the student's own time, even if data gathering may take place during full-time employment. And, of course, in many instances part-time students must confine the whole of their research to their nominal leisure time, realising that this will extend considerably the duration of their studies.

There is much to commend the use of network analysis by part-time students; the ordering of activities being at least as valuable an aid to planning as in the case of the full-time student. The major problem in constructing a control chart from an analysis based on activity durations is the sensible estimation of elapsed times. Although the work content will be similar to that involved in full-time studies the often unpredictable effect of the student's occupation (due to promotion, transfers, special projects, and so on) will render estimates of time much more uncertain. Indeed, it is worth pointing out that if research degree students encounter serious interruption to their plans they should consider requesting a suspension of their registration for a period which may be as long as two years. If students are single-minded about their research though, and the nature of their job permits, control through schedule charts compiled from network analysis is realistic. In other cases it may be more sensible to adopt an approach in which progress is simply marked up on the network. This will enable the part-time student to either take stock periodically or to consider the extent to which milestones are, or (more importantly) are not, being achieved.

If, during the conduct of the research, there is a total disaster in the sense that it becomes impossible (for example, if facilities for fieldwork are withdrawn because of relocation or redundancy) or pointless (for example, if it is discovered that the work has been done before, or if logical errors come to light) it becomes even more essential that the student is able to assess what may be achieved during what time may still be available. The potential value of network analysis in these circumstances is obvious.

CHAPTER SUMMARY

PLANNING: can demonstrate the feasibility of student research within the time available by helping to identify all the activities which will be involved.

NETWORK ANALYSIS: although an additional task for the student, can be of great benefit in showing the interrelationships among activities and in providing the basis for a realistic control chart.

CONTROL CHARTS: enable students to smooth out their efforts when a number of tasks may be addressed in parallel.

NETWORKS & CHARTS: which reflect progress can act as motivational devices as completed work is recorded.

PLANNING IS A CONTINUOUS PROCESS: and is much facilitated by the network analysis approach. It should continue throughout the research to ensure that the work develops logically towards satisfying the aims of the researcher.

4

Literature Searching

INTRODUCTION

Most research work involves substantial use of published literature. Indeed, the ability to ferret out obscure facts is often seen as the primary activity of the researcher and the regulations for research degrees always contain a requirement that the candidate should demonstrate the ability to make proper critical use of relevant literature. Accordingly, the successful researcher needs to be able to do just this.

It is assumed that the reader is reasonably familiar with the use of libraries, particularly specialist and academic libraries. For our purpose the key features of such libraries are:

1. The existence of comprehensive catalogues (usually computer based). The catalogue of book stocks will be classified by author and class number. The latter, in academic Anglo-Saxon libraries, is often based on the Dewey Decimal Classification System together with a classified subject index that

allows the class number corresponding to a particular topic to be determined. In addition, many libraries now catalogue books by title. Catalogues of periodical material will normally consist of lists of journals, and so on, held and information on which issues are available.

2. Substantial collections of:

   a) primary sources – essentially the first publication of a piece of work;

   b) secondary sources – involving the indexing and classification of primary sources and the organisation of the information they contain into the general body of knowledge;

   c) tertiary sources – intended to facilitate the location of primary and secondary sources.

The sources that a researcher can use to carry out a literature search are listed in Table 4.1. Researchers should familiarise themselves with all the sources

---

Primary sources

Journal articles
Conference proceedings
Reports
Government publications
Patents
Standards
Catalogues, specifications, directories

Secondary sources

Monographs
Textbooks
Review series (annals)
Review papers in primary journals
Journals covering specific literatures
Subject abstracts
Indexes of publications
Current awareness/alerting services

Tertiary sources

Handbooks
Guides to specific literatures
Subject bibliographies
General bibliographies
Encyclopaedias

Table 4.1 Some literature sources

likely to be useful at the outset of their research. Academic libraries usually provide excellent tape/slide or film guides to their facilities and the way they are organised.

WHY SCAN THE LITERATURE?

There are two major reasons for carrying out a survey of the literature:
1. As part of the process of topic selection.
2. As part of the research project proper.

Reference has been made in Chapter 2 to a variety of questions that need to be taken into account when selecting a topic. Thus, there is the broad review of reported work in a field in the hope that previous authors will have suggested fruitful studies to be pursued by others. Equally, assessing the novelty of promising ideas will normally involve researchers checking the literature to ensure that the proposed topic has not been tackled before and to define an area of study that they can consider their own.

Having selected their topic, researchers will normally need to carry out several surveys of relevant published literature(s) in rather greater depth. The preparation of a detailed research proposal will require the researcher to define previous work in the proposed field and in those allied to it. Thus, for example, a study of the use of hovercraft in cross-Channel transport would certainly not confine itself to that mode of transport alone. It would be necessary to examine other means of crossing the Channel so as to clarify the unique features of a hovercraft-based service. Again, it would probably be necessary to look at the use of hovercraft in ferry services elsewhere in the world to ascertain whether they are particularly well suited to cross-Channel operations as compared to other means of crossing water. In assembling this wider picture, researchers would be able when presenting the research findings to make proper acknowledgement of the work of previous authors and to delineate their own contributions to the field.

As well as scanning the literatures of their chosen fields and related ones, most researchers find it necessary also to familiarise themselves with a rather different literature dealing with research tools appropriate to their topic. Thus, geophysicists may well find it necessary to employ Fourier Transform methods in analysing and interpreting data signals. A social scientist on the other hand may need to attain a reasonable proficiency in the use of statistical methods.

Most researchers, accordingly, have two broad types of literature search to do: firstly, the specific subject – closely related to the topic of interest – and, secondly, that on research methodology. Usually the former will need to be

74

pursued to considerably greater depth than the latter. It should be noted that some research projects involve the translation of methods devised in one field into another and normally require that an in-depth literature search be carried out for both fields.

A number of different phases can be expected in the course of a literature search in accordance with the various stages of the research plan. Whatever the purpose of a particular phase, only limited resources are available for its execution. Almost always, the restricted time that the researcher can devote to the task is the major constraint.

Often there will be the additional problem that there are insufficient funds to borrow all the desired references from a central library such as the BLDSC (British Library Document Supply Centre), or to pay for unlimited visits to a relevant specialist library. For this reason we shall examine various strategies for literature searching.

LITERATURE SEARCHES AND RELEVANCE TREES

A useful model of the literature searching process is to regard it as an exercise in the construction of a relevance tree of the type described in Chapter 2. At the topic level an initial keyword or subject, selected as a basis for searching, will lead to the discovery of further keywords derived from the early books and journals scanned. Some of these will lead to new literatures not directly related to that dealing with the initial subject. Each of these will in turn suggest further subject headings under which to search.

As an example of a relevance tree, Figure 4.1 shows one set of subjects that might be scanned in defining a topic within the broad framework 'Interviewing in social work'. The figure shows how, starting from the subject 'Interviewing in social work', three broad subject areas have been selected, namely: 'Interviewing in general'; 'The role of interviewing in social work practice'; and 'The Role of interviewing in social work theory'. These three have in turn been used to suggest further subjects.

Though at this stage it is not necessary to pursue any of the subjects in depth it will be assumed that, having advanced the search as shown in Figure 4.1, the researcher has gained sufficient feel for the literature of each to decide that the research will focus on the 'Effectiveness of the casework interview' and that important related subjects will be 'Interview techniques and counselling interviews'. At a later stage each of these subjects will probably form the starting point for another phase of the literature search. This example is, however, typical in that it involves four activities.

1. The generation of a number of alternative subjects/keywords.
2. Deciding which subjects to pursue.

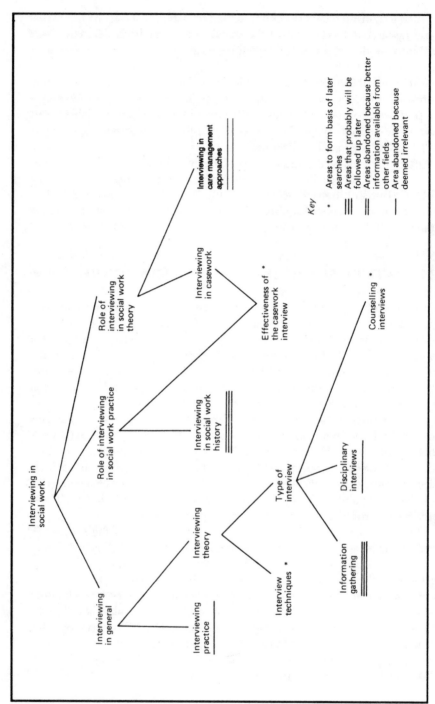

Figure 4.1 A relevance tree for the subject 'Interviewing in social work'

3. Deciding which subjects to abandon.
4. Deciding when sufficient effort has been put in for the purpose in hand so that the process can be (temporarily) halted.

To carry out these four activities effectively we need ways of generating new subjects since, without a touch of inventiveness at the start, our search is likely to be fairly superficial. Conversely, without criteria for abandoning lines of enquiry the literature search rapidly gets out of hand.

The Generation of Alternative Subjects

Once the literature search is successfully under way, finding new, related, subjects ceases to be a problem. In practice, the difficulty of getting started can vary enormously from one subject to another. Thus, researchers who have only a few weeks available to conduct their work should stick to the rule that if they cannot get their literature search beyond the stage of looking for new subject areas within a couple of hours, they should select another topic. They can, therefore, restrict their efforts to looking at four sources of ideas.
1. The alphabetical subject index.
2. Journals.
3. Encyclopaedias/guides and handbooks.
4. Thesauri/dictionaries.

Subject Index
The alphabetical subject index provides a quick and convenient way of finding related subject areas or alternative terms for the same keyword. It also provides a rough and ready guide to the volume of literature in a particular area, since, broadly speaking, a subject area is extensively subdivided only if a substantial amount has been written on it. Once a subject has been identified the subject index will provide its class number. The classified catalogue can then be consulted to provide a list of all books that belong to that particular classification.

A useful trick is, therefore, to find one relevant book, ascertain its subject classification and then consult the classified catalogue for other similar books.

Journals
Usually, journals cover a much wider range of subjects and therefore cannot be classified as precisely as books. Nevertheless, some classification scheme should exist for them that will enable the student to locate journals most likely to be relevant.

In many fields, the PERMUTERM Subject Indexes of the non-computer versions of the Social Science Citation Index, the Science Citation Index, and the Arts and Humanities Citation Index, or a computer search on journal article titles and keywords (as discussed later) provide an alternative way of constructing the relevance tree.

Encyclopaedia

Encyclopaedias provide an excellent method of getting a quick feel for a subject and a picture of knowledge in that field and related areas.

It should be remembered that as well as general encyclopaedias, such as the *Encyclopaedia Britannica*, a variety of more specialist guides and handbooks exist on particular subjects (*cf.* Walford, 1994). Nowadays, many of these sources are available on CD–ROM and therefore extremely convenient to search, if the relevant CD–ROMs can be accessed.

Dictionaries

Where a topic cannot be found in an encyclopaedia or guide, dictionaries are useful for suggesting terms having a similar meaning which can be looked up instead. Note that some fields – for example, social science – have their own dictionaries. A further possibility is to use a thesaurus – that is, a list of alternative terms for the same concept. As well as general thesauri, such as *Roget's Thesaurus*, certain specialist libraries maintain ones specific to the field they cover. The researcher with more time to spare can often profitably make use of additional sources of ideas as discussed later.

Deciding which Subjects to Abandon

Given our broad interest in effective management of student research a word of caution is appropriate at this point. Though many research projects may involve systems that are developing rapidly (for example, the Internet in the early 1990s) researchers must limit the time they spend scanning the literature if they are not to prejudice other activities.

Without mechanisms for deciding which lines of enquiry not to pursue, most literature searches soon get completely out of control. For this reason many researchers adopt the often somewhat arbitrary rule of scanning only 'the literature of the subject'. In some well-defined fields, for example, particle physics, such a strategy is very sensible. In other less clear areas, such as economics, this may be detrimental to the quality of the literature survey. Thus, as well as examining the literature of industrial relations the researcher in the field of wage bargaining might well be advised to consider the literature of conflict theory which might not necessarily be considered relevant to the industrial relations specialist.

If the literature search is not to be confined within the straitjacket of 'the literature', other ways must be found to decide which avenues not to explore.

In practice this means applying one of three rules.
1. Abandon it because it is irrelevant to the area of interest.
2. Ignore it because the literature of some other subject (to be) studied covers the ideas better.
3. Do not pursue it any further for the present since sufficient information has been obtained for that purpose for which the search is being carried out.

Thus, in the example of Figure 4.1, our researcher has not further subdivided the asterisked items because though all will need to be examined further enough work has been done on them for the present. Similarly, the triply underlined items though probably relevant in a later phase of the literature search do not require further elaboration at this stage.

As an example of Rule 2 above, the researcher's decision not to follow up the role of interviewing in care management (doubly underlined) is noted. This is because interviewing plays a far more central role in casework and as such it is unlikely that the literature of care management will provide insights not available from the casework literature. Finally, the singly underlined subjects have been excluded from further study on the grounds that they are probably irrelevant to the subject of interest.

The literature searching strategy embodied in Figure 4.1, whereby the search commences with a very specific subject and is gradually extended into related areas, is of general applicability. The search should always start with the most specific subject definition the researcher is able to supply. Where there is a copious literature the researcher may never need to go beyond this initial subject to amass sufficient references. Where less has been published the relevance tree approach provides a systematic way of expanding the search.

CITATION RELEVANCE TREES

Most articles of a research nature cite previous work and in doing so tend to reference seminal books and articles in the field of interest. Major articles in that field not only provide a useful way into past literature but also with the help of the citation indexes[1], into journal articles published at a later date. The principle of the Science Citation Index, the Social Science Citation Index, and the Arts and Humanities Citation Index is a simple one. For each article by a particular author, the citation index lists articles that have cited it in a particular interval of time. This provides a way of picking up subsequent articles on the same subject. Reference to the index then provides a list of papers cited by those authors. Besides covering articles in academic journals, the citation indexes also cover book reviews in such journals and conference proceedings.

Using a Citation Index

While at higher levels of research there are few subjects for which a literature search can be conducted solely using a citation index, there are many topics for which the use of the Science Citation Index, Social Science Citation Index, or the Arts and Humanities Citation Index forms a natural starting point.

The major knowledge citation indexes assume is the names of one or two important authors in the field or some familiarity with the technical terms used in the broad area of study and a general knowledge of how to use the academic literature. In particular, the paper versions of the citation indexes have the advantage that they are usually to be found on a single shelf within the library, often close to abstracts and other bibliographical material. The researcher can then more quickly build up a bibliography of references than if by deriving them from individual articles in different journals, which might well be in different physical locations and certainly will not follow a consistent set of standards with regard to indexes and so on. Also, searches start from the name of a relevant author and this fits the way in which researchers mentally file details of major papers in their field.

However, the citation indexes do not work equally well in all subjects. Fields where articles make relatively little use of citation of other articles or where references are to personal communications pose problems as do references to works whose relationship to the research being described is tenuous or which have been superseded by better ones. The researcher must expect therefore that their use will lead to a certain proportion of unfruitful references and must decide whether these are likely to be adequately compensated for by the successful ones.

Figure 4.2 shows an example of a forward literature search using the Science Citation Index in the classic way.[2] The general field of interest of the researcher is the topic of computer security. From an article by Landwehr, published in 1983, it is possible to construct a relevance tree extending forward in time. The citation indexes provide an effective way of carrying out a literature search in many fields. Because they deal with recent journal articles, book reviews in academic journals and conference proceedings, they are most useful for subjects that are evolving rapidly. In such fields, most publications of relevance to the researcher are likely to be found in journal articles published in the past few years. Conversely, in fields such as history where articles published several decades ago may well be extremely relevant or in fields where most important reference material is to be found in books, the citation indexes are less useful. Nevertheless, in many fields they provide

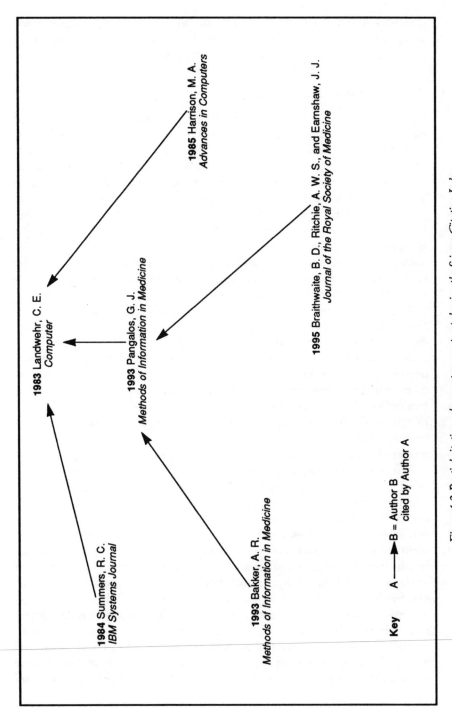

Figure 4.2 Partial citation relevance tree constructed using the Science Citation Index

at a very minimum an important check that no major articles have been over-looked and the reader who is unfamiliar with them is advised to consult the citation indexes themselves for further information on their use.

Closing Off the Citation Tree

Just as it is necessary to restrict the growth of a subject relevance tree so too the researcher needs to find ways of halting the growth of the citation tree. Two ideas are particularly useful here. Firstly, the notion of core references. In any reasonably established field certain articles embody the key ideas of the subject and this is evidenced by the frequency with which they are cited by other authors. Similarly, any particular field of research will have core journals in which any major work in the area is most likely to be published. Defining core books and journals restricts the citation tree by limiting the citations that will be followed up to those publications. Armed with the names of core journals the researcher can rapidly extend the list by using the volume to identify those journals that carry most of the references cited by authors of papers in the journals already known.

The notion of core journals is used by librarians in many subject areas as a basis for bibliographic services such as lists of current contents of journals or for deciding which journal articles should be abstracted. Accordingly, examination of the journals scanned in preparing bibliographic information provides one quick way of establishing the core journals. An alternative method that can sometimes be used is to examine the volume of the Science (Social Science or Arts and Humanities) Citation Index that provides infor-mation on the frequency with which articles in a specified journal cite other journals, though this is becoming more difficult as more and more libraries replace the paper form of the citation indexes by computer databases.

The scope of a search may be reduced by setting a publication date prior to which references will not be followed up. Obviously, the date set must depend on the field. A guide is easily obtained in libraries that date stamp books on issue. The concept of the half-life of journals is well established and finds practical embodiment in many large academic libraries in that only the latest years of a journal are readily accessible. For years which precede the half-life other modes of storage are often adopted – for example, restricted access stacks. Obviously the cut-off date varies from subject to subject. In rapidly changing fields such as particle physics it may be only a few years ago whereas in fields such as economics or social history, publications dating back fifty years or more may well be very useful.

It should be remembered that for a preliminary search in a field the cut-off date need not be set very far back since most authors refer to and summarise the work of their predecessors. The literature of the past ten or twenty years will therefore usually provide a reasonable outline of the field for fifty years or more. If at a later stage of searching it appears that significant work on the subject was published before the cut-off date an earlier date must obviously be chosen. As a concrete instance of this twofold approach we may take the notion of 'continental drift' that was important to the development of the theory of plate tectonics. The student of geomorphology in the early 1960s would have had little difficulty in finding references to the continental drift hypothesis put forward by Wegener, fifty years before. Though summaries of the idea were often sceptical, and frequently dismissive, they nonetheless provided a sufficient basis for understanding the key concepts. Thus, a student carrying out a preliminary search in this field needed only to examine books and articles published, say, up to fifteen years previously. If eventually the student decided that it was relevant to the research topic then it would have been possible to have gone back to the work of Wegener and, indeed, earlier workers. In effect, their cut-off date would probably have needed to be moved back to 1900.

SOME USEFUL SOURCES

Most searches are likely to rely mainly on books and journal articles. Since these are familiar items they need no further comment except to say that in any reasonably rapidly changing field, researchers should expect that most of their references will be to articles rather than books, which are usually less up to date. Other types of source are, however, used much more frequently in some fields than others and therefore their special advantages warrant further consideration.

Reports/Occasional Papers

In many fields, technical reports can be a major source of information. It may well be, therefore, that the more complete account given in a technical report will be of greater use to the researcher than journal articles on the subject. Furthermore, the reports of certain research groups are sufficiently prestigious for the researchers concerned to favour them as a method of disseminating their results. The upshot is that, as well as being more comprehensive, research reports are often more up to date. Similar remarks apply to the occasional papers which tend to be published by many research units particularly in the social sciences. Obviously, this is a special category of material and details of it are usually best obtained through special guides such as those produced by the BLDSC, mentioned earlier, in the UK and through the *STAR Index* (Scientific Technical and Aerospace Reports) in the

USA. In many cases these guides also provide information on how a copy of the report can be obtained.

Theses and Dissertations

At the doctoral level it is necessary to establish that the researcher has made an original contribution to knowledge. Accordingly, it will normally be necessary to check that no theses on the lines the researcher proposes have been published.

Major academic libraries carry lists of theses accepted for higher degrees in various countries, in particular Britain and the USA. For example, the *BRTT* (British Reports, Translations and Theses) *Bulletin* as well as listing reports, translations, theses and so on produced by British government organisations, industry and academic institutions also lists most doctoral theses produced at British universities. The *ASLIB Index* covers theses produced as a result of a research study and is an index to theses with abstracts accepted for higher degrees by the universities of Great Britain and Ireland plus certain others. The *BRITS Index*, published by the British Theses Service, provides another source for theses in the period 1971–87, being last published in 1989. Since the *ASLIB Index* tends to be one or two years behind, it is useful to be able to supplement this by information from *CRIB* (Current Research in Britain) which covers most types of research.

From the appropriate volume of *CRIB* the researcher can identify and contact the workers in UK academic institutions most likely to be carrying out and supervising research in their area.

For theses published in the USA similar information can be obtained from *Dissertation Abstracts International.*

Government Publications

The amount of material published on behalf of governments is enormous and forms an important reference source for many types of research. Indeed, for much UK research this material is a major secondary data source. For this reason it will be considered in more detail in Chapter 6.

Because of the sheer volume of material produced most academic libraries classify government publications separately, very often outside the normal subject index system. Accordingly, researchers need to ascertain whether important material is to be found under government publications and, if so, find how to obtain it in the libraries they use. In the UK, for instance, this will mean consulting the annual, monthly or daily lists of material published by HMSO or the *Catalogue of British Official Publications not published by HMSO.*

In the USA, monthly lists of the US Government Publications Office provide similar information.

Standards/Codes of Practice

Standards can be an important source of information in technological fields since the introduction of new standards may well spawn considerable development activity and in some markets is a major determinant of product performance. For the latter reason, standards and the similar codes of practice may also be important as a data source for the researcher interested in the history of some aspect of technology. In the UK, the most important source of standards is the British Standards Institution (BSI), with similar roles in the USA being fulfilled by the American National Standards Institute, in Germany by DIN standards, in the European Union by EN Standards and, internationally, by ISO Standards.

Outside science and engineering most professional bodies also publish standards or codes of practice with which their members must comply. In the accounting field in the UK, for example, the Institute of Chartered Accountants plays a major role in determining accounting standards.

Patents

In many types of applied research in technology, patents are important either because they indicate new techniques and methods to solve particular problems or because they suggest further inventions that did not occur to the originator of the patent. They also provide an important data source for researchers interested in the history or economics of invention and innovation.

Information on patents appears in a number of indexing and abstracting services. Copies of British patents are available in the UK from regional patent deposit libraries, members of the British Library Patents Information Network. Ideas are usually patented in more than one country, so using a concordance of patents which gives the number assigned to the application for the same patent in different countries makes it possible to find, say, the British application corresponding to a patent that was first taken out in Japan.

Trade Journals and Newspapers

In certain types of research, especially in rapidly changing fields such as information technology, trade journals and newspapers can be important data sources. This is particularly true of the former which often carry information that is not recorded elsewhere.

Practice with regard to the storage of trade journals varies widely in the UK. Few libraries, save the Copyright Libraries[3], take more than a small fraction of those published reflecting the fact that many of them are most unlikely to be used again once they cease to be current. Furthermore, many of those that are taken are not bound, with the result that individual issues may disappear. For these reasons such material is often not all that easy to use and the researcher may well find it worthwhile going to a specialist library for it.

The position is somewhat better as far as UK national newspapers are concerned as there are a number of commercial indexing services available for the quality press at least. For example, *NEWSPLAN* (formerly the *British Newspaper Index*) provides an index to materials contained in *The Times*, the *Sunday Times*, the *Financial Times*, the *Independent* and the *Independent on Sunday*. The *Clover Newspaper Index* covers besides these newspapers, the *Daily Telegraph*, the *Sunday Telegraph*, the *Guardian*, the *Observer*, the *Economist* and the *European*. Microfilm or microfiche copies of major newspapers are available which, though somewhat inconvenient to use, do ensure that copies of fairly recent material are available. Increasingly, abstracts of the text of newspapers are available through online computer services such as Profile or Lexis. The text of a number of newspapers (*The Times*, the *Independent*, etc.) has been available in machine readable form for some time.

Where local newspapers are concerned matters are more complex. It is unlikely that any formal index is available and therefore it may be necessary to work through them systematically for the period of interest if that was some time ago. For relatively current material, however, excellent advice may well be available from the newspapers' own libraries.

Ephemera

Much material is not stored in the library in the usual way and, indeed, may not be catalogued. Examples are company reports, specifications of products, catalogues, price lists, opera programmes, notices of forthcoming sales, applications for planning consents, and so on. Such items are not published in the formal sense and are generally referred to by librarians as ephemera because they are normally useful only for a brief period.

Libraries generally have no obligation to stock ephemera and individual items are likely to be traceable only if they are of sufficient interest to collectors for a catalogue to have been published – for example, Victorian Christmas cards – or they form part of a recognised collection of historical material that has been properly catalogued. However, there is a very large European project called SIGLE (System for Information on Grey Literature in Europe) available online, on CD–ROM, etc. The only useful counsel that can be offered to all but the very experienced researcher is that, if circumstances warrant, an attempt should be made to solicit the support of an expert on ephemera in the field of interest.

Abstracts

Contributors to academic journals are, almost invariably, required to submit an abstract of their articles to be published at the head of the full text. In many fields one or more abstracting services exist that give summaries of the contents of journal articles and/or patents. Such services are reasonably up to date since they tend to be compiled electronically and cover a wider range of journals in the field than are available in all except the very largest libraries.

An example of how this type of service might be enhanced is provided by the *ANBAR Abstracts* in the field of management, delivered in both hard copy and electronically. Independent abstractors, with subject expertise, compile the abstracts and add comments thus providing researchers with an opportunity to narrow the search. A similar facility is offered by abstracting services in other fields.

These services are accordingly of great utility to the researcher who finds a reference to an article in a journal not kept by their own library. Under those circumstances it has normally been necessary in the UK to order a copy from the BLDSC, a process that costs several pounds and which may take up to two weeks. Obviously, there is virtue in studying an abstract, to find out whether the article is likely to be worth reading or merely duplicates material already studied.

An indication of the benefits of developing technology to the researcher is the recent introduction by the British Library and a commercial partner of a document delivery service, via fax or to desktop computers, within seconds of receipt of the request. A similar service is also being introduced to British Universities via the BIDS system, discussed later.

Most abstracting services classify articles in accordance with the subjects they cover; they also provide an indexing service. Services of this type therefore provide an alternative approach to carrying out a literature search aimed at finding articles on a particular topic. Again, the advent of the PC means that abstracts are increasingly available through bibliographic services that are available in CD–ROM format, for example, the business information service ABI Inform.

CARRYING OUT A LITERATURE SEARCH

The major features of literature searching are summarised in Figure 4.3 by use of six flowcharts (see Charts 1, 1a, and 2 to 5).

The variety of subjects and the numerous possible purposes of a literature search inevitably mean that readers will need to adapt the advice given to their particular circumstances.[4] To aid that process each of the charts is now discussed and the major assumptions arising from this discussion are outlined.

Overall Flowchart for a Literature Search (Chart 1)

This gives a broad picture of the process of carrying out a literature search. The first question to be answered is: 'Does the researcher have access to the relevant theses or dissertations?' If so, the search should begin with these. Also the researcher may know a number of references (possibly by author's name) in the field. Where references are known the researcher may wish to be sure that these are comprehensive prior, for example, to putting together the final version of a thesis (this is a special need and is dealt with in Chart 4). If this is not the aim and some key papers are known, the researcher's knowledge of the field is almost certainly sufficient to base the literature search on journal articles (Chart 3).

If none of the above apply, then the researcher is more or less starting from scratch. In that case the alphabetical subject index is usually the best place to begin. This gives the class number of each subject. Once the relevant class number is obtained, the classified subject catalogue should then be consulted to find the names of all books on the subject held by the libraries to which the researcher has access.

If the search is initially to be based on books the researcher may well hope to find bibliographies which list relevant books and indeed journals. Having exhausted these sources of references it may then be appropriate to turn to government publications. At this point, if the library concerned does not list all its own theses and dissertations in the classified subject catalogue, a check should be made using the various abstracts of theses and dissertations to locate any relevant ones available in the researcher's own library. Alternatively, theses and dissertations can be requested from other universities, provided the researcher is willing to wait the necessary length of time for them to be obtained. (The time needed to obtain a thesis may be substantial, particularly one presented at a foreign institution. It is, therefore, worthwhile getting an estimate of the time needed from a librarian.) Finally, if the researcher wishes to broaden the area of search this can be done by returning to an earlier point in the flowchart.

In general, the search will terminate when either the new references being generated are to material already examined or to unimportant sources or where the researcher has reached the limit of the time or money that can be devoted to the particular search. In many fields the complete execution of all

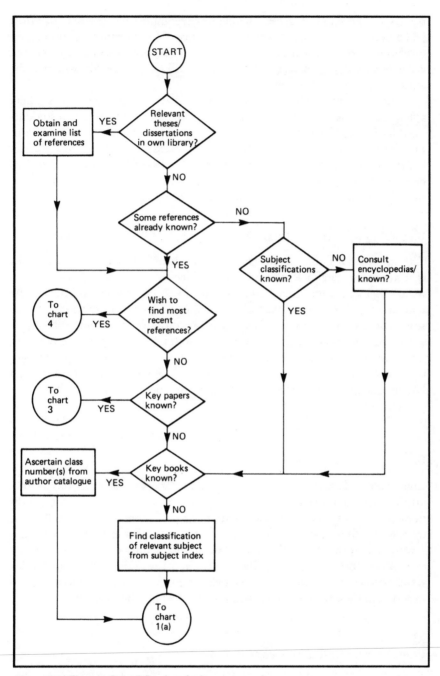

Figure 4.3 Chart 1: Overall flowchart for literature search

the stages shown on this chart would involve impossible amounts of effort and much pointless reduplication of references. In recognition of this fact we have indicated on this chart, and subsequent ones, convenient breakpoints or milestones where the researcher may take stock and decide whether the search has gone far enough.

It should be remembered that in the longer research project, at least, there will usually be several stages of literature searching. Hardly ever will students need to find all references on their chosen subject. Rather, they must continually ask themselves: 'Is this relevant to my research?'; 'For what chapter is this material needed?'; 'Will this article provide sufficient new material to be useful?'

Following up a Book (Chart 2)

The major assumption of this chart is that it is much easier to obtain books that are in the catalogue of a library to which one has ready access than to obtain them via inter-library loans or visits to specialist libraries. Indeed, the two latter sources are increasingly subject to budgetary restrictions. Where some older books are concerned it may be difficult to provide full bibliographic details, that is, title, publisher, and so on. Under these circumstances it will be necessary to consult suitable catalogues such as the British Library General Catalogue of Printed Books or the US Library of Congress National Union Catalog so that the researcher can be confident that the book will arrive if ordered.

Finding Articles (Chart 3)

This chart deals with the broad principles of obtaining references to journal articles given that certain references to them are already known. The conditions under which citation indexes are likely to be useful have already been discussed. Where these are fulfilled and they are available, they are a natural starting place; otherwise, the researcher should identify either a core journal or a set of abstracts with a subject index and find subject headings under which known key articles have been classified. These same subject classifications can then be used as the basis for retrieving other articles.

Finding Recent References (Chart 4)

Again, if applicable, the citation indexes are usually the best way of ensuring

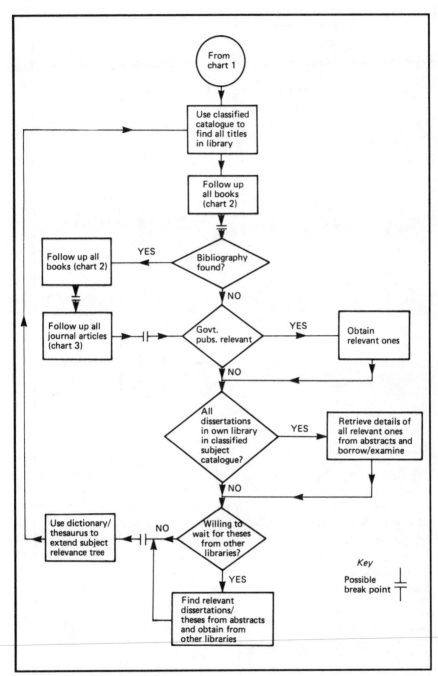

Chart 1a Overall flowchart for literature search

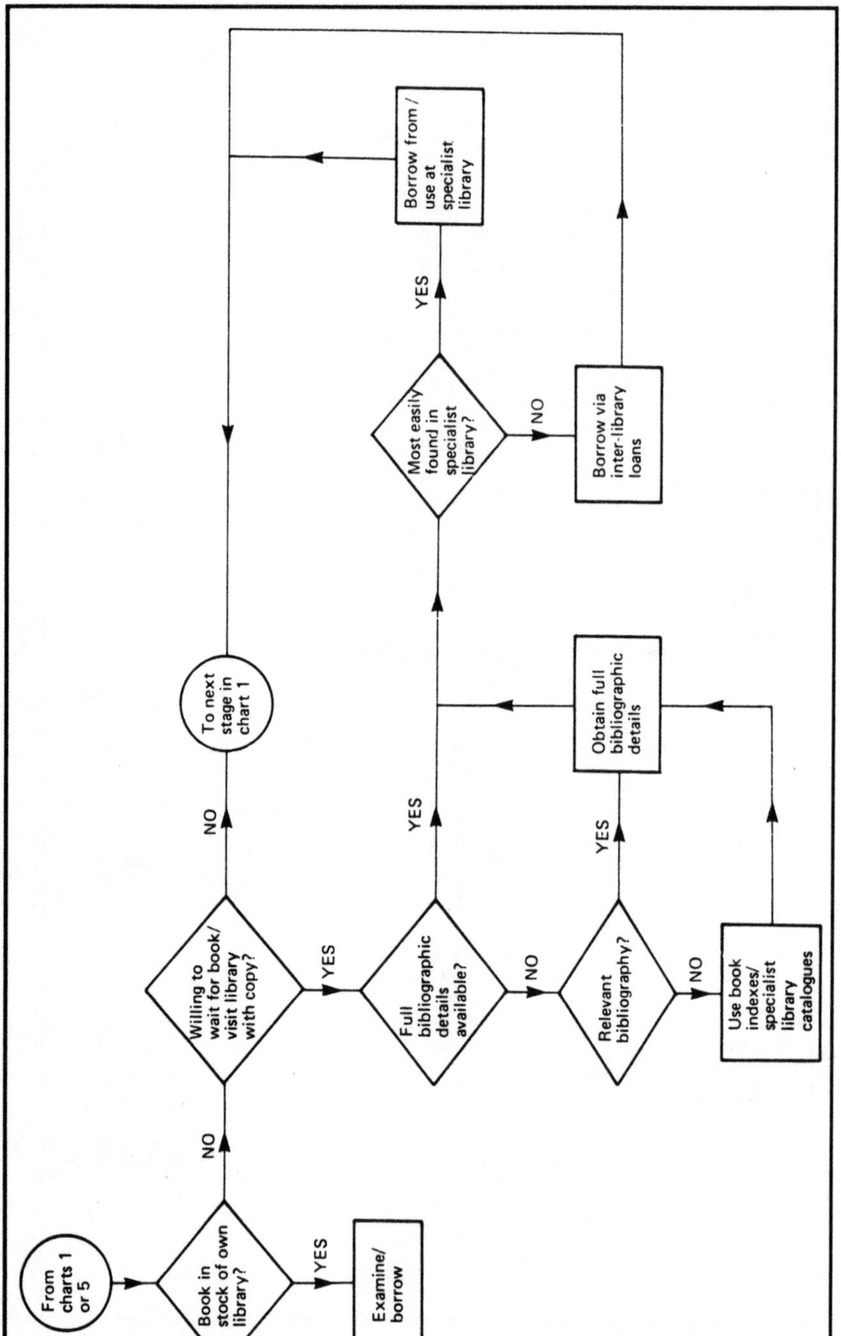

Chart 2 Following up a book

Flowchart contents:

From charts 1 or 5 → Book in stock of own library?
- YES → Examine/borrow
- NO → Willing to wait for book/visit library with copy?
  - NO → To next stage in chart 1
  - YES → Full bibliographic details available?
    - YES → Most easily found in specialist library?
      - YES → Borrow from / use at specialist library
      - NO → Borrow via inter-library loans
    - NO → Relevant bibliography?
      - YES → Obtain full bibliographic details
      - NO → Use book indexes/specialist library catalogues → Obtain full bibliographic details

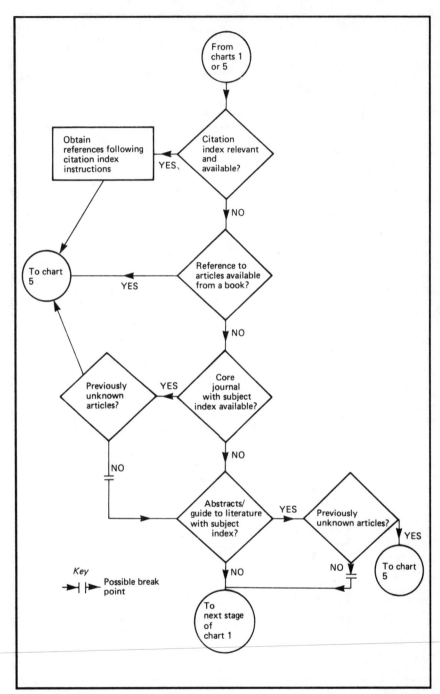

Chart 3 Finding articles

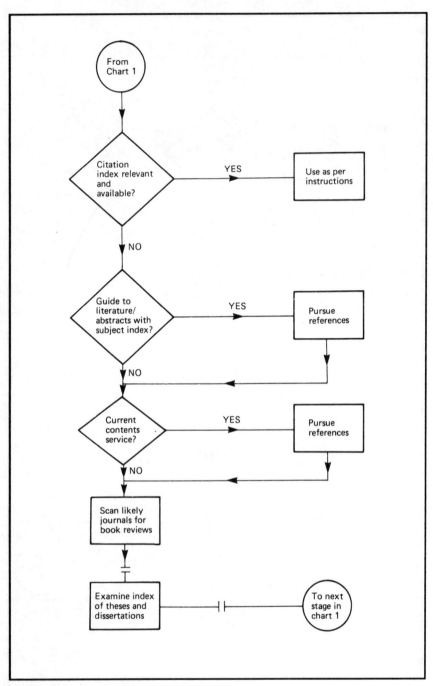

Chart 4 Finding recent references

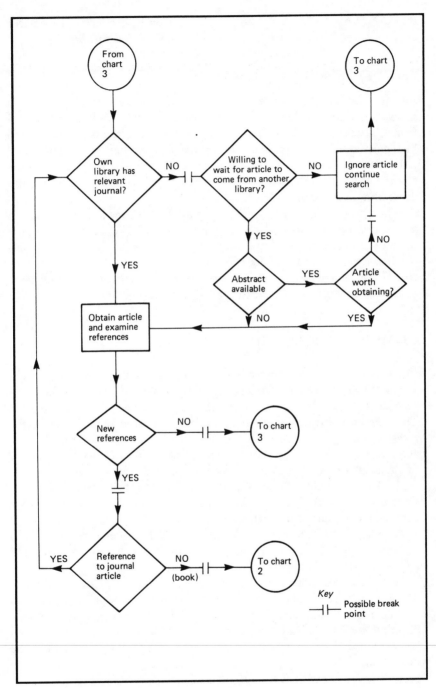

Chart 5 Following up an article

that a literature search is up to date. Alternatively, abstracting or current awareness services if available can be used for the same purpose.

Following up an Article (Chart 5)

As with books, it is far easier to make use of an article in a journal that is stocked by the researcher's own library than it is to wait for it to be obtained from elsewhere. Where the journal is not stocked all the previously noted budgetary restrictions are likely to apply but, since there are usually more articles than books on a topic, perhaps with more force. It follows that the researcher needs to think even more carefully before ordering articles from other libraries than about ordering books.

Whereas the researcher's own library may not stock the journal concerned it may well subscribe to an abstracting or review service which will enable the researcher to gain a good impression of the contents of the article. Usually the article itself will cite various other works, particularly if it is a review article. These, of course, should be followed up in their turn, provided the researcher is happy that the effort involved is worthwhile.

COMPUTER SEARCHES

In the UK, most student researchers are likely to find that their library's subject index and catalogue are actually computer-based – indeed, they will probably have access to the computer based catalogues of other libraries. There are also many bibliographic databases that can be accessed by the researcher using a PC as an online computer terminal to access the database at a remote site (often in another country) or by using a PC to access a copy of the database on CD–ROM.[5] Indeed, the majority of student researchers in the UK probably now employ such an approach to literature searching since paper copies of bibliographic sources such as the citation indexes have become too expensive for many libraries to afford.

A bibliographic database contains a list of articles, patents, reports and so on covering specific fields. Usually, the titles of the articles, their authors, and additional keywords appended to give a better description of the article's contents, are recorded on the database, as well as, in many cases, an abstract of the article. The detailed way in which a search is conducted varies from one database to another. The general principle, however, is that various descriptors are provided by the user and all articles whose titles or associated keywords match these descriptors are printed out by the system. Thus the descriptor:

SEWER and (MAINTENANCE or REPAIR)

will result in all articles whose titles (or keywords) contain the words SEWER(S) and MAINTENANCE in either order, or the words SEWER(S) and REPAIR in either order being printed out.

Such databases have two disadvantages: firstly, it can be expensive for an academic library to gain access to them so not all are necessarily accessible to students, for example, databases of company financial information; and, secondly, they usually contain only relatively recent information extending back perhaps fifteen years. Because it is impractical to separate out a small number of relevant references from a welter of irrelevant ones it is important either to begin the search with a very specific referencing term as described earlier or to request details only of references that cover similar subjects to a key reference supplied by the user.

As already noted, abstracts of articles are usually to be found in computer databases. These are particularly useful in conjunction with the document delivery service that is increasingly available with online systems. Document delivery is either by mail, or more expensively (but quicker) by fax or E-mail. The charge per document delivered is, in the UK, several pounds, so it makes sense to determine from the abstract whether the document is likely to be useful.

Most databases are designed for international use and therefore can spread the very large cost of maintaining them over a worldwide clientele. In many cases databases are capable of generating a wider set of reference material on many topics than would be possible by conventional means. It is for this reason that their importance to researchers has grown considerably as the amount of information held on them has increased. The ability to use such systems successfully ought to be a major benefit that any student should aim to get from a research project.

THE INTERNET

Over the past decade most higher educational institutions (and increasingly those at lower levels) have acquired access to the global computer network, currently referred to as the Internet.

Growing numbers of students are permitted access to the Internet by their institution. That network is of considerable interest to the student researcher because it is greatly accelerating the speed at which information is disseminated for research purposes. There are many thousand specialist mailing lists/bulletin boards where the student researcher is likely to find bibliographies and references related to the subject of the bulletin board.

Bulletin boards often have a relatively short existence while a new subject is developing. At such times, however, they can often host lively debates on contentious issues. In a way, the student researcher becomes party to something like an international conference to which their contributions will be welcomed provided they help to foster debate.

SETTING UP ONE'S OWN BIBLIOGRAPHY

The computer databases embody a principle that is important for the individual researcher – the results of a literature search need to be incorporated in the researcher's own bibliography. Sooner or later some or all of the references will have to be compiled into a list for a dissertation or a thesis or an article in an academic journal. They must, therefore, be recorded in sufficient detail to facilitate this process and preferably in such a way that the multiplicity of different referencing standards – for example, numbered in order of appearance, listed in alphabetical order – are readily accommodated. Furthermore, a good bibliography in any new field is a very tradeable commodity and researchers who possess one are likely to find that if they make it available to other researchers those researchers will in turn make their data available to them. Certainly, for students who come after them (including perhaps their own subsequent research students), such a bibliography is invaluable.

For these reasons we shall now discuss how students can set up their own computer bibliography. Using a sophisticated word-processing package, a spreadsheet, or even a simple communications package, the effort involved in developing such a database is little different from that required to record the necessary information manually. Indeed, there are a number of PC-based packages that are specifically available for this purpose.

A bibliographic database can only be set up if certain standards are adopted. It should be remembered that a system intended for use mainly by one or few researchers need not have the sophistication of a commercial system; the user needs only to adopt a suitable set of conventions. This will usually involve carrying the following information for each reference:

Author(s)/editor(s)
    Type of work; book, paper, thesis, for instance and for example

for a book	*for a journal article*
title	title of paper
edition	name of journal
number of volumes	volume
publisher	issue
place of publication	page numbers
date of publication	year

Research students may well find it useful to produce further information, as:

A set of KEYWORDS describing the contents of the work
Supplementary information

Given that a comprehensive set of details are recorded, the biggest problems likely to be encountered are:
a) spelling errors which can easily be removed if each reference is checked after entry;
b) the transliteration of certain foreign names, where different publishers and writers adopt different conventions – for instance, 'Dostoevsky', 'Dostoevski'.

The remedy for the latter problem is for researchers to adopt one standard and stick to it. Provided they are consistent all occurrences of this name can be edited to some other form at a later date, if desired.

In this connection, it is worth noting that for referencing there are bibliographic standards: for example, in the UK, *BS 4821: Recommendations for the Presentation of Theses*, published (1982) by the BSI.

The practice adopted by the major international databases, for example, the citation indexes referred to earlier, themselves constitute a set of *de facto* standards. It is sensible for student researchers to bear such standards and quasi-standards in mind when selecting a format for their own bibliographies, since this greatly facilitates downloading of information from international databases directly into the student's own bibliographic database.

It is suggested that in the second section of the reference, keywords are given describing the work in question. The individual researcher should give them serious consideration, since their use makes possible much more effective searches within the database. Given the restricted amount of information that can be incorporated in a title (particularly in the case of books), and the fact that titles can mislead as to contents, if searches are based on title alone, a number of relevant references will be missed.

To implement a keyword system the researcher needs to set up a thesaurus of keywords for indexing purposes. This must be sufficiently detailed for a precise description of the contents of any work to be given but should remain reasonably small. It should be remembered that there will often be synonymous terms. In such cases one should be chosen as the thesaurus term and a note should be made under the synonyms of the term actually adopted. In general, for one researcher a thesaurus of a few hundred terms should suffice. Nevertheless, maintenance of the thesaurus is made easier by keeping that on the computer also. Again, it should be borne in mind that international databases may well have relevant terms in their thesaurus and, for obvious reasons, it is useful for the student to conform with these, where possible.

The use of keywords means that the researcher needs to provide a list for each of the references read. This is a useful discipline and is a way of making at least brief notes on a reference and is a check on whether the researcher has understood it. The number of terms used need not be particularly large; the aim, after all, is to categorise the article or book not reproduce it. In fact, in most fields, a dozen or so terms seems quite adequate for all save the exceptional work.

The third section of the record allowing supplementary information to be recorded is usually also worthwhile. It normally causes little trouble to design such a feature into the system from the outset even if, initially, it is not used. To incorporate it later, however, may well be more difficult. This type of facility is useful because most researchers need to record additional information about some references: for example, which libraries hold it, or the researcher's opinion of the work, or quotations from it that may be useful for eventual incorporation into the thesis.

SERENDIPITY IN LITERATURE SEARCHING

The preceding sections have been concerned with the execution of a formal literature search. While at this point the importance of mastering the procedures involved is re-emphasised, it is worth reminding the student that there are also benefits to be gained from relatively unplanned, intermittent and informal searching activities. Browsing in sections of the library where books related to the field of study are stocked provides one such method. Regular inspection of the new titles shelf to be found in most libraries provides another. Casual observation of the books and journals other researchers – perhaps in very different fields – are using is a third way. A lively curiosity about and a good general knowledge of one's own field of study are also very useful and can be promoted by regular reading of book reviews in the quality press and in specialist journals. In the short term, it is unlikely that such activities will lead to a marked benefit in conducting a specific literature research. Most researchers would agree, however, that in the long term they do substantially enhance the quality of their literature searches, and reduce the time required to carry them out.

THE ROLES OF SUPERVISOR AND LIBRARIAN

In practice, the help students receive from both their supervisors and from specialist librarians may well be greater than that they obtain from pursuing the formal literature search discussed above. This is particularly true in the shorter research project or during the early days of research. Usually, a supervisor will know the key references in a field and the most prominent people working in it, so that the research student is saved much preliminary spadework. Similarly, the subject-specialist librarian can be relied on for information about core references and core journals as well as information about pertinent abstracting services. Nonetheless, being able to use the literature effectively is an important part of the researcher's craft. Research students should therefore demonstrate that they have mastered it to the extent that they can pay their way by helping newcomers to their subject to carry out literature searches and by finding references that are useful to their colleagues and their supervisor. If they can do this they need feel no qualms in turn in asking for assistance in those cases where they genuinely need it.

USING THE REFERENCES

Finally, it should be remembered that successful identification of relevant references is only part of the story. Unless the information they contain can be purposefully used, as detailed in the next chapters, the researcher is left with little more than an impressive bibliography – which may well prove counterproductive if the researcher cannot demonstrate the ability to use it competently. It may well be, therefore, that the study of a book such as Fairbairn and Winch (1991) on reading skills – including the improvement of comprehension as well as reading speed – may prove to be a worthwhile investment.

CHAPTER SUMMARY

LITERATURE SEARCHES ARE NECESSARY: for topic selection and as part of the research proper.

SUBJECT AND CITATION RELEVANCE TREES: are effective strategies to adopt in literature searching.

USEFUL SOURCES ARE: abstracts, theses, dissertations, research reports, government publications, pamphlets, newspapers and ephemera.

LITERATURE SEARCH FLOWCHARTS: suggest that a systematic approach to the process can be adopted. Dissertation students who need to pursue literature searches in less depth can usefully confine themselves to the main steps shown in the flowcharts

BIBLIOGRAPHIC COMPUTER SEARCHES: though quite expensive at present are likely to be an increasingly used research technique.

INDIVIDUAL BIBLIOGRAPHIES: set up and maintained by the research student are much to be commended.

Part B

Data Analysis and Gathering

5

Analysing the Data

THE ROLE OF ANALYSIS

As pointed out in Chapter 2, until a feasible outline of the type of analysis to
be undertaken has been determined the research plan must be considered
incomplete. Many students are tempted to embark on literature searches and
massive programmes of data gathering before thinking about how the results
are to be analysed. All too often this leads to considerable wasted effort.
Essential items of data are not collected, or the first attempts at analysis are
too trivial so that a complete rethink is necessary.

One key function of analysis is to communicate the value (whether academic, social or scientific) of the findings. An even more important purpose
is to convince the reader that, through the innate value of the knowledge
gained, the research report makes a sufficient contribution for the level of
research in question and that the research measures up to the necessary standards of academic worth. For this reason at the doctoral level there is a

flavour of the legal process about analysis. It should be seen that it was done for good cause and that it was properly carried out. At the lower levels of a research project, of course, such exalted standards may not come into play. Rather, given the crucial role of analysis in the research process, the primary aim of requiring students to carry out a research project may well be to enable them to develop the ability to evaluate the analysis of other researchers. Such requirements are usually evident, for example, in university regulations for dissertations produced as part of a master's degree, with their emphasis on 'an ordered presentation of knowledge in a particular field' or 'a critical exposition of previous work'.

Of all the stages of research, the related activities of data gathering and analysis (and particularly the latter) demand most intellectual input. Student researchers should recognise this and accept that those with greater skills and insights will be able to achieve a higher standard of work. Just as in any facet of life, those individuals with outstanding gifts and skills are relatively few in number, so too are researchers of outstanding competence. It should therefore be accepted that research into a particular topic will lead to a very different outcome according to who is undertaking the work. Thus, an economics undergraduate may choose to develop a national energy policy model as a final year project. It will, nevertheless, be recognised by both student and supervisor that the output of the research will, in all probability, fall well short of what an experienced econometrician would achieve. We argue that, provided the student is prepared to seek to acquire the skills appropriate to the level of research being undertaken and to identify the depth of analysis needed to satisfy requirements for the programme being followed, successful completion is in prospect. Guidance from the supervisor at this stage is of great importance.

DEFINITION OF ANALYSIS

For the purposes of this chapter analysis will be assumed to involve the ordering and structuring of data to produce knowledge. Structuring will be taken to include summarising and categorising the work of others, which is often the main form of analysis in lower level research projects. Data will be interpreted broadly as information gathered by observation, through books or pictures, field surveys, laboratory experiments, etc. The chapter will cover approaches to analysis that can be applied in a variety of different fields. As such it addresses two topics often separated in texts on research methodology, namely research design and data analysis. In practice, these are closely interlinked – at least in principle – since the design determines the data and what can be done with it, whereas the end purposes of the data analysis are the major determinants of the research design. For this reason we deal here with both aspects.

The definition of analysis proposed is a broad one and it will be presumed to embrace a whole range of activities of both the qualitative and the quantitative type. Nevertheless, there is a discernible tendency for research to make increasing use of quantitative analysis and in particular statistical methods. The latter enjoy a special position in research because they grew up through attempts by mathematicians to provide solutions to problems of scientific investigations noted by philosophers. Furthermore, they reflect the structure of the analysis process in many different fields. Inevitably, then, the bias of this chapter is towards statistical methods. Even so there is still a large number of other such methods. Rather than give a detailed account of some techniques, which would inevitably involve arbitrary selection, we provide here a brief outline of a rather greater number, indicating in particular where they fit into the overall picture and follow this outline with detailed references in the bibliography at Appendix 2. To avoid pointless repetition in what follows it will be assumed that researchers will consult the bibliography for further details of techniques of interest to them.

An overview of some common purposes of analysis is provided in Figure 5.1, noting particular aims consonant with those purposes and certain techniques for meeting those aims.

TYPES OF DATA AND THEIR PLACE IN ANALYSIS

Before commenting on each of the purposes listed in Figure 5.1 it is useful to review the data typology that will be adopted – namely, textual, nominal or categorical, ordinal or ranked, interval and ratio.

The description *textual data* is given to that which records a written or spoken description. Most books and papers are principally composed of material of this kind. Textual data are rich and flexible but much attention needs to be paid to their content and meaning if they are to be properly understood. Usually, they appear in an analysis in summary form as either a precis or as selected quotes. Whilst in some fields – for example, biblical studies – concordances exist so that occurrences of particular words or ideas are easily traced, this is not usually the case and hence data of this type can pose particular problems. Although textual data cannot be used directly for quantitative analysis they may form a basis for it. Such analysis is usually referred to as 'content analysis'.

The use of the term(s) *nominal* or *categorical* data allow classification, for example, 'male', or 'an item of foreign origin'. Such data can be counted and cross tabulated and hence are frequently used.

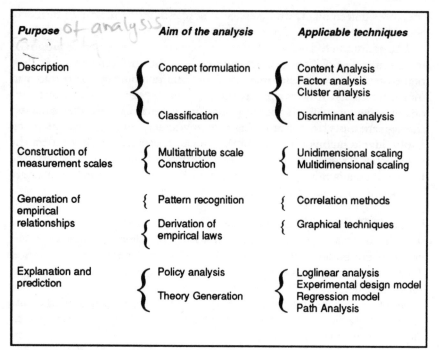

Purpose *of analysis*	Aim of the analysis		Applicable techniques
Description	{	Concept formulation	{ Content Analysis Factor analysis Cluster analysis
		Classification	Discriminant analysis
Construction of measurement scales	{	Multiattribute scale Construction	{ Unidimensional scaling Multidimensional scaling
Generation of empirical relationships	{	Pattern recognition	{ Correlation methods
	{	Derivation of empirical laws	{ Graphical techniques
Explanation and prediction	{	Policy analysis	{ Loglinear analysis Experimental design model
		Theory Generation	Regression model Path Analysis

Figure 5.1 Some common tasks of analysis and some techniques applicable to them

Purely nominal data cannot be effectively compared but it is often desirable to be able to do this. The first type of data that allows comparison is *ordinal* or *ranked* data. Thus, hardness of materials is defined as such a scale by saying material A is harder than material B if it can scratch B. All solid materials can then be ranked in order of increasing hardness on this scale. Note, however, the characteristic feature of such scales in that though A may be harder than B it does not make sense to say A is 1.3 times harder.

A type of scale that enables measurement of the differences between individual values on the scale is provided by *interval* data where an actual numerical value can be given to each point on the scale. Such scales are used for purposes such as the measurement of sound intensity where values are assigned to the difference in intensity of two sounds rather than the absolute intensity of either. Interval scales do not have a meaningful zero although one may be arbitrarily assigned; for example, as in the Fahrenheit temperature scale.

To obtain *ratio* data by which individual items can be evaluated on a scale it is necessary for the measurement scale to have a meaningful zero. Many engineering measurements are of this type, for example, length. In the social sciences, too, they occur frequently, for example, national average wage on a particular date.

Any method of quantitative analysis can be applied to ratio data. Most methods can be used with interval data (basically any technique that uses only differences in values).

The range of methods that can be applied to ordinal data is considerably smaller whereas with nominal data little can be done besides basic enumeration. As far as quantitative analysis is concerned, as we move up the hierarchy from nominal to ratio scales, we can extract progressively more from the data. Usually then it is best to obtain the highest level of data one can for analysis.

THE PURPOSE OF ANALYSIS

Having defined the broad framework within which analysis is located the remainder of this chapter will examine each of the major purposes of analysis in turn. The assumption will be that the purpose of the analysis should be a major determinant of the approach used. In general, the nearer any technique of analysis is to the bottom of the list in Figure 5.1 the more conditions have to be fulfilled before it can be applied. Many research projects are therefore likely to be concerned with purposes nearer the top of Figure 5.1, particularly those in fields that are relatively little developed so that research is likely to be exploratory rather than explanatory in nature. Furthermore, many of the approaches require extended effort and are not suitable for the shorter type of research project. In principle, the type of analysis would be decided taking into account these various factors, but in practice there is an additional significant determinant of the approach, namely the field in which the research is being conducted.

Any subject with a reasonably established tradition will place particular emphasis on certain approaches to analysis. It is hard, for instance, to conceive of research in physics that would involve purely descriptive analysis based on the use of textual data. In addition, it must be remembered that students will normally need to draw on their supervisor for guidance as to how to conduct their analysis. Obviously, this should have some bearing on their choice of approach since otherwise not only may that guidance not be forthcoming but also communication may break down because supervisor and student have no shared language in which to discuss the analysis stage of the project.

Of recent years, there has been a notable increase, particularly in the social sciences, in the view that even at the doctoral level research should be viewed as merely exploratory in nature because of the lack of knowledge in the area of study. Given the explosion that has taken place in the academic literature and the much greater ease with which that literature can now be accessed, this is a somewhat dubious contention. The standards by which analysis is judged will vary by level of research and the subject under study. Students should beware however of not considering carefully what is an appropriate depth of analysis no matter how new their subject. We can only urge students to consider how the field in which they are working should affect their approach to analysis, supplemented by the comments made below about general criteria which must be satisfied if logical inferences are to be drawn from analysis.

LOGICAL INFERENCE AND ANALYSIS

We believe that the laws of logic constitute 'the rules of the game' that must be observed if the researcher's analysis is to persuade others. Although this has become an unfashionable view in some circles as a result of the rise of post-modernism, we feel (as we have argued in the Preface to this second edition) that it is important to understand certain basic principles in the presentation of research findings. For this reason, we would certainly advise the doctoral student to consult some of the texts cited in the bibliography in Appendix 2. Brief comments will be made on some of the more important principles.

Falsifiability

No proposition has value as a basis for research if it cannot be disproved by some data or other. Thus, though the suggestion that Sirius is circled by a planet on which live beings who have mastered the art of communicating without using electromagnetic radiation is interesting it is quite unfalsifiable with our existing technology and therefore is not a valid subject for research.

The Need to Search for Alternative Interpretations

Alternative interpretations of data are not normally difficult to find. In a statistical analysis, for example, one that is often very plausible is that the results apparently obtained are 'data artefacts' – merely a function of the particular set of data collected – which would disappear were other data gathered. On the other hand, research students cannot consider every possible alternative. Rather, what is required is that they deal with one or two highly plausible ones (especially those that may have been advanced by other researchers) and if their analysis plumps for one of them to justify that decision. By its very nature research work tends to lead to a rather narrow perspective and to find this overturned by a rather obvious oversight at the external examination would be a disaster.

Linked to the preceding principle is the notion that researchers in some fields where the potential for application is evident (engineering and the social sciences are examples) recognise that there are a number of options as to the focus of their research. Different options will probably require the gathering of different data. Failure to recognise this in the study design could lead to one of the more frustrating research experiences; realisation at an advanced stage that more data are needed. Thus, a student undertaking a master's dissertation may recommend to an organisation facing considerable pressures on space that it should sub-contract some of its activities rather than move to a two-site operation, having completely overlooked that home-working for some of the staff may have been a better solution to the problem. Limited time available for the research might well preclude the subsequent evaluation of this option and severely reduce the value of the findings.

Simplicity of Explanation

Simple explanations are to be preferred to complex ones; valid explanations that involve few variables are superior to those that involve many. Some research fields lend themselves to powerful theories involving only a few basic concepts whereas in others (for example, the social sciences) this is often not the case. However, even in the latter circumstances it is often possible to find one explanation that involves distinctly fewer variables than another. This is frequently a worthwhile aim since, though an explanation involving very many variables will usually be better for a specific phenomenon, it will usually be of far less general applicability

The Impossibility of Proving Relationships

Outside mathematics, the researcher cannot prove explanations or predictions completely, merely render them more probable. For the student, the practical implication is that a research project with a demonstrable outcome is often a safer bet than one that attempts to predict or to explain some phenomenon, which in the terminology of Chapter 2 may prove to be highly asymmetrical.

The Need for Variables to Take On More than One Value

If explanation and prediction are to be based on the value of a group of variables, it is necessary that those variables be allowed to take on more than one value to demonstrate their effects. Again, the practical implications of this are that what can be extracted from the analysis of a particular set of research data depends critically on what variables have taken on more than one value. If it is required to use the value of a particular variable for predictive or explanatory purposes, information about its value must be obtained at the data gathering stage.

Though the need for variables to vary if anything is to be said about their influence may appear self evident, it is very common to find unwarranted conclusions being drawn about the influence of variables given the values they have taken.

The foregoing six principles show that the conclusions that can legitimately be derived from an analysis depend critically on the data on which it is based. Any piece of research other than that involving the construction of pure deductive theory, as in mathematics, can be viewed as being based on some type of sample from some notional population. It is often difficult to determine just how the results of a particular study can be generalised if sufficient thought is not given to sample selection prior to data gathering. Accordingly, the likelihood of generalising from the results needs to be considered before undertaking the research: a conclusion that will be met again when the problem is examined in the light of the statistical experimental design model which is considered later in the chapter.

A REVIEW OF SOME COMMON PURPOSES OF ANALYSIS AND APPLICABLE TECHNIQUES

Description
Description involves a set of activities that are an essential first step in the development of most fields. Students who can identify a topic about which little is known, of whose importance others can be convinced and for which data can be collected may need to do little other than record them to have their work adjudged satisfactory. Usually, however, knowledge is not so rudimentary and structure must be put on the data by developing or inventing concepts or methods of classification.

Concept Formulation
In order to make any sense of data we need concepts that enable us to focus

on those factors and measurements that are relevant to the field of study. In essence, a concept is a useful idea with a name and concept formulation is thus intimately associated with the idea of language. A concept to be useful must ideally satisfy a number of criteria. It must be unambiguous so that it is possible for different workers to agree whether or not it applies in any given case. Other workers should find it natural to use and it should be unique and not merely a new name for a concept that already exists in some other field.

Relatively little work seems to have been done on how to effectively formulate concepts from textual data (Bolton, 1977). It seems likely, however, that an important method is the use of analogy, for example, the application of the notion of 'half-life', derived from atomic physics, to the declining usefulness of journals with age.

Another very powerful way of developing concepts is the use of pictorial data. The need for the concept of 'crater' in discussing the moon is obvious. In general, seeing provides a very powerful way of getting at concepts, for which reasons many statistical approaches present the results in pictorial as well as numerical form.

It is often the case that the researcher wishes to identify concepts in textual data derived from journal articles or transcripts of interviews or transcripts of the discussion of a 'focus group' on the area of interest. Traditionally this has been done by scanning the different documents and attempting to find common concepts. This may mean allowing for the fact that different authors or interviewees use different terms for the same concept: for example, some may talk of 'new technology scanning' while others talk of 'identifying technological opportunities' while the researcher is happy that for the purposes of the research these can be considered identical. This process has recently been facilitated by the introduction of PC-based packages for comparing annotating different items of textual data – for example, QSR NUD.IST.[1]

A variety of statistical methods are available as aids to concept formation. These are all based on the underlying notion that good concepts are those which enable us to find differences among the objects under study. They accordingly attempt to tease out the major sources of differences in the data to form prototypes, at least, of useful concepts.

One of the oldest sets of statistical techniques are those of factor analysis. These take a number of measurements for each object, for example, psychological test scores, and attempt to select from them a few combinations of these measurements that explain most of the differences between individuals; the so-called 'factors', which can then be named. This approach is applied, for example in intelligence testing, to identify the factors of spatial ability and verbal ability.

Another approach is to compare objects according to how similar they are and then group them in descending order of similarity. This is the basis of cluster analysis. Thus, we might consider grouping people in the light of similarities in educational qualifications. A number of groups would then be expected to emerge naturally: for example, in the UK, those educated to postgraduate level, to graduate level, to A level, and so on.

Classification

The successful development of concepts results in a number of 'pigeon holes' into which individual objects can be classified.

The easiest type of classification procedure to adopt is one that assesses each of the objects to be classified in the light of the concepts to be applied and then assigns it to the category which it most nearly fits. Thus, someone who spends five hours a week playing football for a payment of £20 to cover travel expenses might be assigned to the category 'amateur footballer' rather than 'professional footballer' if the concepts relevant to this classification decision are 'hours spent playing football' and 'whether paid more than £100 per week'. An obvious refinement of this idea is to weight the different concepts according to their importance. Thus, we might assign a weight of 1 to hours per week played and a weight of 5 to amount of money received and then classify as a professional footballer anyone scoring more than 110. With this weighting scheme our footballer would receive a weighted score of

$$1 \times 5 \ (\text{hours/week}) + 5 \times 20 \ (£/\text{week}) = 105$$

and therefore be classified as an amateur footballer.

Rather than derive the weightings subjectively it is often useful to calculate them using the statistical technique known as 'Discriminant Analysis'. The essence of the approach is simple: a number of objects that have already been classified are taken. Measurements of a number of variables for each of them are used to set up a set of predictor functions that will enable future cases to be classified by using a weighted combination of the relevant measurements.

Content Analysis

The aim of content analysis is to put qualitative data into a more quantitative framework. It was originally devised by political scientists for the interpretation of official texts but it can also be used for, say, the analysis of tape recordings from discussion groups.

The essence of content analysis is to:
a) identify the target communications;
b) identify a number of dimensions of the subject in hand;

c) go through each communication assigning statements to it to one or other of the dimensions;
d) count the number of times each dimension is addressed in each communication.

Thus, for a study of the impact of the concept of global warming on, say, the public consciousness in the UK, the target communications might be decided to be the quality newspapers over a specified period of time. A number of dimensions would suggest themselves from the literature, discussion with experts and so on, including issues like the impact on agricultural yields; the impact on biodiversity; the impact on low-lying countries, etc. It is then a straightforward matter to examine the newspapers concerned.

It will nevertheless be appreciated that, firstly, such a process can be very time consuming and, secondly, that it is likely to be expedited considerably by confining attention to those newspapers to which access in electronic form can be obtained. In the latter case, analysis can be considerably expedited by the use of micro-computer based packages for qualitative data analysis such as NUD.IST.

Construction of Measurement Scales

A frequent purpose of analysis is the construction of a measurement scale of the interval or ratio type; such a need occurs surprisingly often. For example, a host of different variables such as height and weight can be measured for a building but none of them provides a direct measurement of the attribute 'earthquakeproofness'.

Traditionally, the approach to the problem of constructing scales has been to adopt surrogate measures: for example, the use of performance on standard flame tests, as a measure of fire resistance. Scales based on the weighting of a number of different attributes or values (as discussed in our footballer example above) have become an increasingly popular alternative: for example, in assessing the fire risk of buildings in the UK.

At a more sophisticated level during the past thirty years, however, a host of techniques have been developed, by psychologists in particular, for constructing scales for which no 'obvious' measurement exists. These may be single (univariate) scales which measure a variable along a single dimension, for example, the measurement of an 'intelligence quotient'. On the other hand, multidimensional scaling techniques apply to situations where more than one concept, or dimension, is relevant. In the case of two dimensions such techniques result in a 'perceptual map'. To revert to our earlier example of the footballer, it might well be that in this case it may be sensible to measure interest in football along two dimensions: firstly, the average hours per

115

week spent playing football; and, secondly, the proportion of the individual's income derived from football. Such a representation would obviously provide a richer measure of the variable of interest than a univariate scale.

Of recent years, the Analytic Hierarchy Process of Saaty (1980) has attracted considerable interest as an approach to the construction of scales representing subjective judgements as to the relative importance of objects of interest, for example, the benefits from investments in different computer systems.

Generating Empirical Relationships

The following section is concerned with the identification of regularities and relationships amongst data. This is an area in which research students can often expect the major results of their analysis to fall. Whilst the sciences and engineering pay considerable attention to the derivation of empirical laws this is less so in the social sciences and humanities. Relatively little seems to have been published on suitable techniques. All in all this area seems underrepresented in texts on research methodology, given its importance in much student research and for this reason will be explored at some length here.

The essence of the problems dealt with in this section is that there is usually no obvious idea of what relationship will be found and the richness of the data need to be displayed in such a way as to suggest fruitful avenues to explore; pictures often provide a good way of doing this. Since pictorial approaches are often considerably facilitated by computer plotting, it may well be worth the student exploring the use of a suitable computer graphics package (see Chapter 8).

Pattern Recognition

The recognition of pattern and order in data is a fundamental step in the development of theories to explain them. Patterns may conveniently be broken down into three basic types:
1. Those showing association among variables.
2. Those showing groupings.
3. Those showing order or precedence relationships between variables.

Association among Variables
Association between two variables is very easily detected using a scatter diagram in which one variable is plotted against another. The quantitative equivalent of a scatter diagram is, in many cases, the correlation coefficient, for which, there is, of course, an extensive statistical theory.

Equivalents of the simple correlation coefficient exist for the case where there are more than two variables. A useful measure is the partial correlation coefficient that measures the strength of association between two variables when the effects of another variable on both of them are allowed for. This is useful, for instance, in cases of spurious correlation such as the relationship between the number of pigs in the USA and US output of cars both of which are substantially associated with the third variable, US gross national product per head. Partial correlation methods are in turn closely related to those of path analysis, discussed later.

Grouping Techniques
Obviously, grouping techniques are closely related to the classification problem discussed earlier. In the present case, however, our interest is in situations in which the number of classifications (if any) is unknown. For this reason, methods such as cluster analysis are appropriate whereas discriminant analysis is not.

Precedence Relationships
Precedence relationships are a type of pattern that occurs in many different contexts. They show order, precedence or priority. Perhaps the simplest instance is one where we search for a pattern in some sequence of activities, for example, in detecting a 'typical' pattern of community growth from hamlet to city.

The quantitative approach to detecting sequences of this type is by the use of cross-correlation coefficients that measure the strength of the relationship between one variable and another a specified number of time units later. They are much used in econometrics and in control engineering for detecting the lag between a change in one variable and the corresponding change in another, for example, an upsurge in orders and the consequent upsurge in deliveries.

Derivation of Empirical Laws

In many fields of technology it is possible to develop empirical laws in the form of simple equations relating one interval or ratio-scaled variable to a few others. Since it is generally possible to find simple relationships between variables there is a long tradition of using graphical methods for their determination, particularly where detailed theoretical knowledge is lacking. Such laws are of considerable practical use in engineering and for researchers in associated fields. To them the methods described may well be very familiar. In the main, however, the picture has been very different in the social sciences. The general belief has been that there is no reason to expect that relationships between variables will be simple and, therefore, there is scant point in trying to establish them using graphical techniques.

Ehrenberg (1975) argued forcefully that a great deal more could and should be done in this direction by social scientists; accordingly, this section is primarily intended for researchers in this field. It is perhaps worth beginning by suggesting why simple laws can be found in the physical sciences and the circumstances under which it might be worthwhile looking for them in the social sciences. Basically simple relationships seem attainable in the physical sciences because they typically describe the behaviour of many millions of entities: for example, where we relate the maximum safe load on an embankment, comprising billions of molecules, to the angle its sides make with the horizontal. This suggests that success in finding simple empirical laws in the social sciences is most likely in fields where the behaviour of a very large number of objects is being described. Thus, as an example, in a number of countries the proportion of companies above a certain size, as measured by turnover or manpower, can be well described by a standard statistical distribution known as the Pareto distribution. This is an excellent example of how a large population (over a million in the UK) can exhibit considerable regularity.

Searching for empirical relationships is best done using certain tricks of the trade. By far the most important are the use of various types of scale that lead to straight line graphs, since a straight line relationship is much easier to fit by eye and lends itself to unambiguous extrapolation.

The starting point of any study of relationships between two variables will be, then, the graphing of Variable A against Variable B on simple linear scales, that is, the construction of a scatter diagram. If a reasonable straight line fit is found no more need be done. Otherwise the next step must be to apply non-linear scales to one or both variables. Graph papers are available with a variety of different scales. Indeed, a glance at the catalogue of a specialist supplier can in itself be a useful way of deciding possible non-linear relationships to explore. Similarly, the manuals for computer spreadsheet packages contain a variety of examples of the different scales provided and examples of their use.

Causal Explanation and Prediction

Traditionally in the Anglo-Saxon world knowledge and research have been equated with the identification of causal relationships and research directed to this end has been accorded the highest esteem. Many fields have not yet been developed to the level where causal explanation is possible or valid predictions can be made. These offer their own special research opportunities as has already been discussed. Nonetheless, where sufficient knowledge exists to make explanation or prediction possible it is not easy to see what benefits would be attained if they were not attempted. In this sense causal explanation and prediction must be seen as involving a higher level of knowledge – though, of course, not necessarily a higher level of research skill.

The meaning of the notions of 'cause' and 'causality' have exercised philosophers for at least three centuries and continue to be the subject of lively debate. Experience suggests that, whereas epistemological considerations of this type are usually too time consuming for the researcher involved in a short project, students undertaking a research degree will often find it necessary to give thought to these matters at some stage in their work. Since the space required to adequately rehearse the philosophical arguments would be substantial the interested reader is referred to the bibliography at Appendix 2.[2] For the purpose of discussion, however, it is necessary to give a more concrete interpretation to the idea of establishing causal relationships.

In practice, this involves the interrelated activities of causal explanation and prediction which are often couched in terms of hypotheses: for example, 'the existence of a close knit Quaker community was an important factor in the early development of the iron industry' (implicit explanation); or, 'the tumbling costs of computer hardware have made software costs a more important factor in developing a computer system' (implicit prediction). Since most tests of hypotheses[3] appear to fall into one or other of these categories and the logical and statistical methods required are the same as those needed for explanation and prediction, they will not be discussed independently.

In what follows, explanation and prediction will be construed as enabling the values of one set of variables to be derived given the values of another. Thus biochemists may direct their efforts to explaining why the body rejects certain types of foreign tissue. Better explanations of tissue rejection in turn enable better predictions to be made about the likelihood of rejection given various forms of treatment. Equally, an important test of a theory is that it makes predictions which can be confirmed by observation or experiment. In pure science, then, explanation and prediction are intermingled. In fields such as engineering this may also be the case but the fact that research is often directed towards the formulation of empirical laws on which predictions can be based means that there also exists the possibility of successful prediction for which no satisfactory explanation can be given. Thus, in hydraulics it is possible to apply standard formulae to relate the flow of a river to its gradient and depth but to give a satisfactory explanation of the basis of the formulae may not be possible. This type of situation illustrates another facet of the interrelationship between explanation and prediction – that is, in practice, we often use the same method for testing out whether we can satisfactorily predict a phenomenon as we do to establish whether we can successfully explain it.

In many social sciences, explanation is often deemed impossible because of the complexity of the systems involved. Frequently, the task of social sciences is, therefore, presented as finding associations between variables that can be generalised to various situations, for example, that urbanisation leads to a growth in reported crimes. Though a variety of explanations of this phenomenon have been offered by criminologists, sociologists, and so forth, none can be said to command general acceptance. Nonetheless, such an association is useful, if it can be established, because it forms the basis of prediction.

Some research students find themselves working in the broad area of policy analysis. The aim of their research is either to carry out an evaluation of the effects of past policies and draw lessons from it (evaluation research) or to formulate, and argue the case for, new policies. Much social science research is of this type as, less obviously, is a considerable amount of research in technology. What differentiates this type of research from those discussed hitherto is that it is primarily aimed at non-academic audiences. Nevertheless, though it has an obvious 'political' dimension it must still meet academic standards and since such research clearly involves explanation and prediction the relevant standards are those pertaining to those topics.

Several techniques which are relevant to explanation and prediction will be examined briefly. As indicated in Figure 5.1 these are loglinear analysis, experimental design, regression, and path analysis.

Loglinear Analysis

The technique of loglinear analysis explains the variations in probabilities of class membership. For example, in the UK, the probability of a person being convicted of a crime before the age of 25 might be explained in terms of variables such as sex, socioeconomic status of the individual's family, highest educational level attained, etc.

Experimental Design

The experimental design model has, aside from its applicability in analysing many different types of research data, considerable virtues as a conceptual model of research directed towards explanation and prediction.

Fundamental to the model is the notion that the variable of interest can be measured on a ratio or interval scale and that the values of the variable to be explained or predicted are affected by a number of other variables usually referred to as factors. Each factor takes on more than one value and each value is called a factor level. Factors may often, however, be measured on nominal scales, for example, fertilizer A, fertilizer B or represent fairly crude groupings – for example, application of less than 100 grams of fertilizer per square metre, application of more than 100 grams per square metre, and so on. Finally, we assume that for each combination of factor levels we have at least one measurement of the variable whose value is to be explained or predicted. The model assumes this value is made up of a number of components: a base value plus various additive effects due to each of the factor levels and also due to interactions between factor levels, plus finally a random term representing errors in measurements, the effects of factors not considered directly and so on.

The virtues of the experimental design model as a conceptual model of the processes involved in explanation and prediction are very considerable even if, for whatever reason, no attempt is made to carry out a statistical analysis. It offers an explanatory framework which is capable of handling complex relationships between the respondent variables and factor levels along with predictions of the effect of any particular set of factor levels. The factor levels can be recognised as independent variables and the implicit requirement of the model that there be at least two levels of each factor enables their effects to be isolated. The experimental design model assumes that the researcher can control the experiment to the extent of selecting the factors and factor levels whose effects are to be examined. This is, of course, not always the case in the social sciences but it may still be possible to approximate to an experimental design by using the fact that particular variables vary between one organisation or country and another or over time. Such applications of the model are usually referred to as 'quasi-experiments' (Cook and Campbell, 1979). The idea of quasi-experiments was originally developed in the context of education research because in investigating the efficacy of, for instance, different reading schemes teachers have only partial control of the classroom situation. The ideas have, however, proved invaluable in a host of organisational and social situations in which it is desired to examine systematically the impact of different policies.

Regression
The regression model has the attraction that it deals with situations where there is no control over the selection of factor levels. In principle, it expresses a dependent variable y in terms of various independent variables $x1$, $x2$, and so on, the precise form of the relationship being derived from the data. Obviously, this model represents a generalisation of the experimental design model since the x's can represent combinations of factor levels/treatments and may be nominal, interval or ratio data. The particular advantage of the regression model is that it does not require observations to be available for specific factor combinations and to a large extent, then, it is capable of utilising the data 'as they are'. On the other hand, this usually means that the rigorous control implicit in experimental design is lost and so

121

the researcher cannot always have the same faith in the results as when an experimental design approach is feasible.

Path Analysis
Another model, and one that is related to the regression model, is that of path analysis. In essence, this attempts to select the set of relationships between variables that is most consistent with the available data. As such it has an obvious bearing on the problem of distinguishing independent, dependent and intermediate variables. As a typical example we might consider two possible explanations for the strong correlation between father's social status and son's social status that is observed in many Western countries. The simple explanation is that the father's status determines the son's status directly. A less obvious explanation is that the father's status determines the level to which the son is educated and the level of the son's education determines his status. Path analysis enables a choice to be made between such competing hypotheses.

TESTING A QUANTITATIVE ANALYSIS

Until now this chapter has been concerned with statistical methods mainly as models of particular types of analysis. For statistical methods of analysis it is, of course, possible to specify procedures for testing results derived from them. Since there are very considerable overlaps in testing procedures for different statistical methods discussion of this question has been delayed to this point. The most common reasons for the rejection of a piece of research are:
a) lack of depth;
b) faulty analysis.

Through our review of common types of analysis we have already covered lack of depth. Faulty analysis relates to inadequate testing of the conclusions by the researcher. Two common reasons for this are:
1. An optimistic assessment of the degree to which the data and analysis support the hypotheses advanced.
2. An erroneous assumption that because of the 'exploratory' nature of the research only very limited testing is possible or, indeed, is required.

Whatever the reason, it reflects insufficient attention to the quality of the results, which in turn shows ineffective management of a key aspect of the research project. For this reason, and because this subject is not so well covered in the literature as are statistical methods, this topic is now examined further.

Most statistical techniques embody methods of testing the results they give for statistical significance. In practice, however, such tests often give an overly rosy picture of the results obtained from them. Basically this is because the test must be based on the notion that some statistical model or other describes reality perfectly, whereas it describes it only imperfectly. It is, therefore, useful, particularly where more complex models are concerned, to supplement the statistical tests with other ways of evaluating the results of an analysis. A number of strategies for testing an analysis, namely, complete enumeration, checking for representativeness, random split half methods, hold-out methods, and checking for missing explanatory variables will be discussed.

Complete Enumeration

As observed earlier, most research involves (notional) sampling and hence sampling error. One strategy available to some researchers however is that of complete enumeration – a census. Thus, many studies of UK companies are restricted to those that are listed on the Stock Exchange since, as far as published accounting data are concerned, complete enumeration of the few thousand companies involved is perfectly realistic where it would not be if the study were to cover the several hundred thousand unlisted companies also.

Checking for Representativeness

As is evident from any textbook, statistical theory relies heavily on the notion of random samples. A frequently adopted procedure for assessing the randomness of a sample is to check how representative it is by comparison with information known about the population being sampled from other sources. Thus, in a UK study of corrosion problems in cars the number of cars of each make and year in the sample could be compared with what might be expected on the basis of information about the actual numbers of cars in each category as recorded at the Vehicle Licensing Agency. Often, several characteristics can be checked in this way. Thus, it would also be possible to check the number of vehicle owners in each social class in the sample against the Registrar General's estimates for the UK population as a whole.

This type of approach has obvious links with the device of quota sampling much used in market research.

Scale Reliability/Split Half Testing

Scale construction can often run into significant problems of reproduction, in that aspects of the scales are very much a figment of the data used and disappear if other data are studied. In essence, this problem is due to an attempt to over-explain the preferences or attitudes being scaled. A useful way of detecting the problem is to split the data randomly into two halves and to carry out the scaling operations on each completely separately. If the two samples give similar results they are combined and the analysis carried out again on the total sample. Where they give different results, attempts should be made to eliminate the problem by simplification, for example, by reducing the number of dimensions in multidimensional scaling.

Usually, data can be split randomly several times and the procedure repeated with a consequent increase in the reliability of the results. Random split half methods are well suited to tests of factor analyses, measurement scales, and cluster analyses, and to the evaluation of discriminant functions and regression models. Their biggest drawback is that large amounts of data are required. The sample size usually recommended for cluster analysis, for example, is of the order of several hundred if split half techniques are to be used.

Split half analysis is built in to many statistical routines in common use, for example, those for measurement scale reliability testing in SPSS (the Statistical Package for Social Scientists).

Hold-out Methods

Where fewer data are available hold-out methods are often attractive. The essence of such a method is to remove the data from one (or a few) object(s) or respondent(s) and derive the scale, discriminant function, and so on, using the remaining data and then with the model obtained compute the relevant values for the held-out data and use these to evaluate the performance of the function in question. Thus, in testing a regression model to be based on n observations, one is removed at random and the model computed on the basis of the other n-1. This model is then used to predict the value of the dependent variable for the held-out data point from the values of its independent variables.

Hold-out methods are, obviously, closely related to testing through prediction (the connection in many cases between prediction and satisfactory explanation has already been discussed). In practice, the hold-out process is repeated a number of times and each of the resulting models are compared. Where the removal of one or a few data points causes a marked change in the model it is a clear sign that the analysis is far from satisfactory. Again, simplification may often resolve the problem: for example, reduction of the number of independent variables on which a discriminant function is based.

For small data sets in particular, hold-out methods are an excellent safeguard against an apparent, though in fact spurious, high degree of success in fitting the model in question.

Again, commonly available statistical packages like SPSS make it easy to use hold-out techniques in conjunction with statistical methods such as Regression or Discriminant Analysis.

In certain fields, such as econometrics, a slightly different approach is possible. Thus, a regression model can be constructed using data for the period 1980-94 and tested on data for 1995. This reflects the fact that extrapolation, that is, prediction for values of the independent variable outside the data set, is always a more powerful test than interpolation where the prediction is made for a value within the original data set.

Checking for Missing Explanatory Variables

Sometimes bias may be introduced into the analysis because important explanatory variables have been omitted. Thus, a study aimed at increasing the amount of time certain equipment is productive where the users were recruited on a voluntary basis might well result in a preponderance of users whose equipment spends an above average proportion of time out of service. In this case the relevant measure of bias would be the average proportion of time the user's equipment is out of service. In such cases the bias can either be reduced or removed by using this variable as a factor in an experimental design model or by formally accounting for its effects through a regression equation. This latter approach is often used, for example, in the assessment of training programmes where participants are given a pre-test and a post-test on a relevant area of knowledge so that the impact of prior learning on the effect of the training can be established.

Another approach to this problem that is useful in longitudinal studies conducted over a period of time is to use time itself as one of the dependent variables. Where it turns out to be an important explanatory variable this is usually a sign that other important dependent variables that have changed in a systematic way with time have been omitted from the study. A similar approach often adopted in studies of organisations is to use some measure of size as an additional variable of the same type.

THE USE OF THE COMPUTER IN ANALYSIS

If researchers wish to use many of the techniques discussed here, as distinct from merely viewing them as providing a conceptual model of some type of analysis, then they will not only need to be familiar with the underlying theory of these methods but also will need to use a computer program to carry out the analysis. There is no doubt that the advent of specialist computer packages aimed at carrying out particular types of analysis, for example, statistical packages, has made a considerable difference to what student researchers are expected to do by way of quantitative analysis, compared with what was feasible for many of their supervisors. In our view this is a fact to be taken into account when deciding on the worth of the analysis contained in a research report or thesis. What might previously have been regarded as desirable but *in*feasible, is now straightforward for the student who has mastered the use of the computer. If this is the case (and there are, of course, still research projects where it is not) then it seems only reasonable that the student be expected to carry out the necessary computer analysis. This needs to be taken into account at the stage of planning the research, since, even if the student already possesses the requisite computing knowledge, it will almost certainly have an impact on the way data are gathered and recorded.

ENSURING THE ANALYSIS IS OF AN APPROPRIATE STANDARD

There are many aspects to analysis and even the somewhat cursory discussion here has necessarily been fairly long. It is worth, therefore, recapitulating the opening remarks. An acceptable analysis is in many ways the key aspect of any research study and students who wish to manage their research effectively must accordingly ensure that their analysis is adequate. Of course, what constitutes an adequate level of analysis depends on both the field of research and the level of the qualification being pursued. Even undergraduate projects in scientific fields are likely to be accompanied by a statistical analysis, whereas this is not necessarily the case in humanities or social sciences, where the emphasis might rather be on the critical analysis of the work of previous authors. Students should be aware that inadequate analysis is one of the commonest causes of unacceptability of a research report at any level of study. It may be helpful to bear the following points in mind:

1. Plan the analysis early in the project so that data gathering can be organised around it and any necessary skills can be acquired.
2. Make sure that you are thoroughly familiar with the methods of analysis usually employed in your field of study, particularly if you wish to deviate from them.
3. Decide on the methods to be used and master the relevant literature particularly that dealing with the snags and pitfalls.
4. Where possible, make the analysis quantitative. Do not avoid employing an appropriate method, for example, a computer package, just because it will require time to learn it. Do not on the other hand, lavish sophisticated

techniques on data of dubious quality. Data can be poor and no amount of analysis can put that right.

5. Make sure that the analysis respects the rules of logical inference given above.

6. Test your conclusions wherever possible, using the methods suggested in the literature and in this chapter.

7. Write down conclusions as you go so it is clear what you are claiming. Expose them to the scrutiny of your supervisor and your friends. If you are pursuing a research degree, review them every month or so as the analysis progresses to make sure they stand the test of time.

8. Where doubts are expressed about either the logic of your conclusions, or whether the analysis has the necessary depth for your level of research, heed them. If nothing more, they show that there is at least one person who is unconvinced about an important aspect of your research.

9. Try to do rather more than is necessary. An analysis that aims at minimum standards all the way through not only runs a considerable risk of rejection by the examiners, it is also unsatisfying to the researcher and means that much of the benefit that should have been derived from carrying out the research is lost.

CHAPTER SUMMARY

THE ROLE OF ANALYSIS: is to supply evidence which justifies claims that the research changes belief or knowledge and is of sufficient value. This is done through the ordering or structuring of data.

THE DIRECT PURPOSES OF ANALYSIS: are description, construction of measurement scales, generation of empirical relationships, and explanation and prediction.

ANALYSIS TO BE CONVINCING: must satisfy the principles of logical inference.

QUANTITATIVE ANALYSES MAY BE TESTED: by a number of techniques besides those usually given in statistics texts.

THE TECHNIQUES OF ANALYSIS THAT NEED TO BE USED: are related to both the field of study and the level of qualification being pursued. Whatever the level, however, inadequate analysis is a common cause of lack of success.

6

Gathering The Data

Almost all research projects involve the gathering of data, both quantitative and qualitative. Indeed, as remarked earlier, that process is often equated with research itself. As a key activity in a research project data gathering must be managed and this has two aspects. On the one hand there is a technical component concerned with why data are collected and how to do so; and, on the other hand, there is a variety of tasks connected with successful data gathering which must be carried out effectively.

Chapter 5 shows that the type of analysis employed and its purpose substantially dictate the nature of the data needed. In practice, however, many types of analysis and therefore of research project are difficult or impossible to carry out because suitable data gathering techniques are not available. The invention of new methods of collecting data or the improvement of existing ones can therefore have a substantial impact on the research done in a particular field. At the higher levels of research just as the development of new methods of analysis is often a good route to success so, too, is introduction of novel approaches to data gathering or of major refinements to techniques already in use.

It is useful in the present context to recognise two categories: primary data which the researcher collects through observation, experiment, and so on; and secondary data that have been collected by others.

The gathering of secondary data can have much in common with literature searching and many of the techniques of Chapter 4 apply here. Furthermore, the literature search – whether it consists of measurements by other workers or statements of opinions and theories – is often the major source of data for fields such as theoretical physics or philosophy where at first sight research can be conducted without data.

Whether the researcher is concerned with primary or secondary data there are a number of general points that apply to either type and these will be discussed before considering the individual types of data in more detail.

ACTIVITIES INVOLVED IN DATA GATHERING

However the researcher chooses to collect the data certain activities will be common. The data must first be located and then arrangements made for their collection. They must be recorded in a form suitable for the intended analysis and checked. Adjustments may then need to be made for errors and omissions or data that for some reason are unusable.

The location of data may often be very difficult and at higher levels the researcher is, at the outset, often unsure as to what the sources will be. Against that data for the short-term research project need to be fairly accessible if the data gathering stage of the project is not to get out of hand. Students undertaking short projects must avoid situations where a great deal of effort is involved in arranging the data collection because, for example, laboratory rigs have to be set up and commissioned, or because considerable training is needed before a particular data collection method can be used.

The gathering of data requires time and there are relatively few fields in which it does not also involve substantial effort. On occasions it may be necessary to await rather infrequent events, as in a study of volcanic eruptions, or the actual process of obtaining the measurements may be long drawn out, as in certain biomedical tests. Whatever is involved in gathering the data, the process by which they are recorded often sets a definite limit on the rate at which they can be gathered and the ease with which they can be analysed. It is no accident that the fields in which most data are gathered, such as radio astronomy, are almost totally dependent on computer methods for gathering and recording data.

In short, data gathering requires time – for acquiring skills and for making the necessary arrangements for collection and to ensure adequate quality – and time is usually the researcher's major resource. Furthermore, it is affected by technology which may place definite restrictions on what can be done in collecting and recording data.

ACCESS TO DATA

Gaining access to data is often a problem for student researchers. They may need to employ special facilities where application to use them must be made long in advance and which may be rationed in other ways. Social scientists often find that the organisations or groups that they wish to study are unwilling for reasons of confidentiality or lack of time to provide them with data.

The student who is involved in a short research project cannot afford such problems and, if access to data is difficult, should find another project. In the longer project, however, where the student is willing to contemplate a period of negotiation it is worth bearing in mind a number of devices for improving the chances of getting access to the data needed.

Firstly, the sponsorship of a prestigious institution and/or of some individual of distinction is extremely useful. Research students are fortunate in that educational institutions do still enjoy high prestige and if the student is sponsored or supported by an official body this may well be of great benefit in obtaining access.

In broad terms co-operation is, of course, most likely where the providers of access gain something in return. If the results of the work are of interest to them, then promise of a copy of any papers that emerge from it may help to secure collaboration. Also, as observed in Chapter 4, many types of data are a tradeable commodity and the researcher may be able to gain access on condition that the data are made available once collected. Researchers have, of course, a responsibility to later researchers. They should observe the elementary politenesses and as far as possible adhere to any bargains that may be struck so that, for example, if a copy of the research report is promised this should be provided.

GATHERING DATA TO AN ADEQUATE STANDARD

It is important that the researcher demonstrates that the data were properly collected. Ideally this means that others would have been able to arrive at the same readings or observations. Where primary data are concerned this is usually not feasible. Instead, researchers must settle for following a procedure that will be adjudged adequate in the light of the level of their research; in particular by the examiners to whom the research report will be sent for assessment. This question is taken up later in the broader context of the assessment of the research report. Here, however, discussion will be confined to a checklist of points intended to secure adequate data gathering standards and which applies to secondary as well as primary data. These are that:

1. The data actually measure what they purport to measure.
2. Proper attention was paid to measurement error and the reduction of its effects.
3. A suitable sample was used, in particular that:
   a) it provided a basis for generalisation; and that
   b) it was large enough for the effects of interest to be detected.
4. Data were properly recorded, in particular that
   a) the conditions under which the data were gathered were properly noted; and that
   b) suitable data recording methods were used and efforts were made to detect and eliminate errors arising during recording.

Not all of these points apply in every situation, and the full list is perhaps only appropriate in the, albeit common, situation where data are to be gathered in some systematic way and are of the nominal, ordinal, interval or ratio type. The researcher's own notes, which we view as textual data and an important data source, would probably need to be judged only against standard 4 above. Nonetheless, the list will now be reviewed point by point, with the greatest emphasis being placed on data recording

Ensuring the Data Measure what they Purport to Measure

In the last chapter it was noted that very often it is difficult to measure the actual variable of interest and instead surrogate measures may be adopted. This is particularly likely to be a problem in secondary data gathering where the researcher may not know just how the data were derived. For instance, there is at least one country whose smooth upward growth in recorded consumption data over the 1970s probably owed more to the predilections of the civil servants who calculated them than to the behaviour of consumption itself.

Errors in Measurement

Quantitative data are often subject to measurement error and the size of that error may have important implications for both the way the data are used and for the scale of the data gathering effort.

Aside from errors due to malfunction of measuring equipment which are of no interest in this context, error may take the form of bias: as in the under-reporting of small company activities in many official statistics; deliberate or instinctive falsehood, as in many answers to questionnaire surveys; or distortion of one form or another, as in the response of a laboratory amplifier to a high-frequency signal.

The practical implication of all three possibilities is the same: information is lost and the data do not fully represent the phenomenon under study. Though it is often easier for the engineer to overcome such difficulties by employing more sophisticated measuring devices, similar opportunities may well arise in the social sciences. Webb *et al* (1966) make a number of creative suggestions for methods of coping with this problem in the social sciences, by the device of 'unobtrusive measurement': for example, measuring the popularity of paintings in art galleries by wear on carpets in their vicinity.

Another form of measurement error that is relevant to quantitative data is pure random error that is supposed on average to fluctuate about zero. Since this is relatively easy to cope with statistically, it is the usual (though not always the most accurate) model of error adopted.

In practice we can attempt to deal with measurement error in one of two ways.

The first is to measure the phenomenon of interest by several different methods. Where each gives rise to random measurement error a combination of the measurements can be expected to give a better estimate of the true value provided the methods are not subject to the same error. Obviously this approach requires more data gathering effort but has much to commend it in those many fields where accurate measurements are difficult. It is, thus, much used in social science research often under the term of 'triangulation' by analogy with the process land surveyors use to fix accurately the location of a particular point on the earth's surface.

The second way of dealing with measurement error that is more or less random is to increase the size of the sample and this is discussed below.

Choosing the Sample

Data gathering normally involves some kind of sampling. The conclusions that can validly be drawn from the sample depend critically on both the population sampled and the procedures used for generating the sample. The first step in choosing the sample is, accordingly, to choose a target population to be sampled that permits interesting conclusions to be drawn and to select a sample in such a way that the conclusions are valid. Though this is unlikely to be a problem for the physical scientist it certainly is in many other fields, particularly the social sciences. Very often, the sheer cost of data gathering pushes the student in the direction of some 'convenience sample' that meets neither of these criteria.

Any statistical method requires a certain size of sample to have a reasonable probability of detecting an effect of interest and in these circumstances the collection of enough data may be quite beyond the resources available to the student researcher. Some social science projects, for example, are very unlikely to produce the hoped for results because they are not based on enough observations. Thus, the effects of positive discrimination programmes such as urban priority areas may be difficult to measure because they are swamped by environmental variables that have a far greater impact. In such cases a large sample is needed if the effects are to be revealed. A crude rule of thumb applicable in a number of situations is that the sample size needed is proportional to the square of the accuracy of the estimates derived from the sample. Thus, to double the accuracy it is necessary to increase the sample size fourfold. It follows that the ideas of statistical power testing that enable the necessary sample size to be inferred before carrying out the data gathering are potentially of interest to many student researchers (*cf.* Kraemer, 1987).

There are many different procedures that can be used for sampling and the reader should consult a specialist text, for further details.

Recording the Data

In Chapter 5 the relevance of the experimental design model to many types of research was discussed. An important aspect of that model is the idea of factors and, by implication at least, the values of all factor levels should be recorded along with the actual measurements of interest. This provides protection against the discovery that further variables, and therefore measurements, are relevant to the phenomenon in question. Equally, notes on the sources of data and time and date of collection can be extremely useful when, many months later, the researcher is attempting to correct an error or to decide whether a set of figures whose origin has long since been forgotten can be used in analysis. Clearly, in both cases the recording of adequate additional information will help to ensure that few data that have been collected will prove to be unusable. Experience suggests that this is by no means always the case. As stated in Chapter 5, researchers do waste effort by having to repeat data gathering activities because certain information was omitted originally. In practice, it is almost always straightforward to collect additional measurements, and so on, when the initial data gathering takes place. In further discussions of data recording it will, therefore, be assumed that consideration has been given to exactly what data are to be recorded and the focus now will be on how to record them.

In primary data gathering, recording may involve two processes. Firstly, data must be captured in some way that is feasible in the context in which they are to be gathered, following which it is often necessary to transcribe or convert the data into a form suited to computer input.

The main concern here is the reduction of data to a form suitable for computer analysis. Ratio and interval scaled data are already in this form and present no problem. Ordinal data can either be input as ranks, or equivalently, using letter codes – for example, A=1, B=2. Pictorial data need to be converted into numbers in some way or other. Nominal data may be recorded by using 1 to denote the presence of some attribute, for example, the item is green, or zero if it does not possess it. For pure textual data there is little choice but to input them as they stand.

Transcription may also be the major process involved when secondary data are being used. This two-stage process is at best somewhat inefficient and at worst may introduce errors at the transcription stage, so automatic data gathering methods that collect the data directly in a form suitable for computer analysis have obvious attractions. To that end it is worth considering the use of computer document scanners to transcribe secondary data that exist only on paper, such as tables in books.

The detection of errors at the data capture stage may, by analogy with data processing terminology, be dubbed validation. The ensuring of accurate transcription will similarly be referred to as verification.

Validation is primarily based on identifying implausible data: for example, a questionnaire that records a pregnant man or more typically, but more subtly, one anomalous liberal response from an individual amidst a host of authoritarian ones. Not all such anomalies will, in fact, be errors and, conversely, such procedures will not identify data that could be correct but in fact are not. Successful validation is heavily dependent on experience and this is one reason why training in the use of data gathering techniques is necessary.

Verification lends itself to more mechanical methods. The traditional approach in data processing, for example, is for two different people to enter the same data into the computer system and then accept the two sets of data if they are the same but otherwise to examine them for transcription errors. This approach relies on the reasonable assumption that the same mistake is unlikely to be made by two different individuals. However, the student researcher is unlikely to be able to afford to pay for this type of verification which is increasingly confined to large-scale professional surveys so needs to think of ways either of approximating to it, or better improving the quality of data entry.

The rejection of data at the validation or verification stage is a somewhat negative process. Though transcription errors are usually remediable, validation errors will not be unless thought is given to making them so. The only way in which this can be done is to introduce redundancy – that is, extra information – into the data gathered so that incorrect or missing data can be reconstructed. If, for instance, the aim is to measure a length the simplest way is to measure it in, say, millimetres and record it. If this is done incorrectly, however, the complete set of measurements related to this length will have to be thrown away. On the other hand, if it is also measured in inches it will be possible to determine the true length if validation checks cast doubt on the recorded figure for the length in millimetres. This example also throws light on the role of 'feel' in validation. Most people in the UK have a far better intrinsic concept of imperial measurements than metric ones and a check of this sort will accordingly have a good chance of detecting the error at the time when the measurement is made.

In many social science applications it may well be possible to approach the respondents again; and in science and engineering studies the measurements can, in principle, be repeated. Nonetheless, both of these approaches require effort and in some cases may for all practical purposes be impossible. Therefore, if the researcher is to avoid throwing away hard-won data it is advisable to devote a little thought to how errors in them can be detected and eliminated.

Though the avoidance of error is a common theme in all types of data capture or transcription there are many different methods that can be used for either or both of these purposes. These differ in the amount of equipment and preparation required to use them, in their costs and in their suitability for dealing with large volumes of data. Though the division is far from being clear cut it is useful to distinguish between methods that are primarily suited to data capture and those that are mainly used for transcription, and that approach will be followed here.

Data Capture

In Figure 6.1 some common methods of data capture are listed. As, with increasing frequency, the data will be subjected to computer analysis the methods are divided into two groups according to whether transcription is needed. They range from 'traditional' methods requiring subsequent transcription through to sophisticated ones that cut out this latter process at the cost of much greater dependence on equipment. The initial discussion will be confined to the data recording aspects of these methods though certain of them, for example, questionnaires, will be considered more broadly later.

The one form of data that will be gathered by all researchers is their own research notes which are worthy of more attention than they are often afforded. Though the researcher who has pursued an almost uninterrupted academic career should have developed effective notetaking practice this may need amendment when, as is often the case, the research is concerned with a

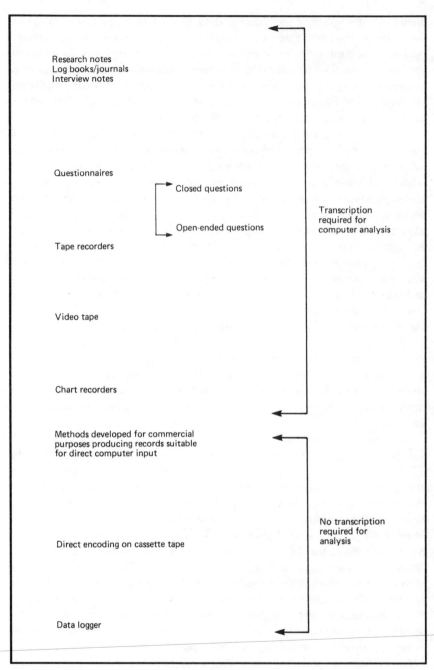

Research notes
Log books/journals
Interview notes

Questionnaires

Closed questions

Open-ended questions

Tape recorders

Video tape

Chart recorders

Methods developed for commercial
purposes producing records suitable
for direct computer input

Direct encoding on cassette tape

Data logger

Transcription
required for
computer analysis

No transcription
required for
analysis

Figure 6.1 Some common methods of data capture

new field of study. The problems of the part-time researcher or of someone returning to academic study after a number of years are likely to be greater.

The basic problem with research notes is that they arise from a variety of activities, from the researcher's own reading through to occasional flashes of inspiration. Usually, they eventually comprise a huge mass of data of many different types. Furthermore, there is no simple way of ensuring that two different pieces of data that should be juxtaposed will be.

As far as notes on books are concerned the most effective practice is probably to make them as the books are read and to produce photocopies of selected passages of particular interest that can be annotated as the student wishes. The selections should rarely amount to more than a few per cent of the work in question unless some form of textual study is being undertaken, so there should be no problem with copyright law. Certainly it is usually a sign that the researcher has not properly digested the contents of a work if it is found necessary to copy most of it and proper cross-referencing soon becomes impossible if the practice is repeated wholesale. Moreover, under such circumstances, problems of copyright law and – even more importantly as far as academic institutions are concerned – plagiarism, are likely to arise. An alternative approach that avoids these difficulties is for the researcher to compile notes using a word processing package as the text is read.

In normal circumstances, researchers will want to produce substantial notes of their own relating to projected analyses, organisation of the research report and so on. These are usually more easy to deal with. For the unexpected insight it is worth carrying a small pocketbook in which sufficient information can be jotted down to enable the idea to be properly worked up later into notes.

Logbooks and journals are the simplest method of data recording available to the experimental scientist or the researcher conducting a field study. Their use is relatively straightforward and is often facilitated by employing a standard layout for each type of observation to be made. Appropriate blanks can be photocopied to be filled in and filed in a binder as required. It should be noted that, nowadays, the logbook will frequently be on a PC, since even in the field notebook and sub-notebook computers provide a more convenient and flexible way of recording notes and observations.

As research is a learning process some students find benefit in viewing the logbook as a chronological record; not a day-to-day diary but a record of key incidents. Examples of such would be: opinions expressed by others during the study; sudden insights gained; and more effective ways of conducting the research. Notes of this type could trigger action and, in some fields of study, assist in the production of the research report.

Interview notes and similar materials are rather more difficult to structure because it is hard to predetermine the course of an interview. Nevertheless, there will in most cases be an interview schedule listing those topics to be covered and this may well serve as the basis of a data gathering instrument with half a page, say, being allocated to each subject heading.

With a little experience it is usually possible for researchers to generate their own 'shorthand' for recording, thus enabling them to come nearer to a verbatim record. In view of the high information content of pictorial data it makes obvious sense for the researcher to record data in that form, where possible.

Questionnaires provide a more structured approach to gathering data of this type. Where closed questions, that is, those which provide for only a limited list of responses are used, subsequent transcription is particularly easy. It pays to design them from the outset with computer processing in mind if it is intended that they should be analysed by computer eventually.

Tape recorders are generally acceptable in most interviewing situations subject perhaps, to certain parts of the interview being 'off the record'. Cassette recorders are sufficiently portable for two to be used, preferably with tapes of different playing time to allow for continuity during changeovers and a measure of backup. It may well be worth carrying both 'narrow' and 'wide angle' microphones so that the most appropriate type can be selected.

One aspect of tape recording which is frequently overlooked by student researchers is the cost of transcription. Six to eight hours transcription per hour of tape recording may well be needed. Moreover, it needs special equipment and is best carried out by experienced staff.

For these reasons and to cope with the situations where they are not acceptable the student still needs other methods of recording. Though the act of taking notes can be useful in pacing an interview, the ideal method is one that the student can carry out while still looking at the interviewee. At a minimum this will usually require some sort of shorthand or code with the ideal being the ability to recall every detail of the interview (remembering that non-verbal behaviour is often very important) an hour afterwards. Certainly the typical student will usually find it useful to write notes on the interview as soon as possible after it has taken place.

Lightweight video cameras are straightforward to use. The largest barrier to their wider employment in research is the difficulty of transcribing relevant parts of the enormous amount of data contained in a video tape into a form suitable for analysis.

Chart recorders are still sometimes used in conjunction with many types of measuring equipment, for example, temperature recording. Since they lend themselves to online connection to the computer they have mainly been replaced by datalogging equipment (that is, equipment which records measurements that can be fed directly into a computer analysis). It should be remembered though that chart records of, say, seismograph readings from past earthquakes may well continue to be important data sources.

Another method is one that enables the data to be transmitted directly to a computer file with the obvious attractions noted earlier. The first group of such methods are those that were developed for commercial purposes, for example, the tally-roll printouts produced by the older type of cash register. Perhaps the most neglected one from the point of view of student research is the mark sense reader capable of recording the presence or absence of a pencil tick in a box in a specified position on a sheet of paper. These are widely used in the US for, amongst other purposes, providing automatic marking of multiple choice examinations.

One commercial data recording method that finds some application in research is direct encoding on to cassette tape. Such recorders were originally developed for stock control in supermarkets where the item code number and a count of the number actually on the shelves were entered on to the tape along, perhaps, with the time at which the data were entered. Similar devices may be used in observation of human behaviour to record the type of behaviour, the time of its onset and the time of its completion.

Finally, for the scientist or engineer there are the 'dataloggers' referred to above. Their use is widespread and growing as microcomputers are increasingly used for this purpose, for example, together with laser rangefinders in field archaeology. However, the user of such facilities may, sometimes, be faced with a somewhat unexpected transcription problem, if, as is often the case, it is wished to carry out the analysis on a different type of computer from that on which the data were originally input. The ease with which data can be transferred from one machine to another varies markedly depending on the computers involved. The researcher is accordingly well advised to explore how best to transfer the data before carrying out the experiments.

Transcription Methods

The standard method of transcribing data for computer input is by entering them using a spreadsheet or word processing package. The process of verification by duplication has already been described and for data sets larger than a few dozen numbers it is advisable to get data verified in this way if possible. Many student researchers are not, however, able to afford this process. The alternative is to employ a variety of checks already discussed in the context of validation. A further useful device is to demand that the data be input in a rigid format. For example, if our numbers are up to four digits long it is possible to fit 16 of them on to the usual 80 character input line leaving a space between each. Provided that where necessary leading zeros are supplied so that '32' is typed as '0032', the fifth, tenth, and fifteenth character positions and so forth should be blank. This can be verified on input, and any input lines that fail the test are then corrected. Such a test detects, for example, accidental double keying, for example, '00322' for '0032'. It will not, however, detect the other common form of transcription error, namely, transposition: for example, '0023' for '0032' which the student researcher will still have to guard against. Many computer packages, for example, SPSS PC make it easy to apply such checks. There should be no trouble in getting data entered into the computer directly from well designed questionnaires or similar documents as long as these have been correctly completed. Pictorial information can be reduced to numbers by using a digitiser. Line information can similarly be converted to numbers by using a light pen.

There are also many circumstances in which the student requires to analyse textual data. An obvious example is in the production of concordances and another is the content analysis of a set of interviews where it is required to find all instances where two or more ideas or variables appear together. Word processing facilities which are extremely useful for such analysis will be discussed further in Chapter 8. However, the reader is reminded that text data can be most easily transcribed into electronic form by the use of a suitable text reader rather than requiring someone to type the text into a word processing package.

PREPARING FOR DATA GATHERING

Though in certain parts of the social sciences, in particular, the view is some-times expressed that all data are inevitably partly subjective, we do not feel that such a view is generally helpful to student researchers whose aim is to complete their research successfully in a reasonable time. Accordingly, we would see the demonstration that researchers have gathered their data in a fashion that could have been repeated by themselves or others at the same time and would have led (allowing for measurement error) to the same results as a matter of practical as well as philosophical importance. Usually, however, this is not a trivial matter. Measuring instruments must be cali-brated and the researcher must become sufficiently familiar with the tech-niques being used to be able to obtain satisfactory results. Even an apparently simple task such as the accurate determination of the relative pro-portions of salt and sand in a mixture can require a lot of practice before it can be carried out successfully. In more complex situations, such as the observation of the interactions of two different groups within a factory, the researcher may well find that perceptions of what, say, constitutes aggressive behaviour changes as the context becomes more familiar. In both cases it is clearly important that researchers allow enough time to 'calibrate' themselves as well as any equipment they may need, and this has obvious implications for planning the research project as discussed in Chapter 3.

Earlier, we pointed out that many student researchers, particularly part-time students find themselves involved in Action Research. Though this may provide ready access to past data, for example, minutes of meetings, it is easy for such researchers to neglect the need to record data about their own interactions with the organisation concerned.

ORGANISING THE DATA

Whichever of the above methods is used to gather data it will normally be necessary to maintain an extensive set of supplementary notes on the sources of the data, the conditions under which they were gathered, their relationships to other sets of data, and so on. These need to be stored in such a way as to offer some reasonable prospect of retrieval when required. The easiest way to do this is on a PC. However, where this is not possible, it is best to store the notes in folders which are then stored in a filing cabinet. Deciding on a list of subject headings under which to file is similar to generating a thesaurus for literature surveying, as discussed in Chapter 4. In many cases it will be obvious that notes could profitably be filed under more than one heading. Where they are brief this is perhaps most easily accommodated by producing several photocopies. Where the material is more bulky, cross-references of the form, 'Note on possible method of assessing the innovativeness of individual engineers, see file on Measuring characteristics of individual engineers' can be filed under the relevant subjects.

Such concerns are perhaps particularly relevant where data are subject to computer analysis. It is often possible to find students repeating a computer run because insufficient information was kept about the original one for its results to be located. Nevertheless, this is an illustration of a far more general point. Effective management of data gathering requires that thought be given to the organisation of the data early in this phase of the project before any retrospective attempt to impose some system and order upon them becomes infeasible. As in many other situations the important thing is to have a workable rather than a perfect system.

COLLECTING PRIMARY DATA

In order to discuss the practical aspects of the collection of primary data it is necessary to break them down into a number of categories, namely: laboratory measurements; field observation; archives/collections; questionnaires, and interviews. Whilst this list is not exhaustive there are important differences between the various sources listed. The brief comments are designed to highlight aspects which are pertinent to the planning and successful execution of this phase of student research.

Laboratory Measurement

Laboratory measurements typically offer researchers the greatest control over their data gathering activities and therefore lend themselves to careful planning. The most important considerations are usually to design the apparatus or experiment to collect and record the necessary data as efficiently as possible, to construct it and to ensure it is working correctly. This can take a great deal of time.

Efficient design is primarily a matter of considering the way in which the data will be used in analysis. To verify that gravity attracts objects towards the earth rather than repelling them needs only very simple apparatus and few observations. To determine the law governing that attraction, however, requires much better equipment and many more measurements. Beyond that it is worth remembering, since extreme measurements always provide a better test of theories, there is much to be said for attempting to design apparatus to cope with a wider range of measurements than it is believed will be needed.

Building a test rig or organising an experimental situation can often be speeded up by formal methods of planning of the type described in Chapter 3. Ensuring that the experiment is functioning as intended and that data are being properly recorded is often harder to plan. The researcher can at least though give proper consideration to the things that might be wrong with the data and ways in which they could be detected at an early stage, for example, by using a duplicate measuring device from time to time to provide a spot check on the main instrument.

Though it is obviously important to detect erroneous data and situations where the experiment is not functioning as planned, the opposite problem also exists of being too willing to abandon data because they are 'not right', or because something must have been wrong with the experiment when they were collected. This can lead to important behaviour being rejected in the name of consistency. All experimenters recognise that there are situations under which data must be rejected for these reasons. Against this, scientific data are often suspiciously tidy with much less error than might have been expected on a statistical basis.

Field Observation

Many types of research, for example, geophysical and ecological, make heavy

143

use of field observation. Where possible it is better to use simple, familiar measuring equipment capable of operating reliably under field conditions for carrying out measurements in the field.

Field observations of human behaviour are of so many different types that it is hardly possible to do more than state some of their major advantages and disadvantages. For a comprehensive discussion of such topics with particular reference to the social sciences the reader is recommended to consult Webb *et al* (1966).

Where the observations cannot be carried out without the knowledge of the subjects as, say, in anthropological data gathering, researchers may well cause unrepresentative behaviour repertoires to be displayed in their presence. Again, there are types of research like Action Research where the researcher's explicit aim is to bring about a change in the situation under study. It follows here that the researcher is an important part of the situation and the researcher's behaviour is part of the experimental data that should be gathered.

For the student interested in this type of observation it is worthwhile consulting the obvious sources of expertise, namely, the cultural anthropologists or sociologists interested in deviant groups. Relevant material can be found for example in Naroll (1962), which also discusses the problem raised earlier of how the researcher's perceptions and therefore the basis of data collection can change as the field observations progress and ways in which it can be overcome. The ideas of Glaser and Strauss (1967) and in particular their emphasis on continual restatement of the theory on which data gathering is based are also of considerable interest in this context.

Field observation need not always be completely passive. Substantial experimental manipulation may be possible even though the complete control of the laboratory situation is not possible.

Situations of this type can often lend themselves to analysis by the statistical experimental design model discussed in Chapter 5. Interpretation of the results is not usually, however, anywhere near as simple as in the laboratory situation and generalisability is often more difficult to assess because of doubts about how typical the field situation is.

Archival Data

Many subjects make extensive use of data available in some type of archive or collection. In many countries, locally maintained records and the minutes of learned societies are important data sources for the historian. The archaeologist is likely to make extensive use of museum collections of artefacts. The accurate astronomical records kept by certain ancient civilisations are of importance in some branches of astronomy and so on.

Public funding for research is often conditional on the data generated being eventually deposited in some publicly accessible collection or, nowadays, online database. In the social sciences in the UK, for instance, such a role is fulfilled by the ESRC Data Archive.[1] Similar bodies exist in other countries.

Less well recognised is the existence of private archives or collections of data. Many private collections of paintings, for example, are not publicised for insurance reasons. On the other hand, there is a mass of material available to the researcher arising from records of normal day-to-day business for which this problem does not exist. If the student can discover the existence of such a collection and obtain access to it then the prospects of producing interesting research findings are well above average.

For recognised collections it is often possible to obtain access for the purpose of *bona fide* research. The problems for the researcher interested in archives of this sort are to obtain sufficient resources to visit them (since there is little prospect of borrowing the material) and then to find some satisfactory way of recording (since the data involved are rarely intrinsically easy to record and there may well be limitations on, say, the photographing of old documents). Some archives of this kind are available as facsimiles – for example, photographs of drawings or microfiches of company accounts – and for these it should usually be possible to find sufficient money to pay for copies of major items of interest. Academic bodies have traditionally looked favourably on the provision of travel grants and scholarships specifically for visiting archives and similarly there may be some possibility of obtaining funds from the sponsor of the student's research.

A number of methods of finding out about private collections have been suggested by Glaser and Strauss (1967) but since they are rarely compiled for research purposes, obtaining access can be difficult. As was stated earlier, students will often obtain access more easily if a request is made on their behalf by someone of suitable academic distinction. Furthermore, it is probably most common for access to non-government material, if granted, to be restricted to a few individuals at most. In broad terms, then, it is rarely worth trying to gain access to private material on which other researchers are already working.

Gathering Data by Questionnaires

Questionnaires have, over the past century, become a common method of gathering information. Their design is a large subject that will not be attempted here, and the reader is advised to consult a specialist text. The concern here is with some of the practical problems that occur in using questionnaires. Since the administration of questionnaires during an interview shares many of the problems of interviewing, we shall concentrate first on the use of questionnaires for postal surveys.

Postal surveys are a favoured way of seeking to acquire data from a large number of respondents. Inevitably, the quality of the data gathered is more superficial than that which can be collected during an interview so the tendency is for the study to be a large one. This in turn means that there will be large quantities of data to process. In almost all cases this favours the use of a computer, the implications of which have already been discussed.

The biggest problem with the postal questionnaire is that it is only somewhat tenuously a primary data gathering method. The investigator may have no direct contact with the respondents who may interpret the questions very differently from the researcher's intention. A pilot survey, however modest, is therefore essential. It need not observe the strict procedures necessary later with regard to sample selection providing it indicates realistically how the questions will be interpreted. Another less used procedure principally employed in cross-cultural studies is that of back translation. The questionnaire is translated from, say, English to Arabic by one person and then from Arabic to English by another and the resulting version compared with the original.

In a postal survey it would usually be considered unwise to have a questionnaire requiring more than about fifteen minutes to fill in or covering more than, say, ten A4 pages. Too long a questionnaire is likely to reduce markedly the percentage of responses and a low response rate always raises questions of bias. As outlined in the last chapter, this problem can to some extent be overcome by including additional questions that enable the researcher to check whether the returns are typical of the sampled population but this, of course, has the disadvantage of increasing the length of the questionnaire. Accordingly, other steps will often need to be taken too. The demand for molybdenum is taken as an example. A small number of responding companies account for the bulk of the behaviour of interest and since they are likely to be large and efficient there may well be definite advantages in eschewing the traditional random sample in favour of 100 per cent coverage of this fairly small group. Where random samples are deemed necessary it may be possible to administer the questionnaire by telephone. Certainly, a telephone call to enlist the cooperation of potential respondents often handsomely increases the response rate. The sponsorship of a prestigious body, such as a professional association, can also improve response considerably. In most circumstances it is usually necessary anyway to send a suitably worded follow-up letter to non-respondents. Since response rates can vary from under 5 per cent to 80 per cent or so, depending on the above factors, it clearly behoves the researcher to consider these points. If this is not done the result may be a small number of possibly biased returns that are insufficient for the purposes of the analysis and the researcher will also be in no position to draw up a realistic budget for the resources required during this part of the study.

Interviews

Most social scientists would see the interview as providing higher quality information that is freer from bias than many other methods available to them. Indeed, in a new field, a programme of interviews may be the only way of obtaining a realistic picture of the way people view it. Such rich potential does of course imply a need for planning and training, if the student is to make the most of the interview programme arranged. Many factors are relevant here: from basic points like the need to be punctual through to considerably more complex topics such as how to probe a particular subject in a non-directive way. A number of texts deal with these points at length, for example, Gorden (1980), and the reader is referred to these for further details.

The major data gathering problems in interviewing are to find adequate ways of recording all the data obtained. These problems in turn relate to the degree to which the interviewer wishes to structure the interview and in fact is permitted to do so (since the research student's control over an interview with, for example, a chief executive is somewhat limited). An interview can, in fact, be just a means of getting a lengthy and complex questionnaire filled in. Usually, however, the student will wish to supplement this by open-ended discussion and a more common model is for the interviewer to define a schedule of topics to be covered and to explore them in whatever order appears natural in the course of the discussion. This situation is obviously more difficult to handle. At a very minimum two things are needed: firstly, some way of discreetly keeping a check that all topics have been covered; and, secondly, an initial icebreaking question that is almost guaranteed to evoke a response from the interviewee. This problem is obviously exacerbated by the fact that, under most circumstances, interviews should probably not take much over an hour and, indeed, researchers may have far less time at their disposal if the subject is one that is of little interest to the interviewee.

Generally, it is not desirable to schedule more than two or three interviews a day which implies that the typical student researcher cannot afford a very extensive programme for reasons of both time and money. This is obviously particularly the case in a dissertation project. Against that, the more modest aims of such research projects generally mean that the results of a few interesting interviews will form the basis of an acceptable dissertation where the topic being studied is relatively novel.

In the longer research project for a research degree, thought also needs to be devoted as to how material gleaned from interviews is to be analysed in the final research report, otherwise the researcher runs the risk of having a wealth of data from a set of individually valuable interviews that collectively are very difficult to generalise from. The preparation of a realistic interview schedule in advance of the first interview is clearly a wise step.

Further Uses for Primary Data

Frequently, primary data gathered for one purpose turn out to be of great value for totally different purposes at a later date. It is by no means unknown for a researcher to return to the data years after the immediate objective of writing a thesis has been achieved. And, like bibliographies, the data may represent a tradeable commodity that will facilitate access to other researchers' data. It follows, then, that where possible primary data should be carefully filed away along with sufficient details to enable them to be used by someone else. Similarly, where some part of them has been transcribed on to the computer those data should be put on to some long-term storage medium, for example, a diskette, so that they are available for future use. If this is done, however, it must be borne in mind that such storage media do not last for ever: there may be physical deterioration or the computer system used to write the data may become obsolete.

SECONDARY DATA SOURCES

By secondary data is meant data collected by others and published in some form that is fairly readily accessible. (See Figure 6.2.) Thus, in these terms company accounts that are published by law are secondary data. In general, the research student will not know too much about the hidden assumptions, corrections or distortions that go into the production of a particular set of secondary data unless trouble is taken to find out what these were. Such data tend to have the beguiling look of the printed page about them and may thus appear far removed from the messy imperfections and inconsistencies that researchers may know to exist in their primary data. For the social scientist it is salutary to read Morgenstern's (1963) compendious review of the myriad ways in which economic and social data can involve error and bias. Whatever the researcher's interest, it is always wise to ascertain the basis on which measurements are compiled since otherwise different sets taken under different conditions or using different methods may well not be comparable. In addition, many data involve substantial measurement error and it may well be important in the analysis to be aware of this.

Source	Type of data
Technical publications (Manuals/handbooks/data sheets/standards)	Physical/chemical constants Technical performance specifications
Books and journals	'Workhorse data' More esoteric quantitative data of all kinds Non-quantitative data
Official publications (e.g. Central and Local Government)	Economic/social data
Trade association data	Technical or economic data
Private data services	Economic/product data
Computer databases	All types of quantitative data Text data

Figure 6.2 Some sources and types of secondary data

On the other side of the coin, secondary data have considerable attractions for students particularly in the social sciences and especially if they are engaged in a short research project. They are usually more quickly available than primary data and much less organisation is required to obtain them. Furthermore, they exist in considerable quantities and may contain information that is fairly easy for a government agency with legal backing to collect; something that would be very difficult for the lone researcher.

A type of secondary data that is increasing considerably in importance with the expansion of research internationally and the trend to storing research data in internationally available databases, is that from previous researchers' studies. If the basis on which previous studies have been conducted has been properly documented, and there has been reasonable standardisation in the way data were collected, then it becomes possible for the researcher to base the analysis entirely on the data from previous studies. This approach, known as metaanalysis, is extensively used in fields such as epidemiology. If the data involved are quantitative, then there are statistical methods that can be applied to enable the data to be analysed efficiently (Hunter *et al*, 1982).

149

Figure 6.2 lists a number of important sources and types of secondary data, and these are reviewed briefly paying attention to some of the main advantages and problems of each source and referring the reader where desirable to more specialist sources for discussions of particular types.

Technical Publications

A host of data, from physical and chemical constants to performance data for particular items of equipment, are to be found in handbooks and manuals. Publications of this type are familiar names to workers in a particular field: for example, *Spon's Landscape and External Works Price Book*. Similar information may be published by equipment manufacturers in the form of detailed performance specifications, or by trade associations or bodies such as the British Standard Institution. Most data of this sort are relatively easily accessible. The basic techniques of literature searching will usually reveal what are available in an academic library.

Books and Journals

For many researchers, books and journals are likely to be the major source of data. Furthermore, they are by far the most important source of what we have called textual data.

One major use of books and journals is in providing certain standard sets of 'workhorse data' that are used by all investigators in a field as test beds for new methods and techniques so that their performance can be compared with well established ones. Very often they will be found in the literature of a subject, for example, the various time series, such as IBM common stock price, used to compare different computer methods of forecasting.

The data presented in a book or paper have typically received more processing and may therefore be subject to more qualifications than other types of secondary data. Indeed, they frequently are based on refinements and reworking of existing secondary data though this may not be readily apparent.

On the whole, unless the research project is short or the data are only of peripheral interest the use of books as sources of other than 'workhorse data' is perhaps best restricted to those which focus on the assumptions and processes by which the data were generated or to those providing expensive or esoteric data not readily available elsewhere.

Official Publications

The volume and diversity of government publications has already been remarked on in Chapter 4. In advanced economies these are a major source of social and economic data of all kinds as well as design and performance specifications for many fields of engineering, and so forth.

The most frequently useful official data are probably the various statistics compiled by government departments. By way of example more detailed accounts of UK Government statistics on population and related matters can be found in Slattery (1986).

Though discovering what official sources are available is usually relatively straightforward, guidance as to how to make effective use of the information is, in our experience, more difficult to come by. Frequently, the researcher needs to carry out further manipulations of the data listed, perhaps by comparing data in one source with those in another. Such are the diversity of uses of government statistics that even the experienced social science researcher is only likely to know a few of the sources well. The student researcher can probably learn much about how to exploit such data from talks and seminars given by those who make regular use of them, that is, market researchers, economists, educational sociologists and so forth.

There are many other public bodies that publish statistics of importance to the researcher. In the UK, for instance, organisations such as the Chartered Institute of Public Finance (CIPFA) publish much material of a statistical nature and the reports of public sector industries go far beyond the provision of statutory accounting data in describing their operations.

The official statistics of other countries are another useful source for the researcher, as are those of international bodies such as OECD and UNESCO, all of which can provide important data for comparative purposes. Many of these find their way into the *United Nations Statistical Yearbook*.

Lists of the official statistics of various countries can also be found, for example, in handbooks intended for market researchers.

Data of this type come in the category of those that researchers could not possibly collect for themselves. Rather, researchers must make the best use of what exists and from the point of view of the research report that means critically appraising the data available to them, assessing their defects and correcting or allowing for them as best they can.

There are many types of research that require historical data. Numerous official statistics have been collected in the past in connection with a decennial census or a particular survey. Certain data series, such as wheat prices, extend back over a substantial period. Two useful guides to UK historical data series are Mitchell and Deane (1962) and Mitchell and Jones (1971). A similar guide to European series also exists (Mitchell, 1975).

Trade Association Data

Trade associations and similar bodies can be an excellent source of both technical and economic data about the operations of their members. For obvious reasons the economic data they publish are more detailed than those available through official statistics. Information on UK trade associations can be found in the *Directory of British Associations* and the availability of data can be checked with the relevant association.

Private Data Services

Data that are of interest to the researcher can often be of considerable use to researchers in general, particularly those working in the private sector in market research, investment analysis, and so on. Data of this type are, accordingly, a commercial proposition and there are many different services available. Sometimes, access to these services is free as with trade catalogues and permanent exhibitions. More usually they cost money. Many are available on a subscription basis, for example, the Extel Service giving details of the accounts of companies listed on UK Stock Exchanges, and are to be found in larger public libraries as well as academic libraries. Some appear regularly – often annually – for example, guides to UK markets. Other data are produced only on a one-off basis and tend to be far more expensive, for example, the multi-client studies produced by certain organisations giving data on various products and markets that typically are intended to be sold only to a few dozen organisations. Often, those services providing information not readily accessible to the academic researcher, for example, details of executive remuneration for different types of post in different countries, are likely to be most useful and for that reason expensive, so their use has to be budgeted for at the planning stage.

Computer Databases

A source of secondary data that is of considerable importance is the computer database. In the UK, many Central Statistical Office Series are available on computer bureaux or on CD–ROM, as are accounting data for listed public companies. The increasing importance of bibliographic databases and the possibility of using them as a data source has been noted in Chapter 4. Similar remarks apply to the databases for products and services now available in a variety of fields. International bodies also maintain important databases, for example, the United Nations database on trade flows. Further information on available databases can be found, for example, in Cox (1991). Many have been developed directly by universities and other institutions for research purposes and will often be available to researchers from elsewhere. Databases of textual information, for example, newspapers, were extensively discussed in Chapter 4. It is worth noting, however, the increasing availability of concordances or specialist literatures (such as the complete corpus of known works in Middle English) in database form.

Where they exist, databases are a very valuable form of secondary data. They usually contain far more observations than the individual student could collect and the basis on which the data have been gathered and the adjustments made is usually explicit. Most importantly, databases are ideally suited to computer analysis and make it quite feasible for the individual student to contemplate types of analysis and research topics that once would have been considered hopelessly ambitious.

Desirably, the student researcher needs free access to the data in order to experiment with different ways of processing them. This usually means transferring the details onto the researcher's own computer system. Nowadays, this transfer can usually be effected directly via a computer network such as JANET in the UK or the Internet internationally, when the database owner is another university (particularly an American one) or some public body. Where the data are provided on a commercial basis the cost may be several hundred pounds (if the owner is willing to make a copy available) because payment is expected for the data themselves. Additionally, there are almost always restrictions on the use researchers may make of the information, for example, it is unlikely that they will be allowed to sell it to others. Whatever the source, it is probable that the researcher will need to budget for further copies of the database at regular intervals so that the version can be kept up to date.

Unless they are familiar with the procedures involved, we would strongly advise students who wish to obtain a copy of a database to consult with the computer department of their own institution since its staff will be in a better position to judge how to do it easily and to liaise with the staff of the computer centre on which the database is maintained. Once students have acquired a copy of the database, however, we would urge them to acquire the skills needed to enable them to carry out their own analyses. At worst, this is unlikely to involve them in more than learning how to handle files in some common computer language such as BASIC; at best, they are likely to find that their installation possesses a file interrogation package that makes the process very straightforward. In either case, they will have acquired a skill that will benefit them in their subsequent careers.

Obviously, conversion of the database to a usable form and the acquisition of the necessary computing skills both require time – and the former may involve expense if it is not carried out by the student. Prospective use of a database has, therefore, important implications for the planning of the research.

CHAPTER SUMMARY

DATA MAY BE DISTINGUISHED AS: primary data – data gathered by the researcher and secondary data – data gathered by others.

THE DATA TO BE GATHERED ARE RELATED TO THE PURPOSES OF THE ANALYSIS: it follows that the type and quantity of data are affected by that purpose and therefore, indirectly by the level of the research project.

DATA MUST BE: located
assessed
collected and checked
recorded in a form suitable for subsequent analysis.

MEASUREMENT ERROR: affects much data and must be reduced to an acceptable level, possibly by increasing the sample size.

DATA GATHERING: is a demanding activity when primary data are involved and time should be allocated for training in collection. Secondary data are usually easier to collect and use although the assumptions on which this type of data are based may be unclear.

DATA ORGANISATION: thought should be given to how best to organise the data and associated notes on them to avoid wasted effort through reduplication of analyses, etc.

DATA RECORDING: usually involves the two processes of capture and transcription. Where possible, means of error checking should be employed at both of these stages.

Part C

Producing the
Research Results

7

Executing the Research

Whatever the level of the research, students should resist the temptation to proceed with its execution until an acceptable plan has been formulated. It would be a mistake, however, to assume that when this plan has been achieved the research will proceed towards its conclusion with as much certainty as the construction of a bridge. Even the smaller project which is planned to be completed within a few months may encounter unexpected obstacles.

This chapter has three main objectives:

1. To identify problems which, with hindsight, could have been avoided and to suggest anticipatory action which should be adopted.
2. To suggest ways of coping with unavoidable or unexpected problems which may arise.
3. To make positive suggestions which will facilitate research progress.

The chapter will tend to focus also on the longer project for a research degree; however, almost all the issues with which we are concerned here are highly relevant to shorter research projects. Indeed, in some instances, for example, illness, some of the problems discussed can be more acute with the shorter project because of its much less flexible time-scale.

AVOIDABLE PROBLEMS

In large part, avoidable problems should be highlighted by the systematic planning process described in Chapter 3. There are, nevertheless, three aspects which should continue to receive attention throughout the course of the study.
1. Overcommitment.
2. Failure to make use of the research plan.
3. Adequacy of supervision.

It is appreciated that supervisors may be appointed at different stages of the research according to the approach used by the particular institution and we have already made the point that in dissertation projects supervision may be very limited. The link between student and supervisor may be established prior to topic selection, between that and the research proposal, or after the proposal. Part-time students may not be accepted in some cases until they have presented a carefully argued research proposal. As, however, most supervision will be undertaken during the execution of the research, the practice is discussed at greatest length in this chapter.

Overcommitment

Reference was made in Chapter 1 to a survey of students which was designed to assess why completion rates were not as good as they might have been. Several activities were identified as competing for available time and certain of these were felt, on balance, to affect progress adversely.

It is not suggested that once students embark upon a research project they should turn their backs on all other types of activity; there should be scope for both leisure and academic related pursuits. This book is not concerned with the former, which must remain the responsibility of the student, but with those opportunities which will present themselves to full-time research students and also which may be perceived as potential contributors to self-development in a career sense, or simply as a means of generating much needed income.

A difficult decision for some research degree students to take is the extent to which they accept tutorial or demonstrating work offered to them.[1] Many such students have inclinations to pursue a career in education and apart from the financial benefits see the experience as being of much potential value. It is important that before accepting a teaching commitment students should investigate the total demand which it will make on their time. A one hour tutorial may involve three hours preparation and two hours marking. Since many research students would see fifty hours of actual work a week as being realistic, ten hours commitment arising from a regular teaching assignment would be a substantial proportion of this total. Certainly, time in excess of this could have a major adverse effect on the rate of progress of the study itself. It is, however, by no means rare for students to acquire a reputation during the course of their research and as a result to be invited to give one-off lectures. In moderation, the acceptance of invitations of this nature are to be encouraged, not least so that advantage can be taken of constructive criticism when they come to writing their thesis.

Students who anticipate that they will from time to time present the findings of their work in a more or less formal setting would do well to read the booklet 'Talking about your research' (Dixon and Hills, 1981); in addition to advice on visual aids and communicating with an audience, the booklet includes a number of useful references on script preparation.

The writing of papers on topics arising from, or very closely related to, the research has much to commend it. In addition to gaining valuable experience of the writing process itself the acceptance of articles for publication is probably the main way in which academic reputations are established. Additionally, a measure of substance is added to research theses if students can reference their own work which has been published in journals of repute. It would therefore be quite reasonable for a student to think in terms of submitting articles for publication at a rate of about one per year of full-time study.

The opportunity for consultancy does not come the way of more than a small fraction of students. Such offers are usually tempting to the impecunious student and may even add considerably to the research, but their acceptance may jeopardise the completion of the project. Perhaps the only advice that can be given is that if students are not prepared to contemplate being unable to finish their thesis on time they should only undertake consultancy if by careful and realistic planning they estimate that the additional work can be accommodated.

The survey referred to above listed 'Other outside work'. This is assumed here to include all extra research activities not so far considered – but which do not qualify as leisure in the usually accepted sense of that word. A good deal depends on the extent to which students are involved in any of the activities already referred to (teaching, writing papers, and consultancy). If they are not greatly involved they could well benefit from doing something to counterbalance research which may be very demanding and at times tedious. The work content of taught degree courses is fairly well defined, research on the other hand can be virtually unbounded. Research students should not be guilt-ridden if they take time off to run a society, edit a student newspaper, or organise a wine tasting.

In practice, the most important determinant of the amount of outside activity in which research students can safely engage is their ability to organise their own time effectively. There are students who manage a substantial part-time commitment to research whilst at the same time occupying very senior positions in large organisations. Equally, full-time research students are known who successfully combine a very active role in research with a part-time commitment to a company as a consultant or as a director. Conversely, many research students, particularly younger ones, find considerable difficulty in organising their own time effectively enough to carry on the single task of research.

A wise student will appreciate that the assumption that during a two or three year study major diversions can be absorbed without prejudicing successful completion is a dangerous one. It is vital that the research should never get out of control. We strongly recommend, therefore, the maintenance of schedule charts that are updated at least once every two weeks, and the avoidance of any binding commitment if that would lead to a high probability that, as a result, the study will be unacceptably extended.

Failure to Make Use of the Research Plan

In Chapter 3 the importance of fixing 'milestones' in the project was discussed, and in particular their use for ensuring that progress is maintained. Experience suggests that many students do not place sufficient weight on meeting the deadlines they identify, or on redefining and replanning the research if for some reason a milestone is missed by any considerable length of time. This is particularly so at the doctoral level where there are few natural markers of the passage of time. The end result can be that each stage takes longer than planned and, eventually, what once seemed a leisurely schedule now seems hopelessly optimistic given the time remaining.

A further and often more serious variant of this problem is to refuse to admit that a significant snag has been encountered. Surprisingly often research students find that a particular stage in the research is more difficult than was envisaged but are unwilling to admit to themselves that the problem is a major one. Instead they begin to look a day or two ahead to the time when the bug will certainly have been removed from a computer program or their apparatus will finally begin to work, and eventually many months can be wasted in a welter of misplaced optimism.

Such situations can be avoided if students realise that they have a problem and seek advice about it. If they continually review their progress against a plan it is unlikely that they will seriously deceive themselves, whereas if they do not they will almost certainly find it far more difficult to seek help given the embarrassingly long time it took to see the need.

Adequacy of Supervision

Students undertaking research projects have a right to expect to receive advice, supervision or direction, though in the case of dissertation projects the 'budget' for such supervision may be very limited. Literal interpretation suggests that the degree of control exercised over the student increases from an advisor, through a supervisor, to a director. All of the latter categories are encountered but the most common in British higher degree research is the supervisor. The word 'supervision' is a fairly accurate reflection of the context in which research is most appropriately conducted, containing elements of both 'advice' when requested and 'direction' when deemed apposite by the supervisor. To some extent, attitudes of supervisors are affected by the fact that demands made upon them differ from those which arise in traditional teaching situations. They may feel a lack of competence in research methodology and in coping with problems which arise in areas with which they are unfamiliar. More fundamental is the degree of obligation which the supervisor carries for the successful completion of a research study. In many courses two conditions need to be met: firstly, the report or dissertation must be handed in by a particular date; and, secondly, minimum standards should be satisfied. Postgraduate degrees are often based wholly or in part on dissertations or theses for which the submission date is flexible within what might be quite an extended period. Although degree awarding institutions define the latest date of normal submission, extensions are usually granted if students can provide evidence that they are continuing to make some progress. On the assumption that few students can obtain finance for full-time study for more than two or three years this points to the research being completed part-time. In these circumstances (even though the student may be paying substantial fees) supervision can become lax and solely reactive. This is, to an extent, understandable as staff members move to new interests and new appointments. Therefore, students taking an inordinate time to complete their projects must expect the initiative for supervision to be largely their responsibility (although this does not absolve the supervisor entirely from action as long as the student continues to be formally registered).

The position of students registered for a part-time research degree is rather different from that of the full-time student. Very often their research will be related to their work in which case they may expect reasonable support from their organisation. In fact some statement to this effect from their employer will often be required by the institution with which they are registered along with formal evidence that adequate supervision will be available. In many cases an industrial supervisor may be appointed or, if the candidate is located overseas, an additional academic supervisor may need to be found locally.

Some academics prefer to supervise part-time research degrees on the grounds that only the highly motivated student will embark on one and that they frequently have access to much richer data sources, such as confidential company records, that are not usually available to the full-time student. The part-time student, moreover, being often more experienced is thus better able to organise the details of the supervisor/student relationship than many full-time students. Indeed, given that their research must be fitted in around the requirements of a job, it is normally best if the part-time student undertakes this responsibility. Meetings and discussions with the supervisor should, desirably, take place at least quarterly; in many cases, these will be supplemented by submission of written material particularly in the writing-up stage. Provided this is done, and the original plans are adhered to, the part-time researcher's chances of success are good, particularly if it is possible to attend courses – or better still register for an extended period (say six months to a year) full-time – once student and supervisor are satisfied that successful completion is possible.

UNAVOIDABLE OR UNEXPECTED PROBLEMS

In addition to those things which the student should plan to avoid it must also be recognised that the research can be threatened by many other factors. It is suggested that the student should be aware of these possibilities but should not 'over-plan' to cover every conceivable contingency which may occur. These problems are described as being unavoidable or unexpected. Figure 7.1 groups this type of problem.

Individual Centred Problems

There are a number of ways in which research progress may be affected by what may be termed 'personal' factors:
a) illness;
b) loss of motivation;
c) occurrence of other opportunities;
d) need to search for a job.

Illness
Illness affecting the student or close relatives is always a possibility. It is likely

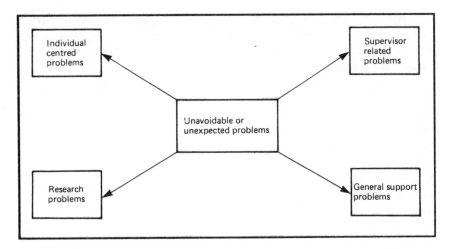

Figure 7.1 Types of unavoidable or unexpected problems

to have an adversely non-linear effect as the duration of illness increases. Probably the maximum of available time which the student can accommodate is 10 per cent; supervisors or examiners should be made aware if 5 per cent of research time is likely to be affected by illness.

Institutions and grant awarding bodies are invariably sympathetic towards students who suffer certified illness and it is much to be preferred that such incidence is notified. If the illness is of long duration the decision to take is clear cut. Students should seek to have their registration suspended and, if they are full-time students, to have part of any support they receive deferred. The decision becomes more difficult if shorter periods of illness are involved when there may be an inclination to absorb the time lost and at the same time retain any grant payment. The proportion of the planned period remaining will obviously be an important factor. If the student is in doubt the inclination should be towards delaying the planned completion date.

Loss of Motivation

Without self-motivation research can be extremely laborious, but no student can maintain the same pitch of enthusiasm throughout a study particularly if it is of several years duration. A range of factors may lead to a loss of motivation. These include tedium, frustration, lack of progress and a reduction in interest. There is little need to give examples, of more importance is how problems of this type may be overcome.

The first recommendation is that these problems should be discussed informally with someone else; preferably the supervisor in the first instance, but also with students who have themselves experienced and overcome similar difficulties. If informal discussions do not bring about the desired outcome then a second possibility is that the student should suggest to the supervisor that an *ad hoc* committee should be set up to review progress. Some institutions use this practice routinely and it is usually found to be very effective. Two or three faculty members (one of whom may have no experience in the field of research) are often able to generate suggestions which indicate how problems may be resolved or which rekindle the student's interest in the topic.

A third possibility which may help in overcoming tedium, in particular during the early stages of research, is to leave aside the task in hand and switch to another element of the research study. Figure 3.2, the bar chart, shows that several parallel activities may have been identified. Unless the activity creating the problem is 'critical' the student can probably find something completely different to pursue and, importantly, will be able to assess how long a task may be deferred before it becomes critical. An example of an activity which can be both motivating and rewarding is the writing of a paper on a distinct phase of the work which has been completed. Even though the paper may be a general one reviewing the current situation in the area, or a descriptive account of the response to a survey, acceptance for publication can be a spur to renewed effort besides having other obvious advantages.

The ability to 'stand back', particularly during the longer studies, and view tedium and frustration as being inevitable from time to time should go some way to overcoming motivational problems. To this end the use of some type of wall chart as described in Chapter 3 will emphasise progress which has been made.

Having tried all means of self-motivation without effect, the student should not lose sight of the responsibility borne by the supervisor. On first being acquainted with the difficulties being experienced the supervisor will no doubt have made a number of suggestions for the student to follow up. If the student is unable to resolve the difficulties unaided, the supervisor should play a much more active role; but this is only possible, of course, if the supervisor is kept fully informed.

Other Opportunities

Those students for whom research is the whole basis of their degree are often confronted with another type of problem: an offer of employment.

Although the whole concern of this book is with the more effective use of time available it would be unrealistic to argue that every study should be completed precisely within one, two, or three years. Students have, therefore, the problem of trying to schedule the transition from study to employment under conditions of some uncertainty. Few prospective employers are prepared to make an open-ended job offer that will allow students to complete their research before taking up an appointment. Rather, more employers will allow some time to be spent during the early months of employment on completing the study, and in some instances (for example, educational appointments) students may feel that they will be able to make time available. Our experience has shown that the completion of research within, say, six months of taking up an appointment is extremely rare. Despite every intention, the demands of a (presumably) responsible position preclude other types of activity. This is a major reason why the completion rates reported by the research councils in the early 1980s and commented upon in Chapter 1 were so poor. Erstwhile full-time students discover that research is not something which can be easily picked up at any time and one consequence is that the longer the period taken the lower the probability of completion.

It is difficult for the young student to make a choice between what might be an attractive job opportunity and the completion of a degree. The attraction of a high salary after months spent at subsistence level whilst working on the completion of a thesis is difficult to resist. But whatever the economic climate the possession of a research degree is likely to continue to enhance the prospects of employment throughout a student's later career.

Part-time students quite often experience a change in employment during their studies; such a change of circumstances is likely to affect their schedules detrimentally. For this reason they need to push ahead rapidly whenever work pressures allow. The only way to ensure that research work does not cause conflict when a plum posting is offered is to have completed it.

Searching for Employment

A rather different employment effect of which research degree students must take note is the increasingly difficult job situation. Whereas until recent times students working for, say, doctorates could be sanguine about their prospects, they must now be prepared to spend considerable time searching for employment. This can have a very damaging effect on schedules during the later part of their research when it is likely that most of their contingency allocation will have been used up. It is therefore sensible that extra time should be incorporated within the research plan to accommodate activities such as the preparation of job applications and attendance at interviews.

Supervisor Related Problems

Ideally, a student should relate to one supervisor throughout the project. For students undertaking two- or three-year projects there exists, however, the possibility that staff mobility, or study leave, will prevent this from being achieved. In these circumstances the supervisor has a responsibility for ensuring that new arrangements are made which will have as little effect as possible upon the progress of the research. If the supervisor is staying in academic life it may be possible for the student to change from one institution to another (research councils will permit this). For a variety of reasons the student may be unwilling or unable to accept a transfer and in these circumstances the supervisor and colleagues should endeavour to effect a move to another member of staff who is able to satisfy the range of requirements. Obviously, the host institution will carry responsibility whatever the reason (for example, retirement, death in service) for the breaking of a supervisory arrangement.

In the unfortunate event that no suitable alternative supervisor can be found the student may be faced with the choice of continuing to work with nominal supervision only, ceasing research altogether, or making an application to another institution.

It is sometimes the case that a supervisor does not have all the necessary skills to advise the student. This situation may be encountered during the analysis phase when knowledge of mathematical, statistical, or computing techniques is required. It is to be hoped that supervisors will not attempt to conceal their ignorance in such matters as these and will direct the student to the appropriate quarters. The student should, however, never be diffident about approaching other members of staff, at the same time keeping their own supervisor informed.

In the longer research project, thesis committees are an effective way of revealing areas that have not received sufficient attention during supervisory meetings and many institutions use them on a regular basis for this reason. No matter how excellent the working relationship it is rare at the doctoral level at least that every need of the student is recognised by the supervisor or that the supervisor is in a position to respond effectively to every request for assistance. Often, the help needed from outsiders is small – a key reference, a suggestion as to methods of analysis – nonetheless, it can well be of major benefit. The thesis committee therefore provides an excellent way of supplementing supervision and in addition may lead to the uncovering of serious difficulties of the type discussed below.

The most regrettable situation arises when a supervisor falls below what is acceptable in terms of both the quality and quantity of supervision. The traditional British 'apprentice model' is so dependent upon an effective relationship between student and supervisor that there must always be a 'fallback' position to which the former can resort. If students feel that their research progress is being marred for this reason they should not hesitate to take informal and then, if necessary, formal steps in an attempt to resolve the situation. All of this assumes that the supervisor has not responded to management and may involve the matter being taken successively higher in the institutional hierarchy in order to find a workable solution. Action of this type though unpalatable, may, if not taken by students, adversely affect their career prospects.

RESEARCH PROBLEMS

The typical research project involves many stages and the chances of running into a snag somewhere along the way are, in the longer project at least, fairly high. The aim of this section is to discuss research problems that may be encountered and, where possible, ways by which they may be overcome. The latter may range from straightforward rectification of small defects to a major reinterpretation of what the research is about. Clearly, the latter end of the spectrum of solutions is only relevant to those carrying out research at the master's level and above.

Two categories of research problem are proposed: those which threaten the continuation of the study and those which seriously delay the study.

Threats to the Continuation of the Study

Although the future can never be predicted with certainty, students who set out on research studies will normally expect (particularly if they have undertaken thorough topic analyses and/or research proposals) to achieve a successful outcome. To some degree the prospects of success are related to the level and duration, and also the nature, of the research (see Chapter 1), with the basic types of research and certain kinds of applied research being more risky in that conclusions which are novel are sought. All types of research may, however, be brought to a halt by factors outside the control of the student. These factors include: the realisation that substantial conclusions cannot be drawn; the withdrawal of facilities; or evidence that some other researcher has successfully covered the same ground.

If researchers find that their efforts are likely to be fruitless there is little point in reminding them that their research design should have been more symmetrical with a low probability of an inconclusive outcome. An example is a student in the marketing area who may have felt quite confident of achieving a valuable outcome from a study of the importance of attitudes of potential customers in relation to the promotion of different makes of car. Having collected a large volume of data and having subjected it to analysis it may remain unclear as to whether any relationship exists; an outcome which would be unacceptable.

In terms of the model of research presented in Chapter 2, the problem in this situation is one where the research has insufficient value. Major changes will therefore probably need to be made to the line of the research and the way it has been viewed, if a rescue is to be effected. These changes include examining why success was not achieved when it was expected, possibly by going outside the original field of research and relating it to other theories; or, alternatively, showing that similar assumptions to those underlying the original research are widely employed by practitioners and pointing out the consequences of their erroneous use. Thus, in the present case the student might well attempt to explore other dimensions of the car buying process. Perhaps the lack of success is explicable in terms of the high percentage of cars purchased by companies rather than by individuals? Alternatively, if the student can show that car design is strongly influenced by similar (incorrect) beliefs then the research has strong implications for the design policy of car manufacturers and this may well make a sufficiently weighty set of findings.

The withdrawal of facilities will primarily affect research studies which depend upon external cooperation. For example, an organisation which hitherto had been collaborating by permitting access to its research and development department may decide to withdraw from the arrangement. In such cases the important question to be resolved is how far the value of the research is dependent on the resource concerned. For example, it is easy to forget, as commitment to a particular path of research develops, the extent to which expediency dictated earlier choices: the support of a company with which the institution has close links; a private collection situated near to the researcher's home. On the other hand, neither is necessarily unique and there may well be other possibilities of carrying out essentially the original research plan but using some other resource. Alternatively, it may be possible to adopt a comparative stance in the research, for example, by looking at several other organisations and seeing how they cope with similar problems to those studied in the original company, or by examining how one sequence of events uncovered in the examination of family papers impinged on others who were involved in them.

A more insidious problem than withdrawal of key resources is the inability of those resources to function as planned. Most engineering laboratories have test rigs that have either never worked at all or have at least required several generations of research students to get them to perform as intended. Computer software, surprisingly often, still refuses to work in accordance with its specification. The difficulty here is that while the student can clearly see that tomorrow the hoped for results will emerge, in the meantime there is little to show for the efforts. Sooner or later, therefore, it is necessary to call a halt and make a decision as to whether to change the direction of the research or focus on getting the resource to function as planned. At the master's level and below the latter is frequently a sensible strategy since the work will probably be of an acceptable standard. At the doctoral level this is more rarely the case and so the decision will probably be to treat the resource as if withdrawn, in which case the earlier remarks apply.

Despite the increasing efficiency of information transfer it is still possible that two researchers will be covering, in ignorance, the same ground simultaneously. If this proves to be so when basic research with its emphasis on generalisability is involved there may be little that the 'second past the post' can do about it. There are, however, relatively few situations where the difficulties are so extreme. Even in mathematics, which might seem the most likely area for it to be so, there is usually scope for alternative methods of deriving results. In the experimental sciences, confirmatory evidence would be considered very desirable and in most situations in the social sciences and humanities exact and irremediable overlap is most unlikely. Much more likely is that the research provides an alternative view.

In each of the above cases, student researchers may initially feel that the ground has fallen away from under them. This will be the case particularly if more than 50 per cent of the period of the study has been completed. Given the catastrophe that appears to have befallen them it is unlikely that their judgement will be sound. Their primary need is for detached, expert advice from outsiders. The first source of help is the supervisor, but it is the nature of these problems that the supervisor may be too closely involved to proffer impartial guidance. Usually, a better plan is for the student to discuss the problem informally with a variety of acquaintances who are also involved in research and then to convene an (*ad hoc*) thesis committee which is primarily composed of researchers with a proven ability in the field of research design who can offer a variety of perspectives on the problem. Ideally, they should all be familiar with the field of research but have related rather than similar interests. Such a committee needs to focus on whether:

a) there is a serious problem; and

b) if so, can it be overcome with as little waste of previous work as possible?

Where the answer to question b) is 'No', the positive options open to the student would seem to be as follows:

a) try to define rapidly a new research topic which will have as much overlap as possible with the redundant topic;

b) consider conversion (in the case of the doctoral student) to an acceptable master's thesis;

c) drop the idea of completing a research degree and write as many papers as possible on the research completed for both academic and (if appropriate) professional journals;

d) write a book on the research area instead.

Much will depend on how much research time is left and on the enthusiasm which the student can retain. The experience gained from undertaking some of the customary research stages should be of considerable benefit if the student has to retrace steps. Which of the options listed is to be preferred will depend on the individual, but if at least one year of the study period remains consideration should be given to working up a new topic despite the knowledge that it may be necessary to write a large part of the thesis on a part-time basis.

It is not easy to make more than general recommendations on the development of a new topic as so much depends on the line of research which has been abandoned. Nor is it suggested that the latter is a common experience. Students may, however, comfort themselves with the thought that the greater the experience they have gained the easier it should be to both define and follow a new direction of study.

One situation in which some consolation may be derived from the frustration of a study arises when a student working for a doctorate has done sufficient work to satisfy the requirements of a master's degree. Much depends on the student's objectives. If, for instance, a future in tertiary education or in research is envisaged the student may be more inclined to use the time remaining to work towards a redefined doctorate. If not, the prospect of a master's degree may be more appealing.

There are few students who would accept that there should be no tangible outcome of, perhaps, three years of study. Most students would see as desirable the establishment of a reputation primarily through publication in academic journals, and perhaps a measure of lecturing or consultancy. If, therefore, the student has made substantial progress but has fallen short of the requirements of a PhD the acceptance of a few well-written papers by academic journals of standing may offer some compensation. In any event, research students are unlikely to communicate with the world at large through their thesis and if it is an academic reputation they seek they must be prepared to write either books or papers or both (see Chapter 8).

Increasingly, similar comments apply to students at lower levels. If, as we have suggested, they have selected their dissertation topic with an eye to their career objectives it may well be of benefit to derive one or more publications from their research project. Usually, however, since the target audience for such articles is likely to be practitioners, the articles would need to be aimed at the professional press.

Some Causes of Serious Delay

The above comments refer to circumstances in which a particular course of study is terminated for unpredicted reasons. More frequently encountered, and linked to poor rates of research degree completion, are those studies which are significantly delayed not so much by inefficient research management but by the occurrence of a specific problem. The most usual hurdle to be overcome faces students who have collected large volumes of data but who are unable to analyse them in sufficient depth. This reinforces the argument that the type of analysis to be employed should be anticipated as much as possible and explains why in this book data analysis precedes data collection.

It is to be hoped that constructive advice will be available from the supervisor on analytical approaches but it should be recognised that in many instances the supervisor may not possess the requisite skills. If this is so the student should not be diffident about seeking assistance from other sources. The academic world has within it many people who can provide guidance and it is a measure of the student's initiative to be able to make effective contact. What can almost be guaranteed is that assistance will be forthcoming on request. This requires that students should be prepared to leave their desks and perhaps undertake some travel, but the effort should be worthwhile.

Another major cause of delay arises from dependence on other peoples' reactions to a researcher's initiatives. The estimated duration of activities used to develop schedules in Chapter 3 assume 'normal' speeds of response but from time to time these will not be achieved. There may be lengthy delays in gaining approval from a collaborating body, items of equipment may not be delivered on time, questionnaires sent out for pilot test may not be returned and so on.

The risk is largely the extent to which parts of the study lie outside the direct control of the student. If there is much of this the need to adopt a formalised approach to planning can only be stressed. It is not so much a matter of normal 'lead time' (the interval between requesting something to be done and its occurrence) but a matter of considering in advance of a specific request whether the ground can be prepared in any way. For example, it would be worthwhile determining the frequency of meetings of an external body which will give approval for a study to be undertaken, or when a key individual is likely to take holidays, or whether an alternative supplier for a piece of equipment can be identified.

The consequences of delays such as those caused by some aspect of the process of the research or the research design may, it is to be hoped, be absorbed during the remainder of the study. But if delay is substantial a student working for a research degree may have to resort to the second and third options (conversion, if appropriate, to a master's degree, or writing papers instead) mentioned above.

Although failure to achieve the prime objective is to be regretted it is highly desirable that there should be some lasting indication of the student's efforts.

General Support Problems

This category includes those problems which arise neither from the individual, the supervisor, nor the research itself. The vast majority of students who commence a research study do so in the expectation that sufficient support will be available for them to achieve their objectives. Thus, they anticipate that appropriate funds will be forthcoming and that at the least they will be provided with minimum facilities such as desk space. Most students would not consider doing full-time research unless funding were guaranteed for the expected period of their study and the sensible student will have established what will be available in terms of accommodation, telephone, filing space, laboratory, library, computer facilities, and so on. The question is whether there is a possibility that any of this support will be withdrawn or will prove to be insufficient.

Students with grants can normally expect to receive, in real terms, a similar level of financial support throughout their studies. The only major problem that might arise under this heading would occur if the execution of the research involved activities that did not qualify for funding (for example, the transcription of interview tapes, or overseas travel). Lack of foresight by the student would at the least require that the student should be able to meet such expenditure from other sources.

If financial support is provided by other types of organisation there may be some risk of discontinuation. This has been a not uncommon occurrence for students from developing countries when political changes have led to a withdrawal of grants. In the UK, many students are funded by private sector organisations and although such incidents are not common economic recession and company closure can lead to similar problems arising.

Many institutions of further and higher education have 'hardship committees' which are often able to give practical support to those students who, through no fault of their own, find that sponsorship is withdrawn, but this support may be limited to fees only.

Although support problems are dominated by issues relating to fees or grants some students continue to experience difficulties through the data collection and analysis stages. Costs and facilities associated with the former should be capable of reasonable estimation and should be highlighted during the assessment of topic feasibility. Thus questions as to whether funds will be available to purchase equipment and materials, to cover travel, or to pay for the mailing of several hundred questionnaires will need to be resolved. Less easy to assess will be whether appropriate support for analysis will be forthcoming. Many students rely heavily on advice from computing departments and it is wise to anticipate as far as is possible the likely extent of what will be needed. Lengthy delays may arise if the student does nothing until on the point of requiring analysis to be undertaken. In large part, therefore, this type of problem should be anticipated at the planning stage and should not fall into the 'unavoidable or unexpected category'. Usually, for example, ample notification will be given of the upgrading of a computer system so that students will be able to reschedule their analysis if facilities are to be temporarily withdrawn or make alternative arrangements if software becomes unavailable.

WORKING WITH A SUPERVISOR

In view of the desirability and importance of high quality supervision of student research projects it is felt that comments are apposite at this point on the type of working relationship which ideally should operate. It is assumed that (at least for research degree students) the supervisor satisfies all of the requirements listed in Chapter 2 and that the student sees a reasonable prospect of a satisfactory relationship. If not, then the student should not hesitate to attempt to find an alternative.

In the initial stages of the research, at least, the student should look to the supervisor for guidance as to appropriate standards. This is an emotive aspect of research and a word of warning is necessary as many supervisors see their role in standard setting as advisory and do not feel it appropriate to direct the student as to what needs to be done to achieve the right level. Rather they see themselves as indicating directions through comments or queries and if these are disregarded they may, eventually, cease to make them. Students, therefore, must make sure that they attempt to meet points which are raised since their relationship with their supervisor will otherwise suffer.

As will be apparent, the supervisor is seen as fulfilling a number of key roles in any research project, though naturally the balance varies depending on the level of research.

In general a supervisor should:
a) get the student to define objectives at each stage of the work;
b) check to see that those objectives are met;
c) verify with the student that the work is of the right standard.

In practice these three aims will normally require a fair amount of guidance as the inevitable snags are encountered. How best to ensure that guidance is obtained is now examined.

Proposed below is what is seen as the ideal supervisory arrangements in

175

the certain knowledge that the actual outcome will, probably, fall short of this. The relationship is considered from the full-time student's point of view, although it is hoped that the suggestions will make sense to the supervisor. The reason for concentrating on full-time research students is that they will normally be supported by some grant-awarding body, which, as pointed out in Chapter 1, will certainly be interested in seeing that the students it supports complete their research degrees within the period nominally required. Given that this changes the pressures on both institution and supervisor it also implies greater conformity on the part of the full-time student than might have been the case in a more relaxed era. Accordingly, the recommendations to the student are fairly strongly prescriptive. It is suggested that both student or supervisor may find them useful in negotiating at its outset the type of relationship they expect to be maintained.

Though for stylistic reasons the term 'supervisor' is still referred to most of what is said applies equally well where the student has more than one supervisor. In fact it may well be that there are relatively few individual supervisors who measure up to the ideal portrayed here. Indeed, those who do may well suffer from an embarrassingly large number of requests for supervision, and under these circumstances might insist on an additional supervisor being appointed to share the task.

It is recommended that the student should:

1. Attempt at the outset to ascertain the supervisor's own views of the staff/student relationship.
2. Agree with the supervisor the routine aspects of the relationship (and take responsibility for their implementation).
3. Produce written lists of queries prior to meetings with the supervisor.
4. Keep written notes of meetings with the supervisor and submit copies.
5. Agree with the supervisor the nature and timing of written material to be submitted.

Each of these points is now discussed in turn.

The Supervisor's Views

Attempt at the outset to ascertain the supervisor's own views of the staff/student relationship. Even though both student and supervisor find a mutual interest in the research the relationship can be soured if, in particular, there are a number of counts on which the supervisor has strong feelings. If, for example, the supervisor has high standards of punctuality, the relationship would rapidly deteriorate if a student was persistently late in keeping appointments or broke them altogether. It is desirable that a student should be able to knock on the door of the supervisor, but if the latter prefers that arrangements should be made by telephone or through a secretary then this procedure should be adhered to.

Establishing Routines

Agree with the supervisor the routine aspects of the relationship (and take responsibility for their implementation). Regular contact between student and supervisor is very desirable. It is accepted that a small proportion of students may have sufficient competence and motivation to complete even a doctorate unaided, but the large majority will rely heavily on expert guidance, mainly from the supervisor. In the latter respect a prime requirement is that the supervisor should not lose touch with progress. Therefore, it should be agreed that the interval between meetings should not exceed a certain period. At some stages of the research frequent discussions will be required but, ideally, routine contact should be maintained with the interval between meetings not exceeding two weeks. The supervisor has a definite responsibility to comply with such an arrangement but as the person to suffer if regular contact breaks down is the student it is the latter who should take the initiative in rearranging dates if a meeting has to be postponed.

Anticipating Queries

Produce written lists of queries prior to meetings with the supervisor. It is helpful to the supervisor if the student submits a brief list of any queries or problems before routine meetings. This serves a number of purposes: it provides a basic agenda for the meeting; it forces the student to properly define what might otherwise remain a vague, unvoiced unease; it prevents the accretion of small difficulties into a single insuperable obstacle, and it fulfils a primary need for successful project management, namely the recognition of problems that need to be resolved. Obviously, in many types of research the student will also need to bring along to meetings supplementary material such as questionnaires or laboratory reports that bear on the queries raised.

Keeping Notes

Keep written notes of meetings with the supervisor and submit copies. Something positive should emerge from most meetings between student and supervisor. This may take the form of questions answered or suggestions to follow. It is all too easy to assume that these will be remembered but the nature of research makes it quite probable that they will not be. Whether or not supervisors keep their own written record of meetings students should certainly do so. Those students who have an aversion to the methodical should learn to accommodate their feelings on this point even to the extent of providing their supervisor with a copy of notes of meetings.

Scheduling and Submitting Written Material

The student should agree with the supervisor the nature and timing of written material to be submitted. Apart from written records of meetings maintained at the initiative of the student it is wise for the latter to gain some idea of the demands for other written material which the supervisor will make.

These demands will fall into two categories: progress reports and draft chapters.

1. Progress reports. Students should be prepared to submit progress reports at a frequency as high as once per month until the writing-up phase proper of the research is entered. They should be as succinct as possible unless the supervisor requests that a particular issue should be enlarged upon. Progress reports should record what work has been done since the previous report and show the relationship of this work to the following:
   a) the latest version of the research plan;
   b) whether a milestone event in the project has been reached;
   c) action points agreed at the last progress meeting;
   d) queries raised by the student or suggestions from the supervisor at routine meetings in the intervening period. Where necessary the assumptions on which the work is based and the ways it was checked should be clearly laid out. This makes it possible to verify at each stage that the work is of the requisite quality and should avoid the disastrous discovery in the final stages that it is based on untenable assumptions. The submission of progress reports is the primary mechanism by which the student ensures that the research plan remains feasible or discovers when it needs amendment. Most successfully managed research projects use some similar formal device as indicated in Chapter 3.

2. Draft chapters. Supervisors vary in the amount of pressure they put on their students to draft out chapters of the report at an early stage in the research. For our example research project (Chapter 3), Table 3.1 and Figures 3.1 and 3.2 are based on a research plan in which the writing of draft chapters is seen to be realistic after only four weeks of the execution phase. What might be attempted here is the 'Introduction' or 'Background to the Research'. In large part, the writing may ultimately be redundant due to a shift in the direction of the research or simply by becoming out of date. The major advantages are that the supervisor will be able to assess

and react to the content of the material submitted, and that the student will be able to gauge the magnitude of the writing-up task, at the same time coming to grips with the demands of format and style.

An obvious point which applies to the submission of any written material is that the supervisor should have had the opportunity of reading it before meeting the student.

Thus far the assumption has been that the student is working with a single supervisor. As pointed out earlier, however, it may be desirable to appoint a second, or indeed the institution may require it. At its best such a supervisory relationship can be of considerable benefit to the student. The calibre of advice received and the additional scrutiny given to the work increase the chance of turning out high quality research. On the other hand such a relationship can create problems that do not exist with a single supervisor. It is easy for each supervisor to believe that the other is carrying the main weight of the supervision. It is more difficult to organise meetings at which both supervisors can be present and additional copies of written material need to be prepared. It follows then that to gain the full benefit of such an arrangement will usually involve the student in more managerial effort.

Students should be aware that the institutions at which they register have obligations to them; obligations which if not properly discharged result in a lowering of reputation and a possible reduction in public funding. There is therefore a downwards pressure on academic faculty to contribute to the overall reputation of the institution through effective performance in the areas of research (including research supervision), teaching and administration. Increasingly, so that the institution may plan and monitor its activities, hours are allocated to staff for the specific work they choose to undertake. Thus a member of faculty with research leanings may have a workload for acting as the director of a particular programme, the teaching of courses, and the supervision of research students. It is the latter point of which the student should be particularly aware. In these circumstances, supervision is not voluntary nor an option but this does not mean that a 'marriage' is inevitable; a measure of 'courtship' will need to take place before a reasonably formal relationship can be established.

Conclusion

This section has been written to advise students how they can get the best out of their supervisor. They should remember, however, that although their research may constitute the whole world as far as they are concerned, this will not be so in the case of their supervisor. Nevertheless, most supervisors are more likely to respond positively and effectively if they are to some extent 'managed' and the student should not be diffident about adopting the courses of action described above.

THE POSITIVE VIEW OF RESEARCH PROGRESS

Virtually the whole of this chapter has been concerned with problems which the research student may encounter, suggesting perhaps that the successful completion of a research project is comparable with the crossing of a minefield. Whilst it is felt that the student should be aware of various types of pitfall and subscribe to the notion that to be forewarned is to be forearmed there is much that can be done to promote progress and that has been the primary aim of this chapter.

Even though students may have drawn up a research schedule they should not be complacent about being on course. If they see an opportunity for completing a stage significantly more rapidly than planned they should do this, and if the saving is significant the schedule should be amended. Many degrees are of fixed duration, this being determined by written examinations. If, however, a research student is able to complete a study more quickly than planned little is gained by utilising all of the originally intended period. Though average completion periods are high (three to four years for doctorates) some students finish in relatively short times and this has obvious advantages. Even if students are ahead of schedule for a limited period only, this will have reduced the likely demand on the time set aside for contingencies and will thus increase the probability of completing on time.

The prime evidence of progress is the writing of parts of the research report. Wherever possible, the student should commence writing draft chapters quite early in the study. Although this comment is more relevant to the longer studies it is an approach which should be adopted whenever possible. By doing this, in addition to resolving issues of style, tangible evidence of progress will be accumulated. As the research progresses the variance between the first and final draft should reduce markedly.

Student research has been separated into a number of distinct phases, with 'execution' falling between the finalising of the research proposal and the writing-up. This has been largely for convenience of discussion and, as has been pointed out on a number of occasions, there is in practice much overlap of activity. As far as students are concerned the execution phase runs from commencement to the moment when the thesis, dissertation, or report is submitted. In many cases the research will be the students' sole academic activity although there will no doubt be many other competing demands on their time. There is much to suggest that despite the fact that successful completion of a study is vital to the self-esteem and career prospects of students, research activities are from time to time ranked much lower than they ought to be. It is not too facile to state that, during their period of study, students' life should be built around their research and that only in exceptional circumstances should a conscious decision be taken to delay a stage of the research in favour of doing something else. The exercising of tight control through carefully planned procedures is much more likely to produce the desired results than is an approach which sees research as something to be done when circumstances permit.

CHAPTER SUMMARY

THE CONSIDERATIONS IN THE EXECUTION PHASE ARE SIMI-LAR FOR RESEARCH STUDENTS AND DISSERTATION STUDENTS: the biggest difference is that the supervisor plays a much less important role in the dissertation project. Because of the short time-scales, problems encountered in dissertation projects can be more difficult to overcome.

RESEARCH RARELY PROCEEDS SMOOTHLY: students will at some stage encounter – and if they are to be successful must overcome – a range of problems.

MANY PROBLEMS ARE AVOIDABLE: careful planning should highlight this type of problem. Two aspects, overcommitment and supervisory arrangements, should be given much consideration.

UNEXPECTED PROBLEMS MAY ARISE: these may relate to the student, the supervisor, the research, or support for it.

RESEARCH PROGRESS CAN BE FACILITATED: by continually adopting a positive attitude towards it and identifying and pursuing activities which are consistent with effective and timely completion.

8

Presentation of the Research Findings

INTRODUCTION

The evaluation of student research is nearly always made through an assessment of the written account of the work undertaken and the conclusions reached. In addition, students are often required to explain or defend verbally their findings. This chapter will be concerned with the two aspects and will consider the steps which need to be taken to ensure that both written and verbal presentation satisfy requirements.

At the beginning of this book it was stated that it was the aim to provide guidance for degree students at all levels who were required, as part of their course, to complete a project. The range thus extends from undergraduate students who have one or two months in which to conduct and report on a project to doctoral students who have three years of full-time study at their disposal. The same policy will, however, continue to apply in this chapter as elsewhere, namely that advice will be given on the preparation and presentation of a doctoral thesis with comments on the needs at other levels where these differ.

The quality of reports on student research may be judged by the criteria listed in Figure 8.1. The figure is consistent with earlier commentary in which the general requirements of research at different levels were indicated. All institutions empowered to confer degrees publish regulations for the guidance of candidates but it is difficult for students to glean what precisely is required of them. It is not easy to identify a sharp divide between the levels and, in the absence of sound advice from a supervisor, the written account may fall short of – or exceed – requirements by a substantial margin. For example, in 1993 a criterion for the degree of Master of Philosophy at the London School of Economics and Political Science was that

> an MPhil thesis shall either be a record of original work or an ordered and critical exposition of knowledge in any field,

whereas the corresponding criterion for the degree of PhD was

> a PhD thesis must form a distinct contribution to the knowledge of the subject and afford evidence of originality, shown either by the discovery of new facts or by the exercise of independent critical power.[1]

It would appear, then, that if students are able to satisfy themselves that the criteria listed in Figure 8.1 for their particular level are met the requisite standard will be satisfied.

Regardless as to whether the written accounts are theses, dissertations, or reports, consideration will need to be given to the structure, style of writing, and process and content.

It should be noted that each of these aspects and particularly the structure and the process and content embody both (to borrow an ice skating analogy) 'compulsory' elements which require students to conform to some standard and 'free' elements where students can display their own approach. Thus, under compulsory elements the need to observe certain typographical standards – for example, that text be typed double-spaced with at least a 40mm margin on the left and at least a 25mm margin on the right should be noted. Similarly, the work of others must be properly referenced; some institutions may even prescribe the form that citation of particular types of work such as journal articles should take.

Where dissertations and theses are involved students should have a right to expect a guidance manual to be available which will state requirements on

Level	Description	Criteria
First degrees and some masters' degrees which require the completion of a project	Project report	1. A well structured convincing account of a study, the resolution of a problem, or the outcome of an experiment
Master's degree by study and dissertation	Dissertation	1. An ordered, critical and reasoned exposition of knowledge gained through the student's efforts
		2. Evidence of awareness of the literature
Master's degree by research	Thesis	1. Evidence of an original investigation or the testing of ideas
	Thesis	2. Competence in independent work or experimentation
		3. An understanding of appropriate techniques
		4. Ability to make critical use of published work and source materials
		5. Appreciation of the relationship of the special theme to the wider field of knowledge
		6. Worthy, in part, of publication
Doctoral degree	Thesis	1. to 6. As for Master's degree by research
		7. Originality as shown by the topic researched or the methodology employed
		8. Distinct contribution to knowledge

Figure 8.1 Criteria to be satisfied by reports on student research

such matters as binding, appendices, margins, figures, and pictures. Probably the most effective way of coming to grips with such requirements is for a student to scrutinise theses or dissertations in their library. It is possible with the introduction of new courses which include a research element that students may not have access to completed reports in their own institution and indeed may find little formal guidance available. If this is the case they may find it of benefit to visit a convenient university library and decide upon their own structure to put forward for adoption at their own institution.

However, the research reports produced by students who were successful in the past can for a variety of reasons be an imperfect guide to present standards. Modestly written reports may have been redeemed by a brilliant defence at an oral examination. The standards of the field may have changed as more research has been done. Students' best guide to the adequacy of their own report is, therefore, the degree to which it conforms to the requirements laid down in the regulations of the institution and the detailed criteria for evaluating a report proposed later in this chapter.

Structure and style are examined first as it is important that students should be able to manage the process of writing in the knowledge of what is required. Structure is held to include the physical characteristics and main components of the written presentation. In large part these will be defined by the regulations of their institution or by the logical breakdown and order consistent with a reasoned account of research work. Within any more or less imposed requirements students have much discretion as to the 'style' of writing and this aspect is given separate consideration as the impact which the writing makes will largely depend on style.

REPORT STRUCTURE

Students must not lose sight of the prime aim of writing-up their research, which is to convince examiners that the students have satisfied the appropriate criteria[2] contained in Figure 8.1. Therefore, it can be said that students are not writing for the world at large but, in the first instance, for one or two individuals who will be acting for the institution or the degree-awarding body in the examining process. Students must structure their writing in such a way that their research is presented in the most effective manner and, at the same time, must also comply with any requirements which the institution lays down.

Other than listing criteria against which writings will be evaluated, most institutions give little indication in their regulations of what is needed in terms of structure. A question frequently asked by students is: 'How long should it be?' If their institution does not prescribe a maximum thesis length, the only real answer to this question at doctoral level is that the thesis should be of sufficient length to accommodate everything which is needed for students to discuss and prove within a context any proposition which they put forward. An examination of university library shelves will show the wide variations in length which have arisen in order to satisfy this general requirement. Experience has, however, indicated that the vast majority of successful doctoral theses do not exceed 500 pages of A4 size typed in double-spacing on one side only. Because of a tendency of some research students towards 'overkill' most universities now place an upper limit on wordage which may be 100,000 or even lower for PhDs with masters' theses being restricted perhaps to 60,000 words. At approximately 250 words per double-spaced A4 page a 100,000 word thesis of about 400 pages, is under half the length of some of the longer theses to be found.

At dissertation and project report level, almost all institutions stipulate maximum and minimum lengths. These limits often assume a notional word count for a figure, for example, 300 words. It is worth noting, in cases where the student runs up against the upper limit (which is frequently the case especially for non-native English speakers), that appendices may not be considered part of the word count in which case limits can usually be accommodated by relegating less important material to an appendix.

Order of Sections

There is a logical order with which (subject to variations imposed by local regulations) most written reports on research should conform:

Title page
Acknowledgements
Preface
Contents
List of Tables
List of Figures
List of other types of materials
Chapters
Appendices
List of references
Bibliography
Index

All of these sections need not necessarily appear. Undergraduate reports, for example, may include only the title page, contents and chapters. Because of the need to relate the research to a body of knowledge a list of references will be a vital element of masters' and doctoral theses. Such a list will include all relevant works which have been consulted by the author and which have been cited in the text. A distinction is made here between a 'List of References' and a 'Bibliography': the latter is, to us', supplied as a comprehensive coverage of books and journals in an area, even though these may not have been cited in the text. Most theses will not carry a bibliography unless the author has publication in mind.

The preface, which precedes the contents, is an important feature of most written accounts and will be discussed in the section dealing with content. Students are often confused by the difference between a table and a figure. The simplest rule is that, apart from the descriptive margins, tables are composed wholly of numerical data whereas, with certain exceptions, all other items of this form are figures. The exceptions are the other materials mentioned in the above list which include such items as photographs or maps. Even in these latter cases serious objection could not be raised if they were viewed as figures, particularly if there were very few of them. It should be remembered that figures or tables which have not been originated by the writer should be acknowledged and full details of sources given within the figure or table itself.

Increasingly, students wish to include computer output in their writings, and this will be discussed in more detail later. It is usually necessary to prune such output drastically and a decision is often needed as to whether selected pages should be incorporated as figures or whether larger quantities should be bound in as appendices or presented as a separate portfolio.

Citation and Quotation

A research report differs from many other forms of writing (a newspaper article, for example) in that it should make clear what material and ideas have been originated by the student and what is owed to the work of others. On the matter of direct quotation it should be remembered that the requirements of Figure 8.1 suggest that, at most levels of research, it is important that students show that they have understood the ideas of others and this they can only do by demonstrating their ability to summarise and present them within their own framework. This means that under most circumstances the amount of direct quotation should be fairly small. For convenience of presentation, we shall defer discussion of the role of summarising until later in the chapter.

Obviously, there are situations where direct quotation is necessary. For example, a study of the impact of Kierkegaard on twentieth-century writers on existentialism would be strange indeed without substantial quotations of Kierkegaard himself and sections of text from later authors that appear to have been influenced by him. Equally, much theory in applied mathematics, say, is of such elegance that it would be foolish to rewrite it in a different notation. There is, however, rarely a case for a research report that consists mainly of quotations from various authors glued together by an occasional sentence supplied by the researcher.

Obviously, quotations should be properly differentiated from the main body of the research report. Indented, single-spaced text is perhaps the easiest way of clearly differentiating the longer passage, though quotation marks are generally adequate for a single sentence. Variations, such as a different typeface (for example, italic), may also be helpful. In either case, the work from which the quotation is drawn should be clearly referenced as discussed below.

Where other authors are drawn on for ideas rather than direct quotation, things can be a little more difficult. Many ideas are in the public domain so that if the researcher is to avoid infelicities such as: *Most chairs have four legs (Adam, 1775; Chippendale, 1778), Similar tendencies have been noted in tables (Hepplewhite, 1782; Sheraton, 1804)*, there is a need to observe certain rules about referencing other work. To some extent this must depend on the customs of the field in which the student is writing. On the whole, though, a defensible approach would be to reference only those ideas which an inexpert reader might think were the researcher's own even though they are not. In such cases the researcher should try to give the original source of the idea provided this can be done without affectation and also the place where it was found, which may, of course be different. Thus, if the researcher has become familiar with, for instance, information theory and the work of Shannon through reading someone else's introduction, academic courtesy would seem to dictate a formula such as: 'As Brillouin's account of Shannon's (1948) work shows (*Science and Information Theory*, 1962) the theory of information has much in common with ideas from fields of physics such as thermodynamics.'

Although it may seem pedantic, students are well advised to treat the matter of citation with considerable care. An external examiner is likely, for instance, to consider that a student who consistently attributes ideas to later workers rather than the person who actually originated them, has conducted an inadequate literature search. Thus, in the example above, attributing Shannon's theory to Brillouin would give a poor impression.

A poorer impression still is created by students who use the ideas of others without attribution. Indeed, if this is done by directly using someone else's writings without due attribution this constitutes plagiarism, which all academic institutions consider a serious offence against academic regulations.

The way in which the work in question is cited must, of course, comply

189

with whatever standards are prescribed by the institution. Often these allow considerable latitude, however. The point made in Chapter 4 may be recalled, namely that it takes little longer to supply all relevant details in the list of references than to use only an abbreviated form of reference. As far as citation in the body of the text is concerned there are two broad schemes in use: the Harvard method as followed in this book (basically author plus date) or the numerical approach in which each reference is given a specific number. The former approach is simpler and permits the insertion or deletion of references at will, whereas in the latter case any references which are introduced or deleted at a later stage will necessitate all of the subsequent numbers being changed. On the other hand, the Harvard method is cumbersome if a particular page is to be referenced.

Flexibility is desirable within the two schemes mentioned, and is linked to style which will be discussed below. Thus emphasis may be given to the idea or to the author, as:

a) ' . . . a strong claim is made that a system of equity must exist within every society (Usher, 1981)'; or

b) 'Usher (1981) has argued that every society should have within it a system of equity'.

It will be noted that in both these cases Usher's initial has not been included. If this might lead to confusion as in the case of numerous Smiths being cited, it would be sensible to supply the surname plus either the initials or one or more forenames – for example, 'Adam Smith'.

If the author adopts the numerical approach it may still be preferred to make reference to a name. For example:

i) 'Usher argued in 1981[34] that every society should have within it a system of equity' may be preferred to

ii) 'It has been argued[34] that, . . .' where, of course, the reference number is 34.

An advantage of a), b) and i) above is that if students are drawing heavily on the ideas of an author they will, for as long as the thread remains unbroken, be able to introduce the surname of the author without repeating date, initials or perhaps the title of the work cited.

In addition to the need within the body of the text to confirm that students are able to relate their thoughts to the body of knowledge, they must also consider the link between individual references and the list which will be positioned at the end of their report. External examiners usually scrutinise the list of references very carefully and will be critical of lists which are not both comprehensive and well presented. In particular, care should be taken to avoid the appearance of plagiarism by not noting in the list of references works by other authors which have provided an important source of ideas.

If the numerical approach is adopted the text and reference can be linked easily in either direction. One limitation is that a reader may not be able to establish quickly whether a particular author has been referenced. With the author plus date approach someone reading through the list of references will not be able to turn immediately to that part of the text to establish what ideas have been taken from the author in question.

It should be apparent that with the author plus date approach the list of references will be presented in the form normally taken by bibliographies, namely that authors will be cited in alphabetical order. In some instances, students adopt the latter approach for their reports as a whole but at the end of each chapter incorporate a separate list compiled in order of appearance.

A standard procedure should be adopted when citing bibliographical references, particularly in research theses. Students should request from their librarian advice as to which method to use. The prerequisite of any system is that the reference should supply sufficient and unambiguous detail. In the main, books and journal articles will be referenced and a commonly employed approach is:

a) for *books*: author and initials (in capitals), title of book (underlined or in italics), place of publication, publisher, date;

b) for *articles*: author and initials (in capitals), title of article in quotes, name of journal (underlined or in italics), volume number, issue, page number, year.

There will be those occasions when other types of reference are made: for example, to theses and separately authored chapters in books. Useful guidance on these and other matters may be obtained from *BS 4821 (1982), Recommendations for the Presentation of Theses*.

Certain Latin words and phrases encountered in scholarly works can be useful in referencing. Sometimes a student may wish to quote something which contains an obvious, grammatical, typographical, or numerical error. In this case '(*sic*)' typed as here within brackets and placed immediately after the error will point to its origin.

It was suggested above that if students wish to make a lengthy and unbroken reference to an author the latter's surname may be used from time to time in the text without involving addition to the list of references. If, however, the points taken from the source are widely scattered or if other authors are cited in between, the following Latin phrases can help in reducing the bulk of the reference list:

a) *Ibidem* (abbreviated to *ibid.*): in the same work allowing successive reference to the same work. This replaces all details in the previous reference,
but should be followed by page number.
b) *Opere citato* (abbreviated to *op. cit.*): in the work cited. This requires the
author's name and page number, and refers to a work already cited.
c) *Loco citato* (abbreviated to *loc. cit.*): in the place cited. This is used with the
author's name and is similar to *op. cit.* but is more precise as it refers to the
same passage in a book already cited.

An example of the use of the three phrases is as follows:

BYNON, T., *Historical Linguistics*, Cambridge University Press, Cambridge,
1977, p. 86.
FOWLER, R., *Understanding Language*, Routledge, London, 1974, p. 31.
Ibid., p. 50. (This is a reference to the previous book – Fowler.)
BYNON, T., *loc. cit.* (This is a reference to Bynon's work above and to
the same page.)
BYNON, T., *op. cit.*, p. 14. (This is also a reference to Bynon's work above,
but to a different page.)

Doctoral theses often contain several hundred references and the work
involved in ensuring that these are systematically presented and are error free
can be formidable. There are obvious advantages at this level of using bibliographic software of the type referred to in Chapter 4 or of utilising some of
the facilities of word processing which will be discussed later in this chapter.

STYLE OF WRITING

The development of an appropriate style (the quality of writing) can be a
demanding task for students. Particularly at lower levels the development of
the student's style is usually an important educational objective. It is unlikely
that more than a small proportion of students will have made a particular
study of the written form of the English language and many are disinclined
to allocate time to such an activity, preferring instead to react to comments
from their supervisor. If the supervisor is able to give advice on style this
approach may work but if not (or, if in the case of shorter projects, the work
is largely unsupervised) the ultimate written account, perhaps weak in other
aspects, may fail because it is not easily readable. Cooper (1990) observed
that:

Writers of reports are fortunately not in the extreme situation of having to satisfy millions of readers to stay in business. If they were they would probably starve.

A short time spent in developing style will be of much benefit both in writing about the research and later in life when it is assumed that the ability to communicate will continue to be needed.

Much has been written about 'readability' and Cooper comments on action taken by government in the UK in response to the writings of Gowers (1954). Cooper also refers to a measure proposed by Gunning (1952) known as the 'fog index'. This description was used because it was felt that long words and sentences made for 'foggy' reading. Briefly:

Fog Index = 0.4 (Average sentence length plus per cent of words more than two syllables in length.)

Words that are capitalised, are combinations of short simple words, or, for example, arise because of the use of the past tense, are excluded from the calculation. According to Cooper, Gunning regarded a 'fog index' of 12 as the danger point, beyond which text becomes difficult to read. An analysis of the writings of classical and popular authors indicated that their fog index did not exceed 12. Widely read magazines of the 1950s, such as *Time* and *Look*, were reported as having a 'fog index' of 10 and 8 respectively, whereas one new highbrow magazine with an index well above 12 ceased to be published within a year. It is probably true that in the modern era, where literature as a source of ideas has declined in importance when compared with television, the maximum acceptable fog index is, if anything, lower than in the 1950s.

As would be expected, writers on style also express views on paragraph length. The general recommendation is that paragraphs should be short, not so much for clarity as for textual appearance. They should, however, be long enough to accommodate a particular idea and very short paragraphs of one or two sentences should be avoided both for reasons of appearance and to avoid the reader having to switch too rapidly from one point to another.

Attention to the suggestions made in this section will not guarantee good style and students should not be under the impression that there is a common style which they should seek to attain. Cooper (1990) states:

Good style is one which makes some impact on the reader. The author's personality comes through. Poor style usually refers to writing which is involved, where there is little attempt to structure the writing, and usually where the vocabulary range is limited.

One aspect of style on which students often seek guidance is the use of personal pronouns. Because student projects are usually of a personal nature there is obviously much scope for 'I' to be used throughout the report. This may be avoided by the use of the passive voice. Thus, 'It was found that . . .' is used instead of 'I found that . . . '.

Traditionally, in most fields of research use of the passive voice has been favoured with the major exception being the use of 'we' in mathematics. In recent times, however, limited use of the first person has been accepted, if only to break up the monotonous effect of continued use of the passive voice.

Writers on style such as Cooper make a number of suggestions as to how impact may be increased. Thus Cooper (1990, pp. 127–36) stresses the importance of analogy, metaphorical language, repetition for emphasis, rhythm, and the avoidance of cacophony and 'phoney' style. Broehl and Shurter (1965, pp. 81–7) argue that writers should make effective use of verbs, be direct, use an appropriate tone, and be specific. Students should give consideration to suggestions of this type and should be aware of the pitfalls which result in poor style.

It may be useful to adopt as a model the writings of a specific author or of workers in a particular field such as economics that maintains a tradition of clear communication of technically difficult subjects. It should be remembered, however, that the research report is typically aimed at a narrower audience and that certain knowledge and predispositions on the part of the reader can be assumed. Thus, though jargon would usually be frowned on in a text that was to have wide non-specialist readership, it may be used in a research report in order that it be clear what the report is about, avoiding the ambiguities that are often associated with everyday language. Similar arguments apply to abbreviations, particularly to entities that have several word names that are mentioned frequently in the text, for example, UN.

PROCESS AND CONTENT

It is assumed that by enquiry and reading students will learn broadly what is required of them in terms of the way in which their report should be structured and presented, and will be aware of factors which make for good or bad style. The student will also have assembled through some of the steps described in Chapter 6 a substantial database, parts of which will have been subjected to analysis. By the later stages of the research the student will have reached some conclusions, and will probably feel under increasing pressure to start to convert all of this into a semblance of what ultimately will be the thesis or report.

We would argue that the process of writing-up a research report, at any level, is probably much more demanding than the average student envisages; to this end, attempts to draft chapters as early in the research as is feasible plus the production of one or more journal articles in the course of a research degree is strongly favoured. This requires some elaboration of the 'chapters' portion of the outline structure of reports proposed in Chapters 2 and 3.

Chapter headings should have been suggested by students as part of their research proposal and will probably be consistent with the following logical order.

Introduction
Survey of prior research
Research design
Results of the research
Analysis
Summary and conclusions

Although the introductory chapter probably suffers more revision than any other, research students should endeavour to write this as soon as is feasible together with chapters which review the current state of knowledge, and describe what the approach to their research will be.

Dissertation students are usually better advised not to start with the introductory chapter but rather with one that is nearer the core arguments of their dissertation. In this way, they can hope to receive feedback at an early stage on whether their style is adequate and, if not, the types of modifications to be made. Because there is a greater commonality between introductory chapters, the dissertation student who elects to start with an introduction is likely to find that less is learnt, if that chapter is written first.

It should be remembered that the order in which chapters or major sections are first written may not be the same as that in which they eventually appear in the report. As will presently be discussed, the structuring of a report so that ideas appear in logical sequence is by no means easy. For instance, a device that is sometimes useful to research students is to write one of the later chapters on some aspect of the analysis, or the conclusions in order to obtain some feel for what needs to be introduced prior to this chapter. Where the research report is written over several months, however, it is most unlikely that certain chapters will not undergo major redrafting both because the researcher's ideas have matured and also to obtain a more logically structured argument. Use of a word processing package greatly facilitates this process.

Effective strategy in report writing requires that the student has a clear picture of the report as a whole. As indicated earlier, however, this will not usually evolve until a great deal has already been written. In reality, then, it is unlikely that the final result will closely resemble the initial structure proposed. Students should expect to have to reorganise some of their material and should therefore allow time for this in their planning.

The process of writing is interpreted broadly to include the following:

a) preparing to write;
b) the writing itself;
c) editing;
d) proof reading.

Some detailed discussion of these elements may be appropriate here.

PREPARING TO WRITE

In one sense, the whole period spent by students on their research before they commence writing is preparation for this activity. However, the time when students feel that there is enough data stored in a filing cabinet, in a computer, on charts, or in their head, to justify tackling a chapter (or at least a major portion of one) is taken as the starting point. It is at this stage that there will be real appreciation of the existence of a systematically compiled set of records with cross-classification where appropriate, as discussed in Chapter 6.

Preparation may be broken down into the five elements of Figure 8.2 from which it will be seen that it is proposed that the first step should be to plan the order of the chapters and the next to plan the detailed order of the sections of each individual chapter.

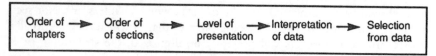

Figure 8.2 Preparing to write: the steps

Ordering the Chapters

There are two aspects at least to obtaining a logical structure. One might be dubbed tactical and involves the organisation of individual chapters in the most effective way; the other is 'strategic' – that is, obtaining a satisfactory interrelationship among the various chapters so that the report as a whole presents a coherent argument; clearly, this issue must be addressed first.

In most research reports there is usually a considerable element of flexibility in defining the interrelationships among chapters. This is a frequent source of problems with material either being repeated in several places or never being properly presented anywhere. Thus, if we consider a student research project that has been concerned with an in-depth study of the use of computer marketing models in four organisations, the end purpose of which is to suggest criteria that distinguish successful from unsuccessful applications, then at a minimum it would probably contain the following material:

1. Prior research on computer marketing models.
2. Prior research on factors affecting the success of computer marketing models.
3. Prior research on factors affecting the success of other computer models.
4. Account of study in organisation A.
5. Account of study in organisation B.
6. Account of study in organisation C.
7. Account of study in organisation D.
8. Analysis of the individual case studies and construction of an overall scheme for the prediction of success.
9. Conclusions.

Though this breakdown is distinctly simpler than that which the student would probably use in the research itself, it illustrates the types of problems that occur. Firstly, it may be noted that before a list can be formulated at all many implicit decisions have to be made about topics that will not be explored. In this case, for example, no reference is apparently made to the literature on the management of innovations, though this might well be relevant. Secondly, there are a number of problems on how this material should be combined into chapters. Should items 1 and 2 be combined into one chapter – probably the best way if the factors affecting success appear to be highly model specific – or should they be separated? If, however, the factors affecting success seem to be relatively independent of the model concerned there may well be a case for combining items 2 and 3. Similarly items 4, 5, 6 and 7 could be run in parallel through several chapters looking at applications of different types of model in each of the four organisations in turn or, alternatively, each item could form a single chapter. The most important determinant of the choice should be the way in which the material will be analysed. For the moment, however, this particular aspect is left since similar problems will be discussed when we deal with the construction of individual chapters. This leaves one further important concern that will undoubtedly exercise the researcher in producing the final version of the report, namely the degree to which the ground will be prepared in earlier chapters for what is to come later. To take but two examples: firstly, some of the previous work on factors determining success will be highly relevant; and, secondly, some of the field observations will be more appropriate than others. In either case it is sensible to highlight these particular aspects as they are dealt with so that the readers know that they should pay especial attention to them.

Ordering the Chapter Sections

The ordering of the sections of each individual chapter is a continuation of the process of logically structuring the report. Take as an example 'Survey of prior research' and consider the number of different ways in which the survey may be presented: chronologically, categorically, sequentially, in order of perceived importance – these are all possibilities.

The case of the student who is researching into factors affecting the success of computer marketing models is taken up again. The chapter on prior research in computer marketing research models could be divided into a whole range of sets of sections, a few of which are indicated in Figure 8.3 (restricted in each case to three sections for simplicity).

Although any of the Figure 8.3 orderings may be acceptable for short student reports they would constitute a poor approach to be adopted by a research degree student. A more appropriate basis might be:

1. The extent and range of computer applications in marketing.
2. Major successes and failures of computer based marketing applications.
3. Suggestions in the literature for new computer based developments in marketing.

A decision on the nature of the major chapter sections will not be sufficient for students to commence writing the body of the text. It will be necessary to continue the process of subdivision once or even twice further. The way in which this is done will have a considerable influence on the impact which the report will make. Again, a number of options are available with, probably, categorical and chronological ordering being most appropriate in the marketing example being used. Thus, major section 1 may be subdivided into market planning, advertising, and logistics, each of which in turn may be discussed under the headings of 'Early applications', 'Applications during the 1970s and 1980s', and 'Recent developments', as suggested by Figure 8.3.

Detailed guidance on format is often provided by a student's institution. Thus, chapter titles may be required to be typed upper case and centred, main sections typed using initial capitals only, and commencing at the left-hand margin, and so on. Probably the most appropriate (and least ambiguous) method of referring to each separate section is to use hierarchical numbering.

Chronological	Categorical		Sequential	Perceived importance
	(a)	(b)		
1. Early applications	1. Applications in North America	1. Market planning models	1. Market research	1. Sales models
2. Applications during the 1970s and 1980s	2. Applications in other developed countries	2. Advertising models	2. Market planning	2. Advertising models
3. Recent develop- ments	3. Applications in developing countries	3. Logistics models	3. Implement- ing marketing decisions	3. Planning models

Figure 8.3 Basis of sections. An example of different section ordering within chapters

This enables students' approach to the logical breakdown of their writings to be clearly seen, particularly in the contents page. Thus, if in our example 'Survey of prior research' is the second chapter of the thesis the early sections of that chapter would appear in the contents page numbered as:

2.   Survey of prior research.
    2.1 The extent and range of computer applications in marketing.
        2.1.1. Market planning.
            2.1.1.1. Early applications.

It is not customary to subdivide chapters further than is indicated in this example; to do this would result in too fragmented an approach causing the reader to be in some difficulty in remaining with the main theme being pro-pounded. The writer, nevertheless, will still have much ordering to do and this, in large part, will be linked to the remaining three steps of Figure 8.2 (level of presentation, interpretation of data, and selection from data).

Report Organisation Charts
An approach that many students find useful for identifying the chapters and breaking them down into subsections is to depict the structure of the report in a 'report organisation chart'.

Figure 8.4 shows the structure already discussed for our marketing models example further elaborated in the light of the possible section ordering in Figure 8.3. Note that only Chapter 2 has been further decomposed in the light of our discussions and even then not completely. In practice, a similar decomposition would need to be carried out for Section 2.2 and for each chapter. Note how the section, subsection and sub-subsection numbering suggested for Chapter 2 translates into levels 3, 4 and 5 of the chart.

Level of Presentation

The 'level of presentation' is determined by the location of the written account on a scale ranging from summary to comprehensive. The point in writing student reports is to demonstrate knowledge and ability but they should aim also for comprehensiveness. The criteria listed in Figure 8.1 imply that, at the level of the research degree, argument must be supported in every detail, leaving students who must comply with a constraint on length in some difficulty as to what can be included. Below research degree level limitations on wordage will also often operate, but in these cases students can resort to the use of 'space precludes' in the text realising that it may be necessary to support any claims which have been made in writing at an oral examination. The doctoral student will have to undergo an oral examination. This, along North American lines, is often viewed as a 'thesis defence'. Doctoral students must always have this in mind during their writing and their draft chapters should include all supportive evidence needed. The defence of their argument should, however, be concerned with the method-ologies which were employed, the value claimed for their findings, and their recommendations for future work, and not with explaining and justifying the omission of corroborative material which should have been included in their thesis. If, therefore, it is felt that the thesis will probably be too lengthy it may be decided to omit whole sections (and justify the omission if called upon at an oral examination) rather than to reduce the level of detail throughout the text.

Students who are unhappy at the thought of taking a prior decision to delete sections may choose to write in an unconstrained manner in the knowledge that, by editing, substantial reductions in length may be needed to comply with word length restrictions imposed by their institution.

Nevertheless, students should not pose themselves an impossible task. Coverage in depth clearly reduces the scope for breadth of discussion and some students do encounter problems by attempting too broad a canvas. As well as leading to excessive length such an approach also carries the risk of superficiality. A page budget specifying the number of pages to be devoted to each section is a useful device for identifying this problem in advance.

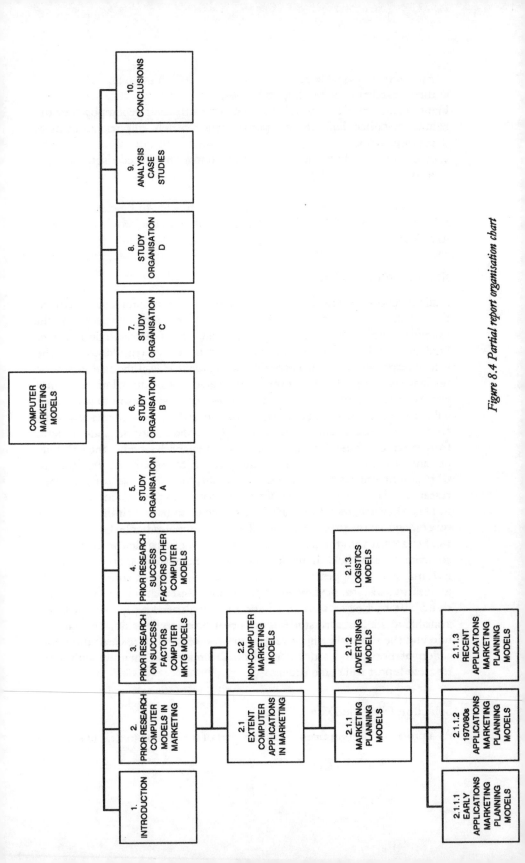

Figure 8.4 Partial report organisation chart

Amongst the possible cures are:
a) the researcher becomes less ambitious;
b) the researcher relies more heavily on summaries and reviews by previous authors rather than attempting to evaluate peripherally related areas of previous work;
c) reference is made to the researcher's own work published elsewhere;
d) whole sections may be omitted.

Obviously, an indispensable aid in this is for students to be clear about the relative importance they assign to the different topics they would ideally wish to tackle.

Interpretation of Data

Student report writing is a very specific form of communication, with the final product initially forming a one-to-one link between the student and the examiner. Particular note must therefore be taken of interpretation of data. Students should always be conscious of the person or type of person who will be responsible for evaluating their work. Obviously, if the examiner is on the staff of the student's institution and there is no external assessment it behoves the student to seek guidance before commencing writing. If external assessment is involved it is part of British tradition that there shall be no contact between student and examiner, but this should not preclude students from making 'behind the scenes' enquiries to establish whether the examiner has any pronounced views on writing or content. Research degree students who accept the advice that writing should commence as early in their research as possible may at that time not know who their external examiner will be. They will, therefore, have little on which to base their interpretation, other than that the person will probably be of some academic distinction and will be familiar with the technicalities and jargon of a particular field. Only if students leave the field should it be necessary therefore to supply definitions.

It may perhaps appear to be a little cynical to give much stress to the need to seek to satisfy the examiner of the report. Research theses in particular should after all be seen as an addition to the general body of knowledge; available to all. Research students are nevertheless undertaking an examination and their primary objective to achieve success is quite clear; the publication of books and articles based on the material contained within the research report will come later.

Selection from the Data

As a process, selection from the data is part of the writing itself, but students may need to take a prior decision on a number of issues. Chapter 6 indicated that by the time students have completed their reading, data collection and analysis this will have resulted in the accumulation of a mass of data held in one form or another. The problem is to transform the data into a well ordered, appropriately interpreted account written at the requisite level.

Although students should have been selective at the data gathering phase some material will probably be superfluous to the requirements of the report. Thus, as stated earlier, if the fieldwork has involved a large sample survey it would be inappropriate to include all completed questionnaires in the report (although these should be retained as primary source material which may be called for at an oral examination). One example of the questionnaire should of course be included. On the other hand if, say, several in-depth interviews have been tape-recorded it would be desirable to include the transcripts of each of these in an appendix. Again computer-based statistical analyses will probably lead to many different outputs. If a representative example of a set of outputs conveys the point the researcher wishes to make then there is no need to include every page of output in the report.

In purely scientific terms an important question with research theses is the degree to which the findings would be repeatable if the work were to be undertaken by another researcher. This implies that as well as an adequate description of the methods of analysis employed (very possibly including computer program listings) primary data should ideally also be made available to the reader. At present, the latter requirement tends to be honoured in the breach and readers are reminded of the observations made in Chapter 6 on how researchers might make their data more widely available.

Taking into account comments made earlier on the level of presentation a reasonable rule for research degree students to follow is that if there is any doubt as to whether a particular piece of data should be included, then include it; deletion is always possible at the editing stage. In reality, the final versions of most theses will omit material that was included at the draft stage. In a lower level research report this may also be the case, although, as suggested earlier, a more likely expedient is to relegate material to appendices.

THE WRITING ITSELF

Student endeavour in all other directions will come to nought if they are unable to transcribe their research experience into a form which will meet the requirements of the qualification they are pursuing. As it could well be the first occasion on which students have tackled a task of such magnitude, and as they will most probably lack the expertise of the professional report writer, it follows that they should provide tangible evidence of their strengths and shortcomings to their supervisors and colleagues as early in the study as possible. Only by putting their thoughts in writing will they be able to generate the constructive criticism which will assist in satisfying the criteria put forward earlier in this chapter. There still remains, however, the problem of what to say, in what order, and how ideas should be expressed. The first two problems are to do with the organisation of the chapters and the last, although obviously involving style as discussed above, will here be considered more broadly as the presentation of ideas.

For the time being we will view 'writing' as taking place along traditional lines. Later in the chapter we will stress the impact that word processing is making.

Writing Individual Chapters

The preparatory stage results in the determination of chapter titles and the planning of each chapter in rather more detail. It was suggested above that it is usually undesirable to divide a chapter into more than sub-subsections. The example used led to 'Early applications' (of the computer in marketing) being a sub-subsection; however, having decided upon their chapter content students should not be tempted to launch themselves into writing without a good deal of further planning. Firstly, they must ask themselves a number of questions.

– What is the purpose of the particular section of their report?
– How important is the section and how much space should be devoted to it?
– How comparative, descriptive, critical should it be?
– Should comprehensive coverage be attempted or would it be sensible to start by deciding that only the USA and the UK will be considered?
– Having selected market planning as a category how should this be defined?
– The implications of a chronological approach, with sub-section 2.1.1.2 covering the 1970s and 1980s means that 'early' refers to the pre-1970 period; is this sensible or should the first period extend to 1975 or even 1980?
– Is segmentation by industry desirable?

What might have seemed at first sight to be a simple and straightforward narrative task is now seen as being far from it. Any attempt by students to write without decisions on structuring will almost inevitably lead to lengthy periods staring into space, followed by much crossing out, insertions and the gradual accumulation of screwed-up paper. To avoid this happening the

student should write down all the points (including *aide memoires*) which may be of relevance, in no particular order, and from them select and order those to be used. The following points are examples which could be used in this exercise:
- Definition of market planning
- Brief account of early computing technology as applied to business
- Adopt a comparative approach as far as possible, USA v UK, industry by industry
- Use as source material leading marketing, management science and planning journals of UK origin, supplemented by private communications.

Having decided the ground to be covered students should then treat each portion of their report which has its own heading as a mini-chapter in which they should:
a) make an introductory statement;
b) provide background information;
c) supply data (often in the form of figures and tables);
d) undertake analysis;
e) summarise the analysis;
f) reach some conclusions.

Even if no further partitioning of the data, by the use of 1, 2, 3 or i), ii), iii) and so on, is attempted the reader will readily appreciate that the student has planned the writing if the sections are organised in this way.

Presentation of Ideas

It is recommended that in order to improve the digestibility of their writing students should try and develop a good style. It is, however, appreciated that style is not acquired easily. Nevertheless, there are a number of factors of presentation with which students should be familiar. Monroe, Meredith and Fisher (1977) refer to these as 'stimulus-response' patterns in their book *The Science of Scientific Writing* which, although addressed to scientists, makes many points of general relevance. Some common patterns which they select are:

Question–Answer: When you generate a question in writing, the reader will expect you to answer the question – soon.
Problem–Solution: If you present a problem the reader will expect a solution or an explanation of why no solution is forthcoming.
Cause–Effect, Effect–Cause: Whether you have mentioned a cause first or an effect first, once you have mentioned one, the reader will surely expect you to mention the other.

General–Specific: When you make a general statement, the reader will expect to be supplied with specifics, which clarify, qualify, or explain the general statement.

Although the presentation of ideas is the very nub of the process of writing there is little that can be added here except, again, to encourage students to devote some of their time to reading literature which has been written specifically on the topic of report writing. It should always be remembered that the research report is a communication and that the response of greatest interest to students will be whether or not it has reached the required standard. At research degree level it will not be possible to assess beforehand the reaction of the examiner and it is therefore essential that a comparable level of criticism is obtained from other sources. Obviously, there will be much dependence on the supervisor but this should not preclude students from seeking expert opinion elsewhere. Though students will certainly wish to take the advice of other researchers familiar with their own field it should be remembered that the layman is often able to spot illogicalities or omissions in the argument and is likely to prove a good touchstone for the evaluation of style. Thus, the acknowledgements to colleagues, spouses and friends that are customary in most research reports are usually far more than a courteous formality.

Students should not be too disappointed if their first attempts to convey their ideas and arguments are heavily criticised. An obvious conclusion is that time is needed to develop the requisite skills and reinforces the need to commence writing as early as is feasible. If the person is an experienced communicator on research then much redundancy would be avoided by leaving the writing until the analysis has been completed; but students will rarely fall into this category.

EDITING

Although notes of guidance for prospective contributors are provided by publishers most of the latter employ editors who modify scripts so that they conform with what is known as 'house style'; however, editors also may often virtually rewrite the material submitted around the ideas it contains.

Earlier in this chapter we advised students to familiarise themselves with the style requirements of their institution but in this section we make a few suggestions about editing in the broader sense. (Further suggestions as to how publication can be facilitated will be found later in the chapter.)

It is not uncommon to find individual supervisors who are prepared to act as editors, but this is not one of the responsibilities that students can expect supervisors to assume. Although the supervisor will normally make comments on a thesis or dissertation before it is sent to the external examiner, such comments may be based on a broad view which is taken of structure and content. We would remind the reader, yet again, that it is the work of the student and not the supervisor which is to be examined. It behoves students to determine their own strategy towards editing.

It is suggested above that in writing a research report for examination students should tend to include rather than exclude material which may support their arguments. If this policy has been adopted it is reasonable to assume that when all the chapters have been written there will be much scope for pruning. It has been found that it is possible to make arguments with the same (even greater) force when papers have had to be reduced in length by as much as 50 per cent. Certainly, there would be very few publishers willing to print doctoral theses in their entirety, being of the opinion that proportionate savings in costs achieved by a reduction in length would much exceed the proportionate force of argument lost – certainly for the first 10 per cent or 20 per cent reduction in length.

Students have control over the length of their reports, subject of course to any overriding word limits imposed by their institution, and if they feel, despite the attractions of conciseness, that there is little scope for reduction that is a decision they may take. Editing is, however, not simply a matter of eliminating text but is designed to ensure that the research findings are rewritten and presented in as effective a manner as is possible. Much of this chapter so far has been taken up in prescribing what students should seek to achieve, but there remains the need to stand back from what has been written and assess it both in broad and specific terms. Although editing will probably be undertaken continuously the two levels of the individual chapter, and of the full report will be considered.

Editing the Individual Chapter

The first draft of a chapter will be either handwritten or produced by the student using a word processing package. Nowadays, many students are competent at word processing but sometimes the final version of the report is completed by a skilled typist. On occasions, too, students may feel inclined to have draft chapters typed; particularly in such cases it is clear that substantial changes to the text should be avoided as far as possible. Before a chapter is passed for professional typing it should therefore be carefully edited.

Monroe, Meredith, and Fisher (1977) have suggested that good style emerges from naming, predicating and modifying. The first two of these suggestions are the basis of the 'core' elements of a sentence, which comprise the subject, verb and object. The core is then expanded by adding modifiers:

a) ' . . . inflation is created' (the core idea);

b) ' . . . inflation is created by excessive wage demands' (the core idea has been modified);

c) ' . . . inflation is created by excessive wage demands rather than by an increase in money supply' (the modifier has been modified).

With each sentence being made up of a core idea and modifiers, Monroe *et al* then proceed to recommend a procedure for editing:

1. Underline the core elements of every sentence. Find the subject, the verb, and the object of the sentence. If there is more than one subject, verb, or object, underline all of them.
2. Look for the core idea. Make sure that the main idea is expressed in the core of the sentence and that this basic idea makes sense by itself.
3. Check for modifiers between the core elements. As a general rule, ten or more words between the subject and the verb is too many.
4. Look for misplaced modifiers. When you come across a potential problem, draw an arrow from the modifier to what it modifies. A long arrow means that you should rework the sentence.
5. Check items for precision. Have you previously defined the specialised terms? Examine all words representing qualitative judgements. Check to make sure that you have used these correctly, that the reader will understand what specific qualities are being summed up in each word.

Monroe *et al* then examine the way in which sentences are assembled to form paragraphs and consider the changes that alterations in one sentence may necessitate in others. Of course, Monroe *et al* are primarily concerned with the writing of articles so, obviously, the sentence-by-sentence procedure they propose above should not be applied to a lengthy report. The proposal's value in the context of the latter is that students could with advantage apply it to their early writing as one way of improving style.

In the above way, readability should be enhanced but it must be borne in mind that this will not in itself guarantee quality of argument. Students should be prepared to undertake a substantial rewrite of sections of a chapter if the whole reads unsatisfactorily. In doctoral or part-time research an interval of perhaps two years may have elapsed between the writing of early chapters on the literature survey and research methodology and the final chapters on analysis and the conclusions. It is assumed that throughout these longer studies supplementary notes will have been appended to chapters as further insights are gained. Editing will include the task of incorporating additional and newer material into the body of the text and revising the structure as appropriate.

Sometimes, so much appears on a fashionable topic that the student finds it almost impossible to keep abreast of what is being published let alone incorporate it into the thesis. Often, such flurries of interest are ephemeral being perhaps occasioned by a centenary or something similar. Under those circumstances, provided they do not fear being 'scooped', researchers are probably best advised to sit it out and hope to complete their work once interest has died down. In other cases the only advice that can be given is to call a halt to further data gathering and analysis and then, as rapidly as possible (that is, within a few months), complete the report and submit it for examination before the researcher's knowledge becomes out of date. The dangers of this type of project particularly for the part-time researcher were indicated in Chapter 2. Some good pieces of doctoral research are never completed for this reason. Furthermore, all students at whatever level face the problem to some degree. The final version of the report cannot be written satisfactorily without a clear view of its structure both overall and chapter by chapter, and this cannot be attained if other research activities are still continuing.

Editing the Full Report

If the procedure recommended above, namely researching and writing simultaneously, has been followed students will eventually have assembled all the sections of their report from Chapter 1 to the list of references. It is to be hoped that students with supervisors will have obtained regular guidance from them and that this guidance will be reflected in the writing. Neither student nor supervisor will, however, be able to assess the whole report until the last section has been written and it is important that plans for final editing are clear.

Depending upon the goodwill of the supervisor and the time budget allowed for supervision it may be that the supervisor will read the final report, make suggestions to the student as to how it should be edited, and then repeat the process through a series of iterations until the product is deemed to be acceptable. If, of course, editing (that is, rewriting) is insufficient and additional analysis is called for, project completion may be delayed significantly. If students cannot expect more than one careful reading from their supervisor it is logical that this should be done after they have undertaken what they see as necessary editing of the full report; albeit that they should expect general rather than detailed comment at this stage. In the absence of a supervisor the whole responsibility rests with the student although it may be possible to prevail upon an acquaintance (including a staff member) to assist.

The research degree student will appreciate that although a thesis will be examined as an exclusively individual effort (unless collaborative work is acknowledged) a bad fail will reflect adversely on the student's supervisor. This would be the case particularly if it is evident that little guidance has been given as, for example, when original conclusions have been poorly presented.

In the later section of this chapter, on preparing for an oral examination, a checklist for evaluating a research report is presented. Many of the questions raised there are pertinent to the editing process.

PROOF READING

The task of proof reading is the final stage of writing before the report is bound into its covers. In publishing, a 'proof' is original text which has been typeset and output for checking. Proof reading is the process in which the typeset material is checked for deviation from the original copy; the proof reader uses various symbols to indicate the nature of an error.

Two types of errors are recognised; firstly, 'author's' when the writer wishes to change material already typeset; and, secondly, 'literals' which are mistakes which have arisen in typesetting. The usual publishing practice is for the proof reader to use different inks to distinguish between the two types of error.

Students will increasingly produce the report themselves using a word processing package. If, however, the final version of the report is to be produced by a typist, students will understand the need to ensure that their instructions are clearly understood. Although each time they re-read their report there is a considerable likelihood that they will wish to edit it further, the concern here is with errors made in typing the report. It can be profoundly irritating to readers if they continue to encounter mistakes of this nature.

Such errors can be divided into two sorts. Firstly, systematic errors: for example, consistent misuse of apostrophes or consistent misspelling of an author's name. Secondly, random errors: for example, the attribution of an article to the wrong author or a one-off misspelling.

Provided that students are aware of systematic errors and how to correct them, they are readily removed from a word processed text by a simple global edit. Most random errors that involve spelling mistakes will be detected by a spellchecker (though care still needs to be taken with word pairs such as 'practice' and 'practise'). It is, therefore, useful as a preliminary to proof reading to spellcheck the text. Unfortunately, 100 per cent sampling of a large number of items (here, words) is not 100 per cent efficient, so other types of random error are more difficult to spot.

Every student who writes a report for presentation should endeavour to ensure that, at least in the typographical sense, the report is perfect. It is not unrealistic to expect that no less than 98 per cent of pages should be error free and that if this figure drops to 95 per cent students can expect adverse comment from the examiner.

Usually proof reading is undertaken by students themselves. The rules are fairly obvious:

a) read each line in turn;
b) recognise that intense concentration is needed and break off as soon as attention starts to wander;
c) read aloud;
d) take a sample (say 5 per cent) of those pages on which no errors have been noted and re-read them.

Particular attention should be paid to: spelling errors; faults in grammar; inconsistencies, for example, where the same reference is cited with a variety of different dates; and to omissions. As an encouragement at this tedious stage of the writing, students should recognise that in contrast to the irritation created by numerous typographical mistakes readers are much impressed by text which is virtually error free.

THE PREFACE

There may be a number of observations which students would like to make which are not part of the research proper. These observations will include introductory or explanatory remarks which students would communicate verbally if the opportunity were available. Most readers prefer sight of a report before discussing it with the writer and it is important to attempt to avoid misconceptions or to pre-empt criticism through the use of a preface, which, it is hoped, will be read before the body of the report itself.

Although the preface provides an opportunity for students to make personal statements it is still necessary to know where the line should be drawn. Thus, although the external examiner may be told that the research was interrupted for three months due to a doctoral student breaking a leg playing rugby, this is not information which will be of relevance to the world at large. It would, however, be acceptable to imply that the time available for the research had been reduced by finding an initial topic unprofitable before turning to the research which is to be reported on. Similarly, it would be in order for a doctoral student to refer to the fact that a foundation for the research had been achieved by the completion of a dissertation in a similar field for the purpose of satisfying the requirements of a master's level course involving taught courses and a short research project.

If joint work has been involved the extent of the collaboration can be clearly stated in the preface. This leads to acknowledgements which as a matter of courtesy should range from academic to material helpers. In the former category would come experts in the subject area who may have carried no responsibility for the student but gave of their time to provide advice, or perhaps computer specialists who put considerable effort into sorting out some of the difficulties which are often encountered in using or developing software. Material help may include the typists who very often will have to struggle with raw and amended copy to an extent well beyond that which any payment might justify. Supervisors should, of course, justify acknowledgement on several counts if they have carried out their responsibilities effectively.

REPRODUCING THE REPORT

Proof reading is, of course, just one aspect of an important last stage of the report. Reproduction from the original text is now put in hand, determined by the several copies required by the institution's regulations and by the students themselves. In most cases the bulk of the report will have been word processed and will then be photocopied as necessary. Since it is one of these copies that will go to the examiner the impression created by it is important. In particular, it makes little sense to devote enormous care to structuring, editing and proof reading the report and then to obscure this by presenting a finished article which has been poorly reproduced.

A number of factors affect the appearance of the final copies. The most important of these factors is the quality of the word processed original. Given the importance of word processing to the quality of the final report and the wide range of additional features that word processing packages offer the student researcher, this topic is discussed in more detail below.

As well as textual material, however, most research reports will contain a variety of tables, drawings and graphs. Where the tables are produced as a by-product of a computer analysis it obviously reduces the chances of error to have them produced directly by the computer. Where possible, therefore, students are probably well advised to design their computer output so that it can go directly into the word processor file containing their report. Whereas many graphs and charts for student reports are most conveniently produced using a spreadsheet package, more complex diagrams such as maps need to be produced on a computer graph plotter. These are available at most larger educational computer systems. Most plotters work in several colours (though without access to a colour photocopier this facility is probably best used sparingly).

Not all diagrams lend themselves to being drawn using the computer.

Traditionally, in scientific work, they are drawn using cartridge or similar pen and mapping ink. However, this is not something that previously inexperienced students can hope to do successfully themselves and therefore if the diagram needs to be drawn this way it will probably be necessary to approach a professional draughtsman. The problems in doing this are that as well as being a fairly costly process it can be a slow one. The alternative approach, and one that can be carried out by students themselves, is to make use of rub-on transfers such as Letraset to produce special symbols, lines, and so on. If produced larger than required and then photo-reduced, this method enables a very professional diagram to be produced quite quickly.

Copying

Once the finished text is assembled it usually needs to be photocopied. Where diagrams are to be incorporated into a mainly word processed text, photocopying may have to be done leaving blank sheets in the word processed original to preserve the report pagination and to allow for gluing diagrams onto these blank sheets afterwards.[4] Provided joins and edges are covered with liberal quantities of proprietary erasing fluids they will not reproduce in the final copy so that the original can well be assembled by gluing several sheets together. What is usually more important to achieve is that the various parts of a composite original be similar in contrast and this may require ingenious preliminaries with the 'light original' button or contrast control on the photocopier to make sure the various sections are of similar density.

It is useful to use a reasonably sophisticated copier as there are often a few pages of the report that cause reproduction problems. Such a copier will also offer photo-reduction facilities which are useful where certain diagrams and computer output need to be reduced in size to fit into the standard A4 format likely to be specified in most sets of UK regulations.

Sometimes a student will wish to include photographs in the report. One possibility is to paste prints into each of the copies produced; alternatively, the photographs may be contained within a folder. To create the best effect students may wish to reproduce the photographs. Photocopying will produce poor results; indeed, printers themselves have to resort to a special screening process for good results. In the latter case, either the prints are photographed through a glass screen ruled with a fine grid which separates the illustration into small dots to simulate the shades of grey or, more likely nowadays, put through an electronic equivalent of this process. If students decide to follow this course they will need to find a printer or someone (probably a graphic designer) with the necessary equipment.

Many students are subject to nightmare visions of draft chapters or even the whole draft report being destroyed by damage to the hard disk on which their word processed file is stored. Such accidents do happen and are perhaps more likely than might be expected in what is often a somewhat stressful period of research. The sensible student will therefore exploit the ease with which back-up copies of word processor files can be produced to insure against disasters of this type. Provided there are at least two copies of the work in different physical locations, one should survive.

Further protection can often be obtained by producing a paper copy for the supervisor. If all computer files are lost, it should still be possible to reconstitute the word processor file by document scanning; providing the supervisor with a copy helps to speed up the process of getting drafts read anyway.

It is perhaps worth noting that in cases where computer files are erased by mistake they can usually be restored quite simply by an expert. Files that have been lost by physical damage to the hard disk can normally also be recovered. If the student is uncertain how to proceed, which will almost certainly be the position in the latter case, it is better to approach an expert in data recovery.

WORD PROCESSING

Word processing provides a way of producing research reports of far higher quality than was possible when reports were manually typed. Good presentation has some impact on almost any external examiner; poor presentation, as noted earlier, certainly does. Therefore, the existence of word processing facilities has increased UK external examiners' expectations of the standard of presentation to be achieved, since, save under very exceptional circumstances, the reports that they see generally are likely to be word processed.

It is convenient at this point to remind the reader of a number of facilities to be found in most word processing packages used in educational institutions, as shown in Figure 8.5. For students and their supervisors the editing functions have considerable benefits. It has already been suggested in the section on style that, at least in the early stages of writing-up, the student or the supervisor may well feel that much rearrangement is needed to enable students to present their arguments as logically and as forcefully as possible. Thus, it is not at all unusual to find that material incorporated in one of the later chapters (which may well have been written first) would in fact be better split and incorporated in one or more earlier chapters. A word processing package allows not merely the movement of sections of text from one part of the report to another[5] but also permits insertion of the bridge passages that this frequently necessitates and the removal of redundant sentences.

Editing functions	Insertion or deletion of text
	Enhancing text by provision of underline, bold and italic typefaces
	Moving sections of text from one part to another
	Spellchecking
	Replacing all occurrences of a word or phrase by another
Typographical functions	Automatic margin setting
	Space adjustment to align margins
	Automatic hyphenation
	Automatic pagination
	Automatic numbering of sections and figures and the ability to renumber if sections are added or deleted
	Provision of footnotes and end notes
	Support for the production of tables
	Compilation of an index and table of contents
	Diagram drawing facilities
Report structuring functions	Outlining

Figure 8.5 Typical word processing package functions

We have already noted above that the ability to correct all occurrences of errors – such as, consistently spelling 'consistent' as 'consistant' – is, again, extremely useful in improving the quality of the text. Such errors often unfairly create a very poor impression of the quality of the research. Luckily, most students have specific spelling problems rather than general ones and probably need at most only to replace the incorrect version of a couple of dozen words. On a more positive note, the global search feature needed to do this is used by the word processing package to provide an index since the word processor can find all occurrences of a specified term in the text and print out the numbers of the relevant pages. Equally, where inspiration strikes late in the day an inferior technical term can be replaced by a more appropriate one.

Some further points to be noted on spellcheckers are:

1. Packages may be geared to USA or UK spellings. Most institutions are willing to accept USA spellings providing that they are used consistently. Overseas students may need to obtain a USA dictionary, if they have learnt USA rather than UK English.

2. Students should be able to add technical terms, and so on, to the thesaurus used by the spellchecker.

The typographical functions enable margins, line spacings, and so on, to be set to whatever standard is required by the institution. The automatic adjustment of spaces between words to align both left- and right-hand margins gives a most attractive 'book like' quality, especially if a proportional spacing font is used to print out the text. As an additional bonus, authors can run their report off in a different format to that specified for examination purposes, for example, single-lined on A5 paper.

The report structuring features of word processing might, more logically in view of our earlier discussion, appear first in the list. However, they have been left until last because they are relatively unfamiliar to most users of word processing. This is a pity since the word processor is extremely useful to student and supervisor alike in the critical early phase of determining the structure of the report.

The principle of outlining is simple. Indeed, the word processing package merely automates the procedure represented in our Report Organisation Chart (Figure 8.4). The student defines a highest level of breakdown corresponding to chapters. Each chapter is then divided by the student into main section headings. These latter are numbered sequentially 2.1, 2.2, etc., by the outliner. Main sections are then divided into subsections that, again, are numbered sequentially 2.1.1, 2.1.2, etc. At any point, the outline can be revised by introducing new subsections or converting, say, a main section to a chapter. All consequential adjustments to section numbering are made automatically by the word processing package.

The outline is usually printed out in indented form like the breakdown shown in Figure 8.6. Once the outline is agreed the student can start creating the report by 'filling out' individual parts of the outline as required. Although decimally numbered sections may well be preferred in the final report, it is not essential. Even if decimal numbering is suppressed, the distinction between,

```
1.    Introduction

2.    Survey of prior research

      2.1      The extent and range of computer applications in marketing

               2.1.1      Market planning

                          2.1.1.1    Early applications

                          2.1.1.2    Applications in the 1970s and 1980s

                          2.1.1.3    Recent applications

               2.1.2      Advertising

               2.1.3      Logistics

3.    Success factors for the application of computer models in marketing

4.    Success factors for application of computer models outside marketing

5.    Case study A

6.    Case study B

7.    Case study C

8.    Case study D

9.    Analysis of case studies to determine success factors in the implementation of
      market models

10.   Conclusions
```

Figure 8.6 The report structure of Figure 8.4, as developed using a word processing package outline function

say, sub-subsections and subsections is still clear, since different typeface styles can be associated with each type of heading.

PREPARING FOR AN ORAL EXAMINATION

It is possible that at all levels of writing, whether report, dissertation, or thesis, students will be called upon to meet one or more examiners in order to defend their conclusions verbally; the award of a doctorate will certainly involve this. However long it may last, the oral examination will only require a fraction of the time that the research project as a whole will take. Nevertheless, it is far from a formality and the wise student will accordingly prepare for it as thoroughly as possible with a view to confirming the high opinion that the examiners should already have conceived of the research from the study of the written report.

The wise student will also, at the earliest possible stage, have done some homework on the examiners and will attempt in the writing of the report to accommodate the implications of any preferences and attitudes which they are thought to hold. It is not too cynical to suggest either, particularly at doctoral level when the examiner will be an expert in the field, that references to the examiner's own work should be made. The academic world is, of course, well known for its conflicts of opinion on topics; doctoral students should accordingly do their best to ensure that there will be no antipathy towards them simply because of the line of argument they have pursued or the way they have presented it.

Students should hope, therefore, that although they will be confronted by examiners who will seek to ensure that academic standards are safeguarded, their examination will be unbiased. So, they can expect that if their writing satisfies the relevant criteria listed in Figure 8.1 they will, given a convincing performance under oral examination, be successful. The listed criteria do not, however, provide sufficient information as to the details of what should have been achieved. Students should, therefore, attempt to place themselves in the position of the examiners and consider the type of question which may be put in order to evaluate the report.

To provide students with a systematic basis for anticipating how their research may be evaluated, a number of questions under each of those eight criteria of Figure 8.1 are posed here which the doctoral student should seek to satisfy. To do this a checklist proposed by Hansen and Waterman (1966) is drawn upon in part. In relating it to their own situation, students may find it useful to remember that for higher degrees individual examiners may well seek the advice of colleagues on particular aspects of the research outside their own sphere of interest or understanding.

Defining Criteria

The eight criteria are listed below.
1. Evidence of an original investigation or the testing of ideas
    a) Was the aim of the research clearly described?
    b) Were the hypotheses to be tested, questions to be answered, or the methods to be developed clearly stated?
    c) Was the relationship between the current and previous research in related topic areas defined, with similarities and differences stressed?

d) Are the nature and extent of the original contribution clear?
2. Competence in independent work or experimentation
    a) Was the methodology employed appropriate? Was its use justified and was the way it was applied adequately described?
    b) Were variables that might influence the study recognised and either controlled in the research design or properly measured?
    c) Were valid and reliable instruments used to collect the data?
    d) Was there evidence of care and accuracy in recording and summarising the data?
    e) Is evidence displayed of knowledge of and the ability to use all relevant data sources?
    f) Were limitations inherent in the study recognised and stated?
    g) Were the conclusions reached justifiable in the light of the data and the way they were analysed?
3. An understanding of appropriate techniques
    a) Given the facilities available, did it seem that the best possible techniques were employed to gather and analyse data?
    b) Was full justification given for the use of the techniques selected and were they adequately described? In particular were they properly related to the stated aims of the research?
4. Ability to make critical use of published work and source materials
    a) Was the literature referenced pertinent to the research?
    b) To what extent could general reference to the literature be criticised on the grounds of insufficiency or excessiveness?
    c) Was evidence presented of skills in searching the literature?
    d) Was due credit given to previous workers for ideas and techniques used by the author?
    e) Is evidence displayed of the ability to identify key items in the literature and to compare, contrast and critically review them?
5. Appreciation of the relationship of the special theme to the wider field of knowledge
    a) Was the relationship between the current and previous research in related topic areas defined, with similarities and differences stressed?
    b) Was literature in related disciplines reviewed?
    c) Was an attempt made to present previous work within an overall conceptual framework and in a systematic way?
6. Worthy, in part, of publication
    a) Was the organisation of the report logical and was the style attractive?
    b) With appropriate extraction and editing could the basis of articles or a book be identified?
7. Originality as shown by the topic researched or the methodology employed

a) To what extent was the topic selected novel?
b) Was there evidence of innovation in research methodology compared with previous practice in the field?

8. Distinct contribution to knowledge
a) What new material was reported?
b) To what extent would the new material be perceived as a valuable addition to a field of knowledge?
c) To what extent do the conclusions overturn or challenge previous beliefs?
d) Were the findings compared with the findings of any similar studies?
e) Was the new contribution clearly delimited and prospects for further work identified?
f) To what extent does the work open up whole new areas for future research?

Students should rehearse their answers to an appropriate selection from the above list of questions. This procedure should indicate what additional evidence will need to be taken into the examination. In the main, any supplementary material will relate to the data gathering and analytical phases, but may also include papers which students have written during their research.

Whatever the level of the examination it should go without saying that students if called upon will be able to defend, explain, elaborate, or even apologise for any part of it. In the last mentioned respect, tolerance which may be extended towards the undergraduate is unlikely to apply in the case of the doctoral student. If an unacceptable weakness is found by such a student after a thesis has been submitted criticism is best anticipated and coped with by preparing a typed statement for distribution at the start of the examination.

THE ORAL EXAMINATION

Though practice varies depending on the level of the research project the oral examination will almost always involve at least two examiners. Usually, there will be at least one external examiner present for a postgraduate project and this may also be the case at undergraduate level.

In most UK universities the supervisor will not be appointed as the internal examiner for doctoral theses. Undergraduate or masters' students may, however, find that their supervisor happens to be functioning as an internal examiner and this will lead to a definite difference in attitude to that to which the student has been accustomed. At doctoral level in most UK universities the role of internal examiner is taken by another member of staff perhaps with the supervisor's formal role being that of 'in attendance'. In addition, for a research project that has involved collaboration with outside bodies, various people not on the staff of the institution may also function as examiners.

It should be appreciated by the research student that the prime purpose of an oral examination is to satisfy the examiners that the report presented represents individual or acceptably collaborative effort. If collaboration has been involved evidence of the degree of cooperation will be considered.

Whether or not the report is a student's own work is fairly quickly established and the main concern of the examiners is to ensure that any claims made in writing can be justified and that the analytical methods used are understood. In part, the examiners are adding credibility to the report by approving it, particularly in the case of the research thesis which will then be included in bibliographies. During the examination, however, students should expect to have to express opinions on topics which they may feel are peripheral to their studies in order to convince the examiners of their expertise in the wider field which includes their area of study. Although well able to defend their written arguments, uncertainty as to where the discussion might lead may give cause for prior concern. In particular, the student's craftsmanship and honesty are to some extent on trial as well as the merit of the research report itself.

As far as preparation is concerned individual students must decide what best suits them. It is obviously sensible to set aside as long a period of time beforehand if at all possible so as to put oneself into the right frame of mind for the oral examination and reacquaint oneself with the details of a research report that may have been completed a significant number of weeks before. To provide such a period may cause difficulty for part-time students or those students who are now working in a full-time job where there are likely to be other demands on their time. Perhaps the best mental preparation of all is for students to be in a position to exploit the strengths of their writing and to pre-empt criticism of its weaknesses. Obviously, the advice of a friend or colleague – or even better a rehearsal for the oral examination – can be of great help here. Doctoral students should be able to remind themselves that insofar as their conclusions are concerned they will be original. They should have developed considerable expertise in their chosen topic area and it should be possible for them to defend their thesis from a position of some strength. They must, however, expect questions which probe the scope of the topic, the nature of the target population, the type of cross-sectional comparison selected, and so on, at whatever level is appropriate for the type of research that has been conducted.

With regard to the examination itself possibly the most important advice that can be offered is that students should not attempt to 'pull the wool' over the examiners' eyes. Very rarely will it be possible to get away with this in front of experts. As suggested above, it is far better that students should admit to their shortcomings even if this means that in part the report will have to be rewritten.

Initially at least, the meeting will be conducted by the examiners with the student playing a very reactive role. At this stage it is important that students answer concisely but completely the questions put to them by the examiners, since the nature of their replies will be taken as a guide to the way in which the research itself was conducted. Therefore, where they are uncertain as to exactly what is meant by a question students should request further clarification before attempting to answer. Nor, where the question is difficult or subtle, should they hesitate to reflect so that they can give a considered reply. It should also be remembered that the examiners are likely to concentrate on what they perceive to be the key strengths and weaknesses of the work in question; various examiners may differ as to what these are. Accordingly, students must anticipate that discussion will range widely and that questions will be posed on many different aspects of the research. If students are confident about their work and findings and when they judge that they have achieved sufficient rapport with the examiners there could well be advantage in students becoming more positive; warming as it were to their theme.

HOW TO PUBLISH YOUR RESEARCH FINDINGS

Once you have successfully completed the research you may wish to think about using it as a basis for publication.[6] Having the results of your research published can be very satisfying. But for most people it is not easy to know where to start in order to work up an idea into publishable form. In fact, most of the hard work has already been done and with a little time and effort it should be possible to transform your report, dissertation or thesis, into a form in which a publisher will be able to use it.

Why Publish?

Getting into print is something that most researchers who care about their work and their ideas look to do at some point. It means that other researchers can see tangible evidence of the effort and intelligence you have put into your research leading, possibly, to recognition both nationally and internationally. It can help in gaining promotion and job-seeking and, if you are interested in becoming a consultant, teacher or speaker at some time, it is invaluable in that publication gets your name and ideas known.

Above all, it can be very satisfying to see our names in print on something that represents much time and effort on our part, and with which we are pleased. We can take professional pride in the achievement; and the institutions or organisations within which we work will share in the esteem.

A number of publication options exist, with by far the most widely chosen being the article submitted to a learned journal. Other possibilities include:
a) articles in practitioner journals;
b) a book;
c) a monograph;
d) a review article or bibliography.

In every case when publishing (other than those rare cases where the author acts as publisher also), consideration and approval will be needed from another party. For journal articles (assuming that they comply with the style requirements of the particular journal), the subject matter will be the dominant concern. This will also be pertinent in the case of a bibliography which is included within a journal. For 'stand alone' bibliographies, monographs, and books, however, commercial considerations will arise.

Journals

Where do I start? As stated, you have already done the hard work in completing the research project successfully. In longer research projects, many institutions demand an abstract or summary of the research for other researchers and practitioners. This provides a basis on which to work. What remains to be done is to:
a) follow the guidelines on format and presentation for the publication of your choice;
b) understand what the editor/publisher of the journal and its readers want;
c) exercise your creative talents within this framework.

The Requirements
The first thing you must do is to gain something of an insight into the requirements of prospective editors/publishers and then seek to tailor your article accordingly. Some of these requirements are discussed below.
a) *Weight*. Your coverage should be substantive and significant. It is to be hoped, however, that you have already crossed that bridge by completing a research report. Remember that in many instances your article will be subjected to review.
b) *Accessibility*. All but the more esoteric journals appeal to practitioners, teachers and students as well as to researchers. Your article must be comprehensible to the main audiences of the journal.
c) *Ease of decision making*. Publishers and editors tend to have many papers

submitted to them; much of the ground covered earlier in this chapter is relevant. Make sure that when they receive your article and covering letter they want to read on.

Choosing Journals

Which journal should be chosen to submit to? In the case of learned journals your literature review should have identified some obvious candidates and, failing that, advice is normally available from supervisors. In the case of practitioner journals, however, there may be more uncertainty. Some publishers will help in the first instance by supplying an up-to-date portfolio of their journals. Look through that and ask for sample copies, if you are not familiar with them already, of the two or three that seem most suitable. Then scan the articles in your target journals to gain a feel for the style. It is most important that you read the 'Notes For Contributors' which appear at the back of most journals. Write to, or telephone, the editor who will usually be delighted that you are interested, and will be genuinely pleased to talk you through the journal's editorial policy and give help and ideas on your piece.

Rules of Writing

How should the article be written? In order to stand a better chance of it being published there are certain 'rules' which you should adopt. These rules of writing articles are largely common sense and apply equally to reports, speeches, presentations, and many other things.

1. Plan. Construct the skeleton of your article before starting the article proper.
2. Introduce. Incorporate the purpose, the objectives and the message of your article into your opening paragraphs.
3. Motivate. Try to catch the reader's attention and interest with a good opening. The novelist Joseph Heller (*Catch 22*, etc.) says he spends much more time and effort on the first two or three lines of his books than he does on any other part.
4. Hold. Do not let your readers reach your second page before they near a point of substance. Many readers have a short attention span so keep the pace up.
5. Discuss. Run through your findings or argument as outlined in your introduction.
6. Break. Use headings and subheadings to break up the text.
7. Illustrate. Use charts, tables or graphs (and/or illustrations) to explain difficult points, present data or simply to make the text more readable.
8. Illuminate. If at all possible bring your points to life by using case examples and accounts of how things happen in the real world. Case histories, quotes and anecdotes can enliven an article.

9. Summarise. Present, clearly and concisely, the key conclusions and recommendations arising from your research.
10.Conclude. Finish with recommendations as to how the conclusions might stimulate eventual application.

Many journals are distributed to an international audience. Ensure, therefore, that a reader on the other side of the world is not confronted with unintelligible acronyms and abbreviations.

What to do next?
Start writing and when you are happy with your article submit it. Nearly all journals now require a short abstract and keywords which will give the editor an overview of the article and allow referees to be selected, if necessary. Invite the editor to contact you with any comments, amendments and suggestions. If possible use a word processor so that additions, deletions and amendments can be made quickly, cleanly and easily.

If you do not hear anything within a month of submitting, contact the editor and ask for a reaction. If you still hear nothing, contact the journal publisher – the editor may have moved, or be away.

If your article is rejected without reasons being given, ask why. Editors will usually offer honest and constructive criticism which can help you in the future. If it is simply because the editor has an overabundance of copy, or does not feel that your article fits the journal, try one of the other publications you identified initially.

It is often possible to prepare more than one article for prospective publication. This may be achieved by dividing up the research report content in order that distinctly different topics can be addressed. Alternatively, a topic may be written up at two levels: one directed towards academics and the other towards practitioners. Sensibly, both editors to whom these articles are sent should be advised of your intentions.

Books

Taking length into account, the longer form of research report may be seen to equate with a book. Before publication of the findings in this form is achieved, however, two major hurdles must be surmounted.
1. A publisher has to be found.
2. The thesis (rarely a dissertation) will need to be rewritten to become 'reader friendly'.

Just one or two instances of a thesis being published as it stands are known to the authors. The researcher will realise that the requirements of the target market for a book will usually differ considerably from those of the examiners. Further, though the publication lead time for an article appearing in a journal may be long, the corresponding period for the publication of a book is usually longer still. But the publisher will be much concerned with the commercial prospects of a book and substantial time may be taken in evaluating what those might be. It behoves the aspirant to plan well in advance if publication in book form is sought and, if a publisher can be found, to recognise the demands of rewriting not long after completing the thesis.

Monographs

The term 'monograph' may be open to a number of interpretations. A monograph may be viewed as a short book to which the comments made in the previous section may apply. Alternatively, organisations which support research may be prepared, for altruistic reasons, to facilitate the production and distribution of a monograph that is synonymous with the research report.

Although, to the general reader, a thesis may appear to contain much 'padding' the author may be reluctant to accept this view. It is, nevertheless, usually accepted, as suggested earlier, that length can be reduced without too much dilution of the argument, albeit that the scope available within a 6,000 word article may be very restricting. Some journal editors and publishers are willing to include 'monographs' alongside standard issues within a particular volume of the journal. Such 'extended articles' of, say, 40,000 words satisfy the publisher's requirements for original copy and the researcher's desire to promote the findings, often in an attractive format, more quickly than would be possible through a book.

Review Articles and Bibliographies

Researchers should, as a routine part of their studies, establish and appraise current thinking in the area that they are exploring. At doctoral level their search of existing literature should be thorough and may well support the production of a review article on the field. Equally, publication may be possible as a bibliography in book form or as a bibliographic article to be included within a journal. As far as bibliographies are concerned, they are more valuable if the compiler presents the material thematically and supplements the list of sources with a synthesis and a critique.

ELECTRONIC PUBLICATION

Most people assume that by 'publication' a book or journal in paper form is implied. There is, however, growing use of the Internet for the publication of electronic journals (E-journals). Dozens of such journals in a range of disciplines (many of which are refereed electronically) are now to be found on the Internet.

E-journals are often located in areas where electronic conferencing has been established. Networks of researchers are able to exchange views through the Internet as though they were attending and participating in a one-site conference.

The major advantage of publishing in an E-journal is speed. The whole process including refereeing can be completed in a day or two. Indeed, the concept of a journal (which for economies of scale will comprise some eight or so individual articles) becomes largely redundant.

There are, as might be expected, problems to be overcome:

a) the transmission of figures, special characters, etc.;
b) the different demands placed on the reader if a printout is not taken (this alone is the main reason why significant technological advances will be needed before E-books become feasible);
c) incorporation in indexes and abstracts (a continuing task, perhaps, for the traditional publisher).

There is, however, little doubt that by the year 2000 much scholarly publishing will be through the electronic medium. For this type of activity the process of electronic conferencing and publishing is recommended for those researchers with the necessary inclinations and facilities.

CHAPTER SUMMARY

EVALUATION OF A RESEARCH REPORT: will involve certain criteria that depend, in part, on the level of the research. Students should be familiar with these.

STUDENTS AT LOWER LEVELS: may have only a very limited opportunity for feedback from their supervisors on their research. It is especially important for such students, therefore, to make as good a job, as possible, of their research report.

STUDENTS SHOULD START WRITING THE REPORT AS EARLY AS POSSIBLE: accepting that initial drafts are readily modified later in the light of comments received.

THE WRITTEN ACCOUNT OF RESEARCH: should be of sufficient quality in respect of: structure;
style;
content.

THE QUALITY OF PRESENTATION: of a report can be an important factor in influencing an examiner and should be given full consideration.

WORD PROCESSING: should be used effectively not only to ensure a high standard of presentation but also as a tool for structuring the report.

AN ORAL EXAMINATION: will certainly be required at doctoral level and may be required at lower levels. As far as possible, it should be carefully planned for and students should rehearse answers to questions which might be put to them.

PUBLICATION: of your research findings, whenever appropriate, should be sought as the final outcome of your research studies.

Epilogue

And now with the student's chosen research topic successfully completed what benefits accrue? Since this has been written for students there should be a tangible reward in the form of a degree or diploma for which the research formed all or part of the requirements. This will undoubtedly have career benefits particularly at the higher levels of research where they will be construed by others as evidence of the student's ability to carry out a substantial study requiring inventiveness, expertise and perseverance.

It is to be regretted that despite the potential for achieving a reputation through the dissemination of a student's research findings these often remain imprisoned in a thesis or a dissertation stored on a library shelf. However, successful students may well wish to make their work more widely available and indeed may be encouraged to seek publication by requests for copies from researchers working in the same field. General advice on how to achieve publication was given at the end of Chapter 8.

At undergraduate and master's levels it is very often possible to publish the results of the research project in a professional journal – for example, for engineers and even in some cases in an academic journal. Supervision of lower level research projects is often seen as a burden by hard pressed academics and the prospect of a publication jointly authored by supervisor and student is a definite incentive to academics to supervise the project well. It offers, equally, significant benefits to the student in their future career in most cases.

Research students in the USA have long had (since 1938) a further option available in the dissertations publishing service provided by University

Microfilms International of Ann Arbor. This service has been available to UK authors since the 1970s. A publication fee is charged which covers the cost of microfilming the thesis to produce a master microfilm copy held by UMI, from which microform or paper copies may then be produced on demand. This system is economical since no initial print-run has to be created as in conventional ink-on-paper publication. In addition, it means that the work need never go out of print and that it is perpetuated in the bibliographical support publications of that programme. Researchers who may wish to publish only an abstract of their thesis can obtain details of submission procedures for UMI's European abstracts journal, *Dissertation Abstracts International, Section C.*

The successful research project can form the basis eventually of a substantial reputation earned through books and articles derived from it and research the student may carry out later. Sometimes it may be many years afterwards that a change of job or a slight alteration in career direction may provide an opportunity to utilise knowledge and skills gained during the research. Be that as it may the immediate and substantial benefit that accrues to any student comes from the learning that is provided to a greater or lesser extent by any research project. For, however good their supervisor and no matter what help they got from others, successful students will have displayed and also enhanced their ability to carry out intellectually demanding work independently.

Appendices

Appendix 1

AN EXAMPLE OF TOPIC ANALYSIS

In this appendix we provide an example of topic analysis as a student would present it in the area of local government studies research, in the initial stage of a research degree.

Topic Analysis

Student's Name: *Date:*

Area of proposed study:

Outsourcing in Local Government in England and Wales

1. Research Objectives or Hypotheses

The objectives of the proposed study are:
a) to describe the growth of outsourcing (that is, the purchase from external suppliers of services previously provided within the organisation) in local government in England and Wales and the main factors that have driven it;
b) to examine experiences with outsourcing to date;
c) to identify the major benefits and drawbacks of outsourcing in local government;
d) to consider the implications of a), b) and c) for future policy on outsourcing by local government.

2. Prior research in the area

Although local government has probably always purchased infrequently used services from outside, the benefits of so doing began first to be urged by commentators in the 1970s. Arguments were usually based on comparison with other countries in Europe and elsewhere in the world where services such as refuse collection had always been let by local government under contract. The theoretical notions behind these ideas, however, derived from the Transaction Cost Economics of Williamson (1975). Williamson argued that organisations that had hitherto carried out their operations internally could benefit considerably by purchasing certain frequently used services, e.g. highways maintenance, from commercial providers. The outside suppliers whose main business was in the provision of the services in question would be subject to competition from other similar suppliers with the result that the market price for the service would be substantially lower than it would cost to provide internally.

With the advent of the Conservative government in 1979, these ideas began to be applied in earnest in local government through a Central Government series of initiatives designed to require services such as refuse collection and direct labour works (building maintenance, etc.) to be put out to competitive tender. The Local Government Planning and Land Act (1980) required local authorities in England and Wales to put out certain maintenance work on buildings and highways to compulsory competitive tendering (CCT) (Greenwood and Wilson, 1994). These moves were encouraged by the extension of CCT in the 1988 Local Government Act (Vincent-Jones, 1994), to refuse collection, grounds and vehicle maintenance, school and welfare catering, sports and leisure management, etc. The majority of the original contracts were won by 'Direct Service Organisations' set up by local councils through redesignating previous internal providers of the services concerned. This led to a purchaser/provider split within many activities in local government. CCT is currently scheduled to be extended to a variety of other more 'white collar' local government services, e.g. IT services, engineering services within the next few years. In fact, however, many local authorities have already voluntarily begun to contract out such services especially in IT, with a number of authorities having opted to purchase all their IT support from outside suppliers.

A number of commentators, e.g. The Audit Commission (1993), have identified problems with the post-1988 round of CCT. One problem was the relative lack of private sector bids for many tenders. However, the major problems identified were in contract specification, contract monitoring and in the enforcement of contract provisions in cases of poor performance.

CCT, however, is just a mechanism for bringing about outsourcing of local government services. Given the trend towards outsourcing in the private sector, it seems inconceivable that it will not remain a substantial issue within local government in the foreseeable future.

Outside the public sector the principal academic interest in outsourcing has been in the area of IT services (e.g. Lacity and Hirschheim, 1993a) reflecting the fact that the phenomenon was first identified in IT though its application to catering services and even legal and engineering services has also burgeoned of recent years. Quinn (1992) and Quinn and Hilmer (1994) argue, however, that outsourcing is a much wider principle that has been growing in importance over the past 15 years in private sector organisations. They advocate outsourcing activities that fall outside the core intellectual properties that distinguish the enterprise from others. Any services that the organisation is unable to perform better than anyone else should be outsourced unless they must be retained to build barriers to entry around its core competences.

A different view of outsourcing as contributing to workforce flexibility is apparent amongst many personnel management practitioners (cf. Harrison and Kelley, 1993). However, the trade press, e.g. in IT, carries regular stories on the problems that outsourcing creates for human resource management in both the public and private sectors.

IT outsourcing has revealed similar problems of contract specification and monitoring to those found with CCT. Fitzgerald and Willcocks (1994) argue that the cost based outsourcing should not be undertaken unless a satisfactory contract can be drawn up and that this is only possible where contract conditions can be tightly specified, as has traditionally been the case in local authority outsourcing. Where there is uncertainty about the outcome as in the more speculative type of system design activity a risk sharing contract is more appropriate. In a similar vein, McFarlan and Nolan (1995) suggest that what they term a strategic outsourcing alliance is the right approach to the problem. Other authors, e.g. Lacity and Hirschheim (1993b), take the view that with relatively little effort the performance of in-house units could be brought up to that of external providers and given the likely deleterious effects of outsourcing on affected personnel and the difficulties of contract definition a bias towards 'insourcing' is more appropriate.

Clearly the problems that exist with outsourcing in the private sector arise in local government also. Moreover, with the extension of CCT to professional services in local government it is conceivable that the difficulties may grow further and that pressures may lead to the retention of insourcing. Even were CCT to be abolished, however, the attractions of workforce flexibility and low cost supply by external providers who specialise in the type of service being sought will remain. Local government will still need to consider under what circumstances outsourcing is appropriate, where it should be used, and how it is best managed.

3. Value of the research

Within IT, outsourcing is a major business with a high growth rate (Fitzgerald and Willcocks, 1993). There appear to have been few systematic studies of outsourcing outside IT. Outsourcing within local government has received even less attention, with academic work being mainly concentrated on the impact of CCT. The results of the proposed research would appear to be of clear value to the academic community.

For the reasons given, it is bound to be an important issue in local government in the future. The findings of the research would similarly appear to be of value to practitioners both within central and local government and amongst providers of outsourced services.

The study would be of personal value to the researcher, since it is linked to anticipated career development.

4. Proposed Methodology

An interview based study would be conducted across the same 3 departments in each of 4 local authorities. One department would be amongst those subjected to CCT by the 1980 Act, possibly highways; one department would be one subjected to CCT by the 1988 Act, possibly refuse collection; one department would be in the professional services area, possibly IT to facilitate comparison with the bulk of the outsourcing literature. Two of the local councils would be metropolitan authorities and two would be county authorities. In each pair one authority would be chosen because it was enthusiastic about outsourcing, whilst the other would be chosen because it was unenthusiastic. It is expected that appropriate access can be gained via personal contacts.

Based on discussions with other researchers in local government, it is anticipated that around 10 individuals will need to be interviewed in each department giving around 120 respondents. Interviews are expected to take under two hours each. At 5 interviews per week this suggests around six months will be required for basic data gathering.

References

Audit Commission (1993) Realising the Benefits of Competition: The Client Role for Contracted Services, Audit Commission, London

Fitzgerald, G., and Willcocks, L. (1993) Market as opportunity? Case studies in outsourcing information technology and services, Journal of Strategic Information Systems, 2 (3), 223-242

Fitzgerald, G. and Willcocks, L. (1994) Contracts and Partnerships In The Outsourcing Of IT, Proceedings of the Fifteenth International Conference on Information Systems, Vancouver, December 14th-17th 1994, 91-98

Greenwood, J. and Wilson, D. (1994) Towards the Contract State: CCT in Local Government, Parliamentary Affairs, 47, 3, 405-419

Harrison, B. and Kelley, M.R. (1993) Outsourcing and the Search for Flexibility, Work Employment and Society, 7, 2, 213-235.

Lacity, M. and Hirschheim, R. (1993a) Information Systems Outsourcing, Wiley, Chichester

Lacity, M. and Hirschheim, R. (1993b) The Information Systems Outsourcing Bandwagon, Sloan Management Review, 35 (1), 73-86

McFarlan, F.W. and Nolan, R.L. (1995) How To Manage An IT Outsourcing Alliance, Sloan Management Review, 36, 2, 9-23

Quinn, J.B. (1992) Intelligent Enterprise, Free Press, New York

Quinn, J.B. and Hilmer, F.G. (1994) Strategic Outsourcing, Sloan Management Review, 35, 4, 43-55

Vincent-Jones, P. (1994) The Limits of Near-contractual Governance: Local Authority Internal Trading Under CCT, Journal of Law and Society, 21, 2, 214-237

Williamson, O.E. (1975) Markets and Hierarchies, Free Press, New York.

Appendix 2

A SELECT BIBLIOGRAPHY ON STUDENT RESEARCH

Topic Selection and Development

Ackoff R. L., *The Art of Problem Solving accompanied by Ackoff's Fables*, Wiley, New York, NY., 1978.

Buzan T., *Use Your Head*, BBC Books, London, 1989.

de Bono E., *Teaching thinking*, Temple Smith, London, 1976.

Tarr G., *The Management of Problem Solving: Positive Results from Productive Thinking*, Macmillan, London, 1973.

Theory of Knowledge

Cohen M. R. and Nagel E., *An Introduction to Logic and Scientific Method*, Routledge & Kegan Paul, London, 1934. A standard text on scientific method. Considers both experimental and observational studies and history. Useful discussion on principles of measurement.

Gardiner P. L., *Theories of History*, Free Press, New York, NY., 1959. Comprehensive set of readings on what is meant by historical knowledge with applications to other fields also.

Kuhn T. S., *The Structure of Scientific Revolutions*, University of Chicago Press,

Chicago, Ill., 1962. The classic text on the role of paradigm shifts in scientific discovery.

Popper K., *The Logic of Scientific Discovery* (2nd Edition), Hutchinson, London, 1968. The classic logical positivist account of scientific method including the notion of falsifiability.

General Texts On Research Methodology

Behavioural Research

Kerlinger F. N., *Foundations of Behavioural Research: Educational, Psychological and Sociological Enquiry* (3rd Edition), Holt Rinehart & Winston, New York, NY., 1986. General discussion of the underlying philosophy of behavioural and related research plus useful introduction to discriminant analysis, factor analysis, experimental design, etc.

Thines G., *Phenomenology and the Science of Behaviour*, George Allen & Unwin, London, 1977. An account of psychological research from the phenomenological perspective of the philosopher Husserl.

Educational Research

Fox D. J., *The Research Process in Education*, Holt Rinehart & Winston, New York, NY., 1969. Comprehensive coverage of a variety of research methods for use in the social sciences and humanities ranging from content analysis to the experimental design model. Particularly good on practical aspects of carrying out research of this type.

Maruyama G., and Deno S., *Research in Educational Settings*, Sage Publications, London, 1992. A more recent text on a major area of student research.

Health Care Research

Crabtree B. F. and Miller W. L. (eds), *Doing Qualitative Research: Multiple Strategies*, Sage Publications, London, 1992. Discusses the application of a variety of research methods in the health care context.

Management Research

Easterby-Smith M., Thorpe R. and Lowe A., *Management Research: An Introduction*, Sage, London, 1991. An overview of a variety of different approaches to management and organisational research and issues in their application in practice.

Elfring T., Siggaard Jensen H., and Money A. (eds), *European Research Paradigms in Business Studies*, Handleshøjskolens Forlag, Copenhagen, 1995. A variety of perspectives on and paradigms of business research, many grounded in continental European philosophical traditions other than those of logical positivism.

Policy Research

Struening E. L. and Guttentag M. (eds), *Handbook of Evaluation Research*, Vols 1 and 2, Sage Publications, Beverley Hills, Calif., 1975. A guide to research in the evaluation of social policy, taking in many types of analysis and data collection methods particularly the experimental design model.

Texts on Specific Aspects of Research Methodology

Burrell G. and Morgan G., *Sociological Paradigms and Organisational Analysis: Elements of the Sociology of Corporate Life*, Heinemann, London, 1979. A classic account of types of knowledge about social systems.

Dubin R., *Theory Building*, Free Press, New York, NY., 1969. An examination of the construction of various types of theory in the social sciences but relevant to many other fields.

Glaser B. G. and Strauss A. L., *The Discovery of Grounded Theory: Strategies for Qualitative Research*, Weidenfeld & Nicholson, London, 1967. A key reference for the student engaged in exploratory research. Distinguished by its insistence on the interaction between data gathering and theory development. Also contains novel ideas on data sources. Intended for social scientists but of interest to all researchers making use of field observations.

Kvale S. (ed.), *Psychology and Postmodernism*, Sage Publications, London, 1992. Despite its title, the various contributions in this volume provide a good overview of the relevance of postmodernist ideas in both the humanities and the social sciences.

Strauss A. L. and Corbin J., *Basics of Qualitative Research: Grounded Theory Procedures and Techniques*, Sage Publications, London, 1990. Grounded theory approaches have become very popular in the social sciences of recent years. An up-to-date account of the ideas.

Warwick D. P. and Osherson S. (eds), *Comparative Research Methods*, Prentice

Hall, Englewood Cliffs, NJ., 1973. Excellent set of readings on methodological problems in an important area of social science research.

Data Sources and Data Gathering

Many of the sources listed in this section are serial publications. Because many serial publications, such as dissertation abstracts, are now available in CD–ROM form we have not given frequencies of publication, since these are generally higher for the CD–ROM form than the paper form but may vary depending on the precise nature of the library subscription.

Research In Progress

Current Research in Britain: the humanities, British Library, Boston Spa.
Current Research in Britain: the biological sciences, British Library, Boston Spa.
Current Research in Britain: the physical sciences, British Library, Boston Spa.
Current Research in Britain: the social sciences, British Library, Boston Spa.

Theses

INDEX TO THESES WITH ABSTRACTS accepted for Higher Degrees in the Universities of Great Britain and Ireland, ASLIB, London.
British Theses Service, *The BRITS index: an index to the British thesis collections held at the British Library Document Supply Centre and London University (1971–1987)*.
Dissertation Abstracts International, Part A: Humanities and Social Sciences. Part B: Science and Engineering. Part C: European Abstracts, University Microfilms, Ann Arbor, Mich.

Official Publications

British reports, translations and theses received at the British Library Lending Division, British Library, Boston Spa.
Catalogue of British Official Publications Not Published By HMSO, Chadwyck-Healey, Cambridge.
STAR (Scientific Technical and Aerospace Reports), NASA, Washington, DC.
Central Statistical Office, *Guide To Official Statistics*, HMSO, London.

244

EUROSTAT, *European statistics: official sources*, Office for Official Publications of the European Communities, 1993.
United Nations Statistical Year Book, United Nations, New York, NY.

CD–ROM Material

CD–ROMS in Print, Mecklermedia, Westport, Conn.

The Internet

Gilster P., *The Internet Navigator* (2nd Edition), Wiley, New York, NY., 1994. How to find your way around this increasingly important source of contacts with other researchers, etc.

Surveys and Questionnaire Design

Fink A. and Kosecoff J., *How to Conduct Surveys: A Step-by-Step Guide*, Sage Publications, Beverley Hills, Calif., 1985
Fowler F. J., *Survey Research Methods* (2nd Edition), Sage Publications, London, 1993.
Singh D., *Theory and Analysis of Sample Survey Designs*, Wiley, New York, NY., 1986.

Less Conventional Data Gathering

Webb E. J., Campbell D. T., Schwartz R. D. and Sechrest L., *Unobtrusive Measures: Non reactive research in the social sciences*, Rand McNally, Chicago, Ill., 1966. A compendium of imaginative approaches to gathering social data without causing bias in the observations.
Simpson D. K., *Psychology, Science and History: an introduction to historiometry*, Yale University Press, Yale, New Haven, Conn., 1990. The methods are mainly conventional statistics as used by psychologists but applied to a field (history) where data are usually seen as primarily qualitative.

Analysis and Analytical Techniques

We have attempted, somewhat arbitrarily, to distinguish analysis techniques which are not necessarily statistical in nature from those that undoubtedly are. However, many of our 'non statistical' techniques make extensive use of statistical methods.

Content Analysis

Holsti O. R., *Content Analysis for the Social Sciences and Humanities*, Addison Wesley, Reading, Mass., 1969. Comprehensive account of purposes of and techniques for analysing the content of text material. Clear discussions of a variety of applications with particular reference to the overall place of content analysis and the problems encountered. Good discussion of the principles of use of the computer in content analysis.

Krippendorff K., *Content Analysis: an introduction to its methodology*, Sage Publications, London, 1980.

Metaanalysis

An approach to the consolidation of data from a number of studies conducted by previous researchers. Increasingly used in medical research and in the social sciences.

Hunter J. E., Schmidt F. L. and Jackson G. B., *META-ANALYSIS: cumulating findings across studies*, Sage Publications, London, 1982.

Noblit N. and Hare R. D., *Meta-Ethnography: Synthesising Qualitative Studies*, Sage Publications, London, 1988.

Pattern Recognition

McLachlan G. J., *Discriminant Analysis and Statistical Pattern Recognition*, Wiley, New York, NY., 1992. A statistical approach.

Everitt B., *Graphical Techniques for Multivariate Data*, Heinemann, London, 1978. A statistical approach supplemented by pictorial techniques.

Qualitative Analysis Techniques

Silverman D., *Interpreting Qualitative Data: Methods for Analysing Talk, Text and Interaction*, Sage Publications, London, 1993. As the title implies a good account of a variety of approaches to the analysis of qualitative data.

Quasi Experiments

The idea of quasi-experimental designs is important to researchers in areas where control of all the experimental factors is not possible – for example, education, organisation studies.

Campbell D. T. and Stanley J. C., *Experimental and Quasi Experimental Designs for Research*, Houghton Mifflin, Boston, Mass., 1966. Clear non-statistical discussion of ideas underlying experimental design model and of ways of extending it to field studies where not all factor levels can be controlled.

Cook T. D. and Campbell D. T., *Quasi Experimentation: Design and Analysis Issues for Field Settings*, Rand McNally, Chicago, Ill., 1979. Later, more comprehensive, examination of methodological problems of causal explanation based on field observations and ways of overcoming them.

General Statistical Texts

Reference is made to a number of statistical texts of a comprehensive nature. The level of mathematical/statistical knowledge required to use a text varies widely from one text to another in an era when statistical analyses are almost always carried out by students using a computer package.

Bagozzi R. P. (ed.), *Advanced Methods of Marketing Research*, Blackwell, Oxford, 1994. A discussion of a wide variety of recent, multivariate statistical methods and their application. Of interest to social scientists, information systems researchers, etc.

Box G. E. P., Hunter W. G. and Hunter J. S., *Statistics for experimenters: an introduction to design, data analysis, and model building*, Wiley, New York, NY., 1976. A standard text on statistical methods for experimental scientists.

Green P. E., Tull D. S. and Albaum G., *Research for Marketing Decisions* (5th Edition), Prentice Hall, Englewood Cliffs, NJ., 1988. Requires knowledge of elementary statistics but otherwise little mathematical expertise. Remarkably comprehensive coverage of the underlying concepts and marketing applications of many different multivariate techniques including regression, experimental design, discriminant analysis, cluster analysis, etc. Particularly good on multidimensional and other scaling techniques. Very useful to researchers in any field who are willing to make the effort to translate the examples into a context relevant to their research.

Statistical Techniques

Analysis of Variance

Bray J. H. and Maxwell S. E., *Multivariate Analysis of Variance*, Sage Publications, London, 1985. A guide to applications in the social sciences.
Edwards A. L., *Multiple Regression and the Analysis of Variance and Covariance* (2nd Edition), Freeman, New York, NY., 1985. Broader coverage of the subject taking in its relationship with the regression model.

Cluster Analysis

Anderberg M. R., *Cluster Analysis for Applications*, Academic Press, New York, NY., 1973. Self-explanatory title.
Everitt B., *Graphical Techniques for Multivariate Data*, Heinemann, London, 1978. Describes a number of different techniques of clustering with a strong emphasis on visual presentation. Also of interest from the point of view of pattern recognition.

Discriminant Analysis

Klecka W. R., *Discriminant Analysis*, Sage Publications, London, 1980. Covers practical application of classical techniques of discriminant analysis in the social sciences.
McLachlan G. J., *Discriminant Analysis and Statistical Pattern Recognition*, Wiley, New York, NY., 1992. Applications in computing and electronics.

Experimental Design Model

Cox D. R., *Planning of Experiments*, Wiley, New York, NY., 1959. Clear description of the statistics of experimental design methods with a range of applications in the physical, biomedical and agricultural sciences.

Keppel G. and Saufley W. H. Jr., *Design and Analysis: A Student's Handbook*, W. H. Freeman, San Francisco, Calif., 1980. A guide to the use of experimental design methods in practice with particular reference to applications in psychology.

Factor Analysis

Bartholomew D. J., *Latent Variable Models and Factor Analysis*, Griffin, London, 1987.

Lewis-Beck M. S. (ed.) *Factor Analysis and Related Techniques*, Sage Publications, London, 1993.

Loglinear Analysis

A technique for the analysis of tabulated data that has grown greatly in popularity in recent years.

Agresti A., *Categorical Data Analysis*, Wiley-Interscience, New York, NY., 1990.
Hagenaars J. A., *Categorical Longitudinal Data: Log-Linear Panel, Trend and Cohort Analysis*, Sage Publications, London, 1990. Applications in the analysis of social surveys.

Regression Analysis

Allen D. M. and Cady F. B., *Analyzing Experimental Data by Regression*, Lifetime Learning, Belmont, Calif., 1982. A book aimed at experimental scientists.
Doran H. E., *Applied Regression Analysis in Econometrics*, Dekker, New York, NY., 1989. Econometricians are amongst the largest users of regression methods. Furthermore, the applications of the technique are often sophisticated.
Jaccard J., Turrisi R. and Won C. K., *Interaction Effects In Multiple Regression*, Sage Publications, London, 1990. An important topic in the practical application of the regression model.
Kerlinger F. N. and Pedhazur E. J., *Multiple Regression in Behavioural Research*,

Holt Rinehart & Winston, New York, NY., 1980. Good discussion of applications of regression in the social sciences including path analysis.

Scaling

van der Ven A. G. G. S., *Introduction to Scaling*, Wiley, Chichester, 1980. Clear account of both unidimensional and multidimensional scaling techniques.

Green P. E., Carmone F. J. Jr. and Smith S. M., *Multidimensional Scaling: Concepts and Applications*, Allyn & Bacon, Boston, Mass., 1989. Account of the uses of multidimensional scaling in marketing and allied fields.

Writing Research Reports

Becker H. S., *Writing for Social Scientists: How to Start and Finish Your Thesis, Book or Article*, University of Chicago Press, Chicago, Ill., 1986. An excellent guide on writing longer research reports in the social sciences. Particularly strong on the process of writing.

Ebel, H. F., Bliefert C. and Russey W. E., *The Art of Scientific Writing: From Student Reports to Professional Publications in Chemistry and Related Fields*, VCH, Weinheim, 1990. Guide to writing research reports in the physical and biological sciences.

Williams J. M., *Style: Toward Clarity and Grace*, University of Chicago Press, Chicago, Ill., 1990. A very practical guide to effective scholarly writing based on theoretical considerations.

Turabian K., *A Manual for Writers of Research Papers, Theses and Dissertations*, Heinemann, London, 1982.

Appendix 3

BOOKS AND ARTICLES CITED IN THE MAIN TEXT (EXCLUDING THE TOPIC ANALYSIS)

Because many serial publications, such as dissertation abstracts, are now available in CD–ROM form we have not given frequencies of publication, since these are generally higher for the CD–ROM form than the paper form but may vary depending on the precise nature of the library subscription.

Ackoff R. L., *The Art of Problem Solving accompanied by Ackoff's Fables*, Wiley, New York, NY., 1978.

ANBAR Abstracts, MCB University Press, Bradford.

Arts and Humanities Citation Index, Institute for Scientific Information, Philadelphia, Pa.

Bakker A. R., 'Access to Medical Databases: Theory and Practice', *Methods of Information in Medicine*, Vol 32, No. 5, p. 357, 1993.

Bolton N., *Concept Formation*, Pergamon Press, Oxford, 1977.

Braithwaite B. D., Ritchie A. W. S. and Earnshaw J. J., 'NATALI – A Model for National Computer Databases in the Investigation of New Therapeutic Techniques', *Journal of the Royal Society of Medicine*, Vol 88, No. 9, pp. 511–15, 1995.

Brillouin L., *Science and Information Theory*, Academic Press, New York, NY., 1962.

British reports, translations and theses received at the British Library Lending Division, Britisb Library, Boston Spa.

British Newspaper Index, London.

British Theses Service, *The BRITS index: an index to the British thesis collections held at the British Library Document Supply Centre and London University (1971–1987).*

Broehl W. G. and Shurter R. L., *Business, Research and Report Writing,* McGraw Hill, New York, NY., 1965.

Catalogue of British Official Publications Not Published By HMSO, Chadwyck-Healey, Cambridge.

Clark P. A., *Action Research and Organisational Change,* Harper and Row, New York, NY., 1972.

Cook T. D. and Campbell D. T., *Quasi Experimentation: Design and Analysis Issues for Field Settings,* Rand McNally, Chicago, Ill., 1979.

Cooper B. M., *Writing Technical Reports* (2nd Edition), Penguin, Harmondsworth, 1990.

Clover Newspaper Index, London.

Cox J. J., *Keyguide to Information Sources in Online and CD–ROM Database Searching,* Mansell, London, 1991.

de Bono E., *Teaching Thinking,* Temple Smith, London, 1976.

Directory of British Associations, CBD Research Ltd., Beckenham.

Dissertation Abstracts International, Part A: Humanities and Social Sciences. Part B: Science and Engineering. Part C: European Abstracts, University Microfilms, Ann Arbor, Mich.

Dixon D. and Hills P., *Talking About Your Research,* Primary Communications Research Centre, University of Leicester, 1981.

Ehrenberg S. C., *Data Reduction: Analysing and Interpreting Statistical Data,* Wiley Interscience, London, 1975.

Fairbairn G. J. and Winch C., *Reading, Writing and Reasoning: A Guide for Students,* Open University Press, Buckingham, 1991.

Glaser B. G. and Strauss A. L., *The Discovery of Grounded Theory: Strategies for Qualitative Research,* Weidenfeld & Nicholson, London, 1967.

Gorden R. L., *Interviewing: Strategy, Techniques and Tactics* (3rd Edition), Dorsey Press, Homewood, Ill., 1980.

Gowers Sir E., *The Complete Plain Words,* HMSO, London, 1954.

The Grants Register: postgraduate awards in the English-speaking world, St James Press, London.

Grinyer P. H., Classification suggested at the 5th National Conference on Doctoral Research in Management and Industrial Relations, University of Aston Management Centre, 6/7 April 1981

Gunning R., *The Technique of Clear Writing,* McGraw-Hill, New York, 1952.

Hansen K. J. and Waterman R. C., 'Evaluation of Research in Business Education', *National Business Education Quarterly,* Vol. 35, pp. 81–4, 1966.

Harrison M. A., 'Theoretical Issues Concerning Protection in Operating Systems', *Advances in Computers,* Vol 24, pp. 61–100, 1985.

Howard K. (ed.), *Managing a Thesis*, University of Bradford Management Centre, Bradford, 1978.

Hunter J. E., Schmidt F. L. and Jackson G. B., *META-ANALYSIS: cumulating findings across studies*, Sage Publications, London, 1982.

INDEX TO THESES WITH ABSTRACTS accepted for Higher Degrees in the Universities of Great Britain and Ireland, ASLIB, London.

Kraemer H. C., *How Many Subjects?: Statistical Power Analysis in Research*, Sage Publications, London, 1987.

Landwehr C. E., 'The Best Available Technologies for Computer Security', *Computer*, Vol 16, No. 7, p. 86, 1983.

Lock D., *Project Management* (4th Edition), Gower, Aldershot, 1988.

London School of Economics and Political Science, *LSE Calendar 1995–96*, London.

Mitchell B. R., *European Historical Statistics, 1750–1970*, Macmillan, London, 1975.

Mitchell B. R. and Deane P., *Abstract of British Historical Statistics*, Cambridge University Press, 1962.

Mitchell B. R. and Jones H. G., *Second Abstract of British Historical Statistics*, Cambridge University Press, 1971.

Monroe J., Meredith C. and Fisher K., *The Science of Scientific Writing*, Kendall Hurst, Dubuque, Ia, 1977.

Morgenstern O., *On the Accuracy of Economic Observations* (2nd Edition), Princeton University Press, Princeton, NJ., 1963.

Naroll R., *Data Quality Control : A New Research Technique*, Free Press, New York, NY., 1962.

Office of Public Service and Science, *Realising Our Potential: CMND 2250*, Government White Paper on UK Science Policy, HMSO, London, 1993.

Pangalos G. J., 'Medical Database Security Policies', *Methods of Information in Medicine*, Vol 32, No. 5, 1993.

Recommendations for the Presentation of Theses: BS 4821, British Standards Institution, London, 1982 .

Rummel J. F. and Ballaine W. C., *Research Methodology in Business*, Harper and Row, New York, NY., 1963.

Saaty T. L., *The Analytic Hierarchy Process*, McGraw Hill, New York, NY., 1980.

Science Citation Index, Institute for Scientific Information, Philadelphia, Pa.

Shannon C. E., 'A Mathematical Theory of Communication', *Bell System Technical Journal*, pp. 370–432 and pp. 623–59, 1948.

Simon J. L., *Basic Research Methods in Social Science*, Vols I and II, Random House, New York, NY., 1969.

Slattery M., *Official Statistics*, Tavistock Publications, London, 1986.

Social Science Citation Index, Institute for Scientific Information, Philadelphia, Pa.

Spon's Landscape and External Works Price Book, Spon, London.

STAR (Scientific Technical and Aerospace Reports), NASA, Washington, DC.

Tarr G., *The Management of Problem Solving: Positive Results from Productive Thinking*, Macmillan, London, 1973.

United Nations Statistical Year Book, United Nations, New York, NY.

Universities Funding Council, *Circular 5/92*, Research Assessment Exercise 1992, Bristol, 1992.

University of Kent, *Regulations for Degree of Doctor of Philosophy*, Canterbury, 1995.

Usher D., *The Economic Prerequisite to Democracy*, Blackwell, Oxford, 1981.

Walford A. J., *Guide to Reference Material*, (3 vols, 6th Edition), Library Association, London, 1994.

Webb E. J., Campbell D. T., Schwartz R. D. and Sechrest L., *Unobtrusive Measures: Non reactive Research in the Social Sciences*, Rand McNally, Chicago, Ill., 1966.

Notes

Chapter 1: *Research and the Research Student*

1. This unpublished survey was carried out by the authors at the University of Bradford Management Centre.

Chapter 2: *Selecting and Justifying a Research Project*

1. Office of Public Service and Science, *Realising Our Potential*, 1993.
2. For some sources of support for student research in the English-speaking world see *The Grants Register*.
3. Office of Public Service and Science, *Realising Our Potential*, 1993.

Chapter 4: *Literature Searching*

1. The citation indexes were originally produced in book form, albeit from a computer database. Nowadays, citation indexes are available in many academic libraries, either on CD-Rom or by online access to a national or international provider. Such a service is currently (1996) available to most UK universities via the BIDS system at the University of Bath.
2. We have retained this example to illustrate the original principle of citation index searching when using the paper-based citation indexes. Nowadays, however, the citation indexes are likely to be encountered in computer form. Most researchers, therefore, are more likely to achieve similar results via a title/keyword search (see

later). However, a forward search of the type shown here can perfectly well be carried out with the computer version.

3. The Copyright Libraries are those libraries entitled under UK law to a copy of every book published in the UK. They are: The British Library; the libraries of Oxford University and Cambridge University; the library of Trinity College, Dublin; the National Library of Scotland. In addition, for some books, the National Library of Wales, Aberystwyth.

4. For instance, it will be apparent that in Charts 1–5, many of the search activities (for example, carrying out a subject index search) may well involve the use of a computer. Readers are advised to familiarise themselves with the operation of the appropriate computer systems in their own libraries.

5. In most UK academic libraries, bibliographic sources such as abstracts are most likely to be found on CD–ROM. For a listing of the enormous range of material now available on CD–ROM, see *CD–ROMs in Print*.

Chapter 5: *Analysing the Data*

1. Recently (1996) launched by Sage Publications, London.

2. Causal explanations in history, for example, can be problematic. In fields such as ethnography that involve the identification of belief systems and inferences about their effects, the notion of causality is even more difficult.

3. By 'tests of hypothesis' in this context the evaluation of the credibility of some hypotheses like those above is meant and not the narrower definition employed in elementary statistics.

Chapter 6: *Gathering the Data*

1. The ESRC Data Archive is located at the University of Essex.

Chapter 7: *Executing the Research*

1. In the UK, the Research Councils, which play a major role in the public funding of university research, encourage graduate students to undertake teaching providing that not more than six hours a week (including preparation) is spent on this activity. Also permitted is a small amount of other paid work providing that the supervisor's approval is obtained.

Chapter 8: *Presentation of the Research Findings*

1. LSE Calendar, 1995–96.

2. At the time of writing (1996), the particular thesis requirements (if any) of the new

MRes degree in the UK had not yet emerged. Similarly, in the UK, the new-style doctoral qualifications – for example, the DBA – with a taught course component had not been clearly differentiated in terms of thesis requirements from those of a PhD. We have, therefore, not explicitly covered these and students following such qualifications may need to modify somewhat our recommendations to fit their own circumstances.

3. Some institutions use the term 'Bibliography' to denote what we describe as a 'List of References'. We would suggest that where possible the student restricts the use of 'Bibliography' to a general list of books and journals consulted, but not explicitly cited.

4. This is one reason why photocopying is necessary. Another is that the economics of photocopying compared with laser printing mean that, even if the text has no diagrams that need to be pasted in, the student will still find it considerably cheaper to photocopy one laser-printed master rather than produce on the laser printer the several copies required by the institution.

5. A problem with word processed text to be avoided is that, because re-ordering of sections and even chapters is very easy, when rearrangements are made to the text the result can mean that items such as abbreviations end up being defined considerably after they have first appeared in the text.

6. The first part of this section is based upon K. Howard and J. Peters, *Managing Management Research*, MCB University Press, Bradford, 1960, pp. 62–3.

Index

267